S0-AHM-333

Simply *in* Season

TENTH ANNIVERSARY EDITION

"What you read here comes from a voice that is pastoral, not judgmental . . . expect to be lovingly challenged in your decision to eat what is fresh and in season."
—Graham Kerr, former host of *The Galloping Gourmet*

"Our debts to other colleagues and writers are as numerous as the books in our library . . . and the kitchen bookshelf: Alice Waters, Deborah Madison, Mary Beth Lind, and Cathleen Hockman-Wert."
—Barbara Kingsolver, in *Animal, Vegetable, Miracle*

"I've tried a few cookbooks that were advertised as 'seasonal,' but the only one to live up to its cover blurb has been *Simply in Season*."
—*Green Living Ottawa*

"A treasure trove of culinary delights centered around local and seasonal foods, that goes easy on the wallet and the planet."
—Katrien Vander Straeten, Suite

"Practical, not preachy. It's down-to-earth and useful to everyone, regardless of faith."
—Melinda Hemmelgarn, *Columbia Daily Tribune*

"An essential kitchen companion . . . This is a book I will turn to over and over again. They've put the recipes in the most organized, easy-to-use cookbook I've seen."
—Catherine Walthers, author of *Raising the Salad Bar*

"In this era of the 'locavore,' *Simply in Season* offers creative and nutritious recipes that will inspire experienced cooks and initiate culinary newcomers alike."
—Lisa Weasel, author of *Food Fray*

Library of Congress Cataloguing-in-Publication Data
Lind, Mary Beth.
Simply in season : a world community cookbook / Mary Beth Lind and Cathleen
Hockman-Wert ; commissioned by Mennonite Central Committee (MCC) to
promote the understanding of how the food choices we make affect our lives
and the lives of those who produce the food. — Tenth anniversary edition.
       pages cm
Includes bibliographical references and indexes.
ISBN 978-0-8361-9912-3 (hardcover : alk. paper)—
ISBN 978-0-8361-9913-0 (pbk. : alk. paper)
1. Cooking, American. 2. Seasonal cooking. I. Hockman-Wert, Cathleen. II. Title.
TX715.L7575 2015
641.5973--dc23
2015003304

Scripture is from the *New Revised Standard Version Bible*, © 1989, Division
of Christian Education of the National Council of the Churches of Christ in the
United States of America. Used by permission. All rights reserved.

All rights reserved. This publication may not be reproduced, stored in a
retrieval system, or transmitted in whole or in part, in any form, by any means,
electronic, mechanical, photocopying, recording, or otherwise without prior
permission of the copyright owners.

SIMPLY IN SEASON (TENTH ANNIVERSARY EDITION)
© 2005, 2009, 2015 by Herald Press, Harrisonburg, Virginia 22802
       Released simultaneously in Canada by Herald Press,
       Kitchener, Ontario N2G 3R1. All rights reserved.
First edition printed 2005. Expanded edition printed 2009.
Tenth anniversary edition printed 2015.
Library of Congress Control Number: 2015003304
International Standard Book Number: 978-1-5138-0167-4 (paperback layflat)
Printed in United States of America

Design by Julie Kauffman.
Food styling by Cherise Harper. Food photography by Melissa Hess.
Cover photograph of Plum Tomato Galette, p. 160. Other photographs,
including photos on p. 110 and 306, from Thinkstock.

To order or request information, please call 1-800-245-7894 or visit
www.heraldpress.com.

20 19 18 17 16   10 9 8 7 6 5 4 3 2

TENTH ANNIVERSARY EDITION

Simply
in
Season

Mary Beth Lind
Cathleen Hockman-Wert

*Commissioned by Mennonite Central Committee (MCC)
to promote the understanding of how the food choices we make
affect our lives and the lives of those who produce the food.*

*MCC, a worldwide ministry of Anabaptist churches, shares
God's love and compassion for all in the name of Christ by
responding to basic human needs and working for peace
and justice. MCC envisions communities worldwide in right
relationship with God, one another, and creation.*

*Royalties from this cookbook support the work of MCC
(www.mcc.org and www.mcccanada.ca).*

Herald Press
Harrisonburg, Virginia
Kitchener, Ontario

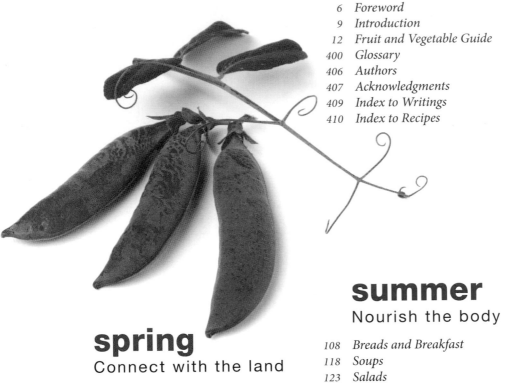

spring
Connect with the land

summer
Nourish the body

autumn
Slow life down

all seasons
Consider your neighbors

winter
Reflect on values

Foreword

We are watching a revolution take place. It's not about politics or world domination. It's not about economic equity or social justice. It's about food. It's about the simple idea that many people in our country want good, fresh, and nutritious food. Somehow, over the past fifty years or so, corporations hijacked our menus. Profits trumped flavor. Convenience trumped cuisine. Shelf life trumped nutrition. Salt and fat trumped seasoning. Gordo trumped gourmet. We were urged to grab a box of rehydrated, microwavable, corn syrup–sweetened convenience foods, readily available and cheap, cheap, cheap. Many fell into the appeal of this approach, buying into the apparent ease.

Many . . . but not all. As the corporate world took over our food, a small but dedicated voice continued to keep real food alive. That voice has continued to this day, reviving and strengthening support for nutritious eating. Here's what that revolution looks like: A strong interest in food diversity and heirloom plant varieties. Awareness of saving rare breeds of animals for their charm and flexibility. A zest for getting dirt under the fingernails. Concern for local production, healthy soil, regional foodsheds, and flourishing neighborhoods.

Wisdom and skills for putting food by, canning and storing for a rainy day or a colder season. And most importantly, a passion for cooking. Not the style of cooking that starts with a recipe and sends us out shopping, but the other way around. In the new food revolution, seasonal food availability tells us what's best for dinner. If that's a revolution you wish to join, then you are looking at the perfect book.

When my family and I embarked on our Year of Local Eating about ten years ago, we were delighted to discover the first edition of *Simply in Season*. Within its pages we found kindred spirits, offering something along the lines of a how-to manual. Ten years after we wrote *Animal, Vegetable, Miracle*, we are still actively following the local food path, and *Simply in Season* has remained one of our favorite resources. Since then I created a restaurant, the Harvest Table, to build the local economy and bring fresh local cuisine to our region. What we prepare is in sync with local growers, and our menus track the food seasons. Our chefs always start with what we find, and many variants of the recipes in *Simply in Season* can be found in our dining room.

This tenth anniversary edition is an incisive new vision of the original book, and I am pleased to participate in its launch. Many excellent cookbooks have come along in support of the local food revolution, but there is still not a better one than this.

—Steven L. Hopp, coauthor, *Animal, Vegetable, Miracle*

I am immensely grateful to be part of an intergenerational family farm on which we grow grain, bison, sour cherries, vegetables, rainbow trout, and children. I include children because we are not agribusiness people but rather agriculturalists. And this piece of land along the South Saskatchewan River holds a piece of our identity. We love our children, and we also love this land.

One autumn evening three generations of my family were planting cherry trees. The air was deliciously warm, with a spectacular harvest sunset in the western sky. A great blue heron came soaring lazily over us, gracing us with his presence. A beautiful evening—hands in the earth, working together, children running about.

I glanced over at my dad and saw tears on his weather-worn face. "Daddy, what?" I asked.

"This," he said, sweeping the vista, "this is what I have hoped for."
—*Eileen Klassen Hamm, Saskatoon, Saskatchewan*

Simply in Season explores the

complex web of factors that bring food to our plates. Along with recipes, it shares stories: personal stories of connection to food, stories of communities and the foods that sustain them, and stories from farmers' markets and farms. Each chapter centers on a theme that reflects each season. You may find yourself reading through this cookbook twice—once for the recipes and once for the stories. Or read these stories as you cook, pausing a moment while the onions sauté, the soup simmers, or the bread bakes. You'll hear the voices of our neighbors who farm as well as gardeners and cooks who find joy in eating with the seasons.

Before the advent of modern transportation and storage systems, eating local food was the norm—as it still is in much of the world. Within our memories we see our parents and grandparents with hands full of fruits and vegetables from their gardens or gardens nearby. Eggs, milk, and meat also came from local sources.

Today the average food item travels more than fifteen hundred miles before it arrives on our tables. We have become distant from our food, and not just in terms of geography. Who grows our food? What are their lives like? How is the soil cultivated and prepared for the next year? How are the animals treated in life and in death? How does the production of the foods we eat affect the land and the people who raise them? Does any of this really matter if we have plenty of food on our table?

It matters a great deal. For food production systems are not all the same—any more than the taste of a vine-ripened, homegrown tomato equals one picked green. Each food purchase we make is like a vote for the way we want food to be produced—and for the world in which we want to live.

Simply in Season does not offer all the answers. It does offer a starting point, encouraging us to feed both body and spirit with nutritious food and challenging ideas about the world around us. The stories in Spring explore the environmental impact of modern agriculture. Summer stories offer thoughts on health; the stories in the Autumn section focus on time; and Winter follows with thoughts on the economic factors of food. The final recipe chapter, All Seasons, presents a vital overview of food production and food security issues, bringing us full circle in our understanding of the meaning and place of food in our lives.

Connecting all the seasons are invitations at the beginning of each chapter encouraging you to live fully in the particular time (season) and place (location) in which you find yourself.

Simply in Season also remains a cookbook filled with delicious recipes. Part of the fun of cooking with the seasons is learning to use what's locally available. That often means taking recipes as starting points: a theme on which to playfully improvise rather than a blueprint to follow precisely.

For easy reference, seasonal chapters are designated by color. The beginning of each chapter lists recipes by type, such as salad and main dish, along with a few menu ideas. If you come across a term you don't know, try the glossary in the back.

This tenth anniversary edition includes new elements, including colorful photographs of many of the dishes and updated statistics and terms. To make the cookbook more useful for people on special diets, the publisher has included vegetarian Ⓥ and gluten-free ⒼⒻ recipe labels. As fruits and vegetables are the centerpiece for eating locally, an expanded guide offers you information on how to select, store, and prepare many. Yet this edition retains all the richness of the original in its blend of seasonal recipes and compelling stories from around the world. (The contributors are still listed in the locations where they lived when the cookbook was first published in 2005.)

A work created with the help of hundreds of volunteers, *Simply in Season* is a community cookbook about good food: foods that are fresh, nutritious, tasty, and in rhythm with the seasons. Whether they come from a farmers' market, a CSA (Community Supported Agriculture) farm, or your own garden, fresh, local foods are good for the earth we share. Ultimately, they nurture our spirits as well as our bodies.

Whether you have long cherished local food or are new to these ideas, we hope you are encouraged in your journey with food choices. The path is long and continuous, with innumerable points of entry. None of us has "arrived," and all of us will have to decide what choices are right for our own circumstances. But it is a delight to share the stories—and recipes—of fellow travelers who love good food. Welcome! And enjoy!

—Mary Beth Lind and Cathleen Hockman-Wert

They shall all sit under their own vines and under their own fig trees, and no one shall make them afraid. (Micah 4:4)

Fruit and Vegetable Guide

Offering a vast array of color, flavor, and nutrition, fruits and vegetables are a cook's delight. So it seems a shame to destroy broccoli's bright green by overcooking, or lose tomatoes' flavor of warm summer sun by refrigerating. The following pages give you some tips on how to choose, store, prepare, and use selected fruits and vegetables.

NEW TO THIS EDITION

Tips on how to use the whole vegetable, especially those you find at the farmers' market. Learn how to use carrot or turnip greens. There are also suggestions on how to use discarded vegetable peelings and leftovers to flavor soup stocks. Use your favorite soup stock recipe and add/substitute any of the suggested vegetables when you make your broth.

NUTRIENTS

Nutrients listed are those for which one serving of the food is a good source (providing 10–20 percent of the FDA recommended daily allowance) or a very good source (providing more than 20 percent). The latter are **bolded** in the text. Unless otherwise noted, a serving is one cup raw; cooking may alter the nutrients. Complete nutrient information is available at www.nutritiondata.com.

Keep them fresh

CHILLING slows down the metabolic activity. Most fruits and vegetables store best at refrigerator temperatures of 30–40° F / -1 to 4° C. A few like it warmer: potatoes like 40–50° F / 4–10° C. Pumpkins, winter squash, and sweet potatoes like 55° F / 13° C, and tomatoes like room temperature.

LIMITING OXYGEN reduces oxidation-tissue breakdown. This is most often accomplished by storing in an airtight container. Place the fruit or vegetable in a plastic bag and gently squeeze out all the air before closing. Or vacuum seal: Close the bag except for a small space into which you insert a straw, use the straw to suck out all the air, quickly remove the straw, and close the bag. If, however, the fruit isn't completely ripe, you will want to allow it to be warm and breathe. Store ripening fruits at room temperature in a paper bag. Add a piece of already ripe fruit, such as an apple, which gives off ethylene gas.

MAINTAINING MOISTURE avoids wilted and limp fruits and vegetables, most of which are 70–95 percent water. However, excess moisture can cause mold growth and rot. So remove excess surface moisture—for example, with a lettuce spinner—and then store in a tight plastic bag to avoid additional evaporation.

Keep them nutritious

When cooking or microwaving, use only a small amount of water to assure the best retention of flavor and nutrition.

When microwaving, use only glass dishes. Plastic compounds from plastic containers can migrate into the food. Foods cook more evenly in round dishes than square or rectangular ones.

Save cooking liquid to use as soup stock or broth. It contains concentrated soluble vitamins.

Apples

YEAR-ROUND

Description: These familiar round fruits are classified as eating, cooking, or all-purpose. They can be sweet or tart and come in various colors. Summer apples do not keep well, while other varieties keep all winter. Find out what varieties are grown in your area and become familiar with their attributes.

Selection: Apples should feel firm and crisp, not soft or spongy. Avoid those with cuts or bruises. Surface blemishes do not harm fruit quality.

Storage and handling: Apples will stay fresh at room temperature for 2 days, and in the refrigerator for 2 weeks or more. Wash in a bowl of cold water before eating.

Preparation: Halve or quarter lengthwise through stem end. Cut away stem, core, and seeds. Remove peel if desired. **Cook** and mash for applesauce. **Bake** alone (p. 322) or in dessert recipes.

Serving suggestions: Eat raw apples plain, topped with peanut butter, or chopped or shredded and added to salads (p. 299). Cooking apples lend themselves to baked desserts—pies, crisps, cakes, and muffins (p. 282).

Comments: Most apples discolor quickly after cutting, so use them quickly or toss them with an acid source, such as diluted lemon juice, to stop browning.

Nutrients: Vitamin C; anthocyanin antioxidants (red-skinned varieties); fiber.

1 lb raw = 2¾ cups
1 lb cooked = 1¾ cup

Asparagus

SPRING

Description: A perennial, asparagus are spear-like shoots that come in three main varieties: green, the most common; white, for which the green variety is field blanched; and purple, an extra sweet and tender variety that turns green when cooked.

Selection: Look for spears with tight buds and smooth skin. Asparagus should not be withered, brown, or limp. Smaller spears are especially tender.

Storage and handling: Store asparagus upright with water at its base for 2–3 days in the coolest part of the refrigerator. Rinse well before using, especially around the scales.

Preparation: Snap the stems where they naturally break to remove the woody bottom portion. Cut into pieces or use whole spears. **Steam** (or cook in a little water) about 5 minutes, until crisp tender. **Microwave** about 5 minutes in a covered dish with a little liquid. **Roast** with garlic (p. 67).

Serving suggestions: Serve raw asparagus in salads (p. 61) or on a vegetable tray. Season cooked or roasted asparagus with balsamic vinegar or lemon butter. Use peeled stems to flavor soups.

Nutrients: Vitamins A, C, **K**, thiamin, riboflavin, folate; iron; fiber.

1 lb raw = 3 cups
1 lb cooked = 2 cups

Beets

Description: Beets are a root crop with round red or gold flesh. Beet leaves are also edible.

Selection: Choose beets with tops attached. Bunches with beets of similar size will cook more evenly. Very large beets are sometimes woody and tough; those that are about 2 inches in diameter are just right.

Storage and handling: Remove the leaves and treat them like other greens. Store beets in a plastic bag in the refrigerator produce drawer for 2–3 weeks, or in a root cellar. Before eating, scrub with a brush and remove dangling roots and all but an inch or so of the tops.

Preparation: Boil for 20–30 minutes, drain, cool, and peel. **Microwave** 1 pound of whole 2-inch beets by placing in covered dish with ¼ cup water and cooking 10–11 minutes. **Pressure-cook** for 12–20 minutes, depending on size. Skins will slip off easily after cooking. **Sauté** peeled, shredded beets, covered, for 10 minutes.

Serving suggestions: Peel and shred raw beets for use in salads (p. 296). Season cooked beets with butter and salt. Beets marry well with a sweet and sour flavor and are often pickled (p. 332). Use beet greens like spinach in salads or soups, and use beet stems to flavor stock for beet soup.

Nutrients: Vitamin C, **folate**; potassium; fiber.

1 lb raw = 4 cups
1 lb cooked = 2 cups

Blueberries

Description: These are round berries with a firm, smooth skin. Similar round berries include **saskatoons**, **elderberries**, **gooseberries**, and **currants**.

Selection: Look for firm, plump, richly colored berries with no soft spots or discolorations. All berries should be dry with no mold or signs of juice leaking on the container. They will not ripen after picking.

Storage and handling: Blueberries will last up to 10 days, covered, in the refrigerator as long as they are kept dry. Just before using, wash and drain well.

Preparation: Remove any stems. Use in recipes as desired.

Serving suggestions: Raw blueberries are delicious plain or added to smoothies. Eat any of these berries in baked goods—muffins, pies (p. 188–89), cobblers, and crisps. Use in jellies and jams or on top of cereal. Elderberry flowers can be added to salads or batter-dipped and fried like fritters.

Nutrients: Vitamins **C** and **K**; anthocyanin antioxidants; fiber.

1 lb raw = 2 cups
1 lb cooked = n/a

Broccoli

SPRING, SUMMER, AUTUMN

Description: Broccoli grows in thick green stalks topped with umbrella-shaped clusters of dark green florets.

Selection: Look for firm stalks and tightly closed florets. Florets should be blue-green or purplish-green; yellow-green broccoli is older and likely to have a strong flavor and odor. Very wide stems may be too woody to eat.

Storage and handling: Refrigerate in a loosely sealed plastic bag for up to 3 days. When ready to cook, separate stalks from florets and wash thoroughly. Trim ends and peel stems with paring knife, and cut into bite-sized pieces.

Preparation: Steam in basket over water by covering and cooking 7 minutes, depending on size and age. **Microwave** bite-sized pieces in a covered dish with small amount of water, 5–7 minutes. To avoid loss of the bright green color do not cook broccoli for longer than 7 minutes.

Serving suggestions: Use raw broccoli florets in salads (p. 231) or for dipping. Peeled raw broccoli stems can be sliced and used in place of water chestnuts in recipes. Dress steamed broccoli with vinaigrette, lemon butter, olive oil, garlic, toasted nuts, or cheese. Steam young broccoli leaves and use as garnish.

Nutrients: Vitamins A, **C**, **K**, folate; cancer-preventing compounds sulforaphane, isothiocyanate, and indoles; fiber.

1 lb raw = 5 cups
1 lb cooked = 2 cups

Brussels sprouts

AUTUMN, WINTER

Description: These tiny cabbages grow on tall, thick stalks.

Selection: Choose bright green sprouts smaller than a Ping Pong ball. They should feel firm and crisp and be tightly closed. Sprouts on the stalk will keep longer.

Storage and handling: Store in a loosely sealed plastic bag in the refrigerator for no more than 2 days. Before serving, remove from stalk, peel off the outer layer or two of leaves, and take a thin slice off the stem end. Rinse in cold water. Cut an *X* in the core for even cooking.

Preparation: Steam small brussels sprouts 6–8 minutes, medium ones 8–10 minutes, large ones 10–12 minutes. **Boil** in small amount of water until just tender, 4–5 minutes for small sprouts, 5–8 minutes medium, 8–12 minutes large. **Sauté** thinly sliced sprouts in a flavorful fat (butter, olive oil, bacon grease) for 4–5 minutes (p. 239). **Microwave** a half pound of sprouts in a covered dish with ¼ cup water; small sprouts take 2 minutes, medium ones 4 and large ones 8. **Roast** (p. 239).

Serving suggestions: Use raw, small, tender sprouts, halved lengthwise, in a vegetable tray. Top cooked sprouts with vinaigrette, toasted nuts, or a white sauce flavored with cheese or Dijon mustard (p. 389).

Nutrients: Vitamins A, B6, **C**, **K**, folate; potassium; cancer-preventing compounds sulforaphane, isothiocyanate, and indoles; fiber.

1 lb raw = 3½ cups
1 lb cooked = 2½ cups

Cabbage

SUMMER, AUTUMN, WINTER

Description: Cabbage's tightly layered leaves form a compact head surrounded by darker outer leaves. Common varieties are green, red, crinkly Savoy, Chinese, bok choy, and Napa. Cabbages are generally interchangeable in recipes, although Chinese cabbages cook in less time.

Selection: Choose vividly colored, tightly closed heads that appear unblemished and feel crisp and heavy for their size.

Storage and handling: Refrigerate in a loosely sealed plastic bag. Cabbage heads stay fresh 1–2 weeks; sliced cabbage keeps 5–6 days. Cabbage can also be root cellared.

Preparation: Remove tough or dry outer leaves and cut head into four wedges through the stem end. Cut the hard, white core off each wedge and chop or thinly slice the rest of the wedge if desired to add to dishes or snack on raw. **Stir-fry** tender (Chinese) cabbages. **Steam** wedges of cabbage 6–9 minutes, slices 5–6 minutes. **Boil** wedges in small amount of water 6–9 minutes.

Serving suggestions: Toss shredded raw cabbage with a vinaigrette or creamy dressing to make coleslaw (p. 294) or add to tossed green salads. Season cooked cabbage with butter or herbs, or bake in a cream sauce (p. 302). Make sauerkraut (p. 331).

Nutrients: Vitamins **C** and **K**, folate; anthocyanins antioxidants (purple varieties), cancer-preventing compounds sulforaphane, isothiocyanate, and indoles.

1 lb raw = 3½–4½ cups shredded
1 lb cooked = 2 cups

Carrots

YEAR-ROUND

Description: Carrots come in orange (by far the most common), yellow, purple, and red varieties. They vary from long tapers to small round balls.

Selection: Choose crisp, firm, small to medium carrots. Dark orange carrots have more vitamin A.

Storage and handling: Refrigerate in produce drawer for up to 2 weeks. Remove any greens attached to the carrots and store separately. Before eating, wash in a bowl of cold water and scrub with a vegetable brush if not peeling. Rinse carrot tops in a bowl of water to remove dirt.

Preparation: Trim stem end and any dangling roots. Peel if desired and cut or shred. **Steam** sliced carrots in a basket over boiling water, covered, 10–12 minutes. **Boil** sliced carrots, covered, in a small amount of water, 8–10 minutes. **Roast** with other vegetables (p. 307). **Microwave** a pound of carrots, cut into 2- to 3-inch lengths, in a covered dish with 2 tablespoons liquid, 7–8 minutes.

Serving suggestions: Eat raw carrot sticks plain, or slice or shred for slaws (p. 294) or salads (p. 297). Top cooked carrots with olive oil and herbs, butter, honey, or brown sugar. Cook and mash with potatoes (p. 303). Add shredded carrots to sauces and baked goods (p. 329). Use carrot tops as a garnish for salads and soups or use a moderate amount in smoothies.

Nutrients: Vitamins **A**, **C**, **K**; potassium; alpha- and beta-carotene antioxidants; fiber.

1 lb raw = 3–3½ cups
1 lb cooked = 3–3½ cups

Cauliflower

Description: Cauliflower grows in a compact head shielded from sunlight by its outer leaves, so it doesn't develop chlorophyll and thus remains white. **Broccoflower**, a cauliflower-broccoli hybrid, grows in a head like cauliflower but is green like broccoli. It cooks more quickly and has a milder flavor than white cauliflower.

Selection: Firm, crisp florets indicate freshness, as does a creamy white color with no discolorations. Leaves should be green and not limp.

Storage and handling: Refrigerate in a loosely sealed, dry plastic bag for 2–4 days. Before eating, cut off the thick stalk and leaves on the bottom of the cauliflower and reserve. Cut around the thick core, remove, and save. Separate florets if desired, then wash and shake to remove excess water.

Preparation: Steam a whole (trimmed and cored) cauliflower by placing it right side up in a basket or colander over boiling water, covered, 20 minutes for a 1½-pound head; florets steam in 6–10 minutes. **Microwave** in covered dish with ¼ cup liquid, 8–10 minutes for a whole head, 6–8 minutes for a pound of florets. Slice and simmer tender leaves.

Serving suggestions: Eat raw cauliflower florets with or without dip, or add to salads. Top cooked cauliflower with browned butter, lemon butter, or cheese. Try cauliflower in a curry (p. 248).

Nutrients: Vitamin B6, **C**, K, folate; fiber.

1 lb raw = 4 cups
1 lb cooked = 1½ cup

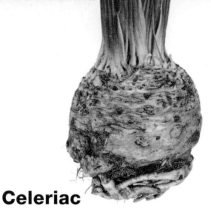

Celeriac

Description: Celeriac is a globe-shaped root vegetable with a celery-like flavor.

Selection: Small to medium roots (about 1 pound) have the best flavor and texture. Look for roots that are heavy for their size and appear relatively smooth.

Storage and handling: Refrigerate for up to 1 week. Just before using, scrub with a vegetable brush while holding under cold water.

Preparation: Cut a thin slice from each end of the root. Reserve stalks and leaves and use moderately to flavor soup stocks. Place the root side down and cut around the root to remove the tough, stringy skin. Once the white center is exposed, it can be sliced, diced, or shredded. **Boil** a whole peeled celeriac 25–30 minutes, slices 8–10 minutes, cubes 5–8 minutes. Or boil whole with skin on; a 1-pound root will take 45–50 minutes.

Serving suggestions: Raw celeriac makes an excellent base for coleslaw-like salads. Use to season soups and stews. Purée cooked celeriac with cooked potatoes or other root vegetables and serve in place of mashed potatoes. Use finely chopped leaves for seasoning.

Comments: Celeriac discolors quickly after cutting, so use it quickly or toss with an acidic dressing (if using for salad).

Nutrients: Vitamins B6, **C**, **K**; potassium; fiber.

1 lb raw = 2 cups
1 lb cooked = n/a

Celery

SUMMER, AUTUMN

Description: Celery is a tall, green stem with small, feathery leaves.

Selection: Firm, crisp stalks and healthy dark green leaves attached to celery indicate freshness. Avoid celery with browning on the outer stalks or hollow stalks.

Storage and handling: Refrigerate celery in a loosely sealed plastic bag for a week or longer. When ready to use, separate the stalks. Discard any that are past their prime. Wash thoroughly and dry. Remove the leaves, wash thoroughly, and dry or freeze to use in soups. To re-crisp celery, place in ice water in the refrigerator for a few hours.

Preparation: Trim any tough parts from stalk ends. If desired, strings may be removed by running a vegetable peeler over the ridged side of the stalk. **Sauté** chopped celery in a little butter or oil for about 5 minutes. **Microwave** 2 cups sliced or chopped celery by adding 2 tablespoons liquid, covering, and cooking 8–10 minutes.

Serving suggestions: Enjoy raw celery sticks as a snack, or slice to use in salads. Add celery to stir-fries and soups (p. 52). Add celery leaves to salads and casseroles.

Nutrients: Vitamins A, K, folate; antitumor compound allicin, bioflavonoid antioxidants.

1 lb raw = 4 cups
1 lb cooked = 2½ cups

Collards

AUTUMN

Description: Collards are smooth, broad, dark green leaves. They have a hearty, chewy texture and an assertive flavor that mellows with long cooking. Collards are hardy enough to withstand a hard frost, and their flavor actually improves afterward.

Selection: Greens should look fresh and crisp. Avoid those that are wilted or yellowed.

Storage and handling: Collard stalks are too tough to be edible, so remove stalks before using. Wash greens thoroughly, checking for insects and dirt clinging to underside of leaves. Greens should be wrapped in a damp paper towel, placed in a sealed plastic bag, and refrigerated. Stored this way they will last up to a week.

Preparation: Chop into bite-sized pieces and **sauté** or **boil**. **Microwave** washed greens in a covered dish for 6 minutes.

Serving suggestions: Collards are not often eaten raw. They are tastiest sautéed with garlic and onion or boiled in broth or salted water. Try them in a peanut sauce (p. 233).

Nutrients (when boiled): Vitamins **A**, B6, **C**, **K**, **folate**, riboflavin; **calcium**, **iron**; lutein and zeaxanthin antioxidants; **fiber**.

1 lb raw = 7–8 cups
1 lb cooked = 2–3 cups

Corn

SUMMER, EARLY AUTUMN

Description: Sweet corn (as opposed to field corn) may be white, yellow, or bicolor, with a sweetness level of regular, sugar enhanced, or super sweet.

Selection: Freshness is crucial. Choose ears with full, plump kernels. Avoid ears with wilted or dry husks.

Storage and handling: Refrigerate ears still in their husks for 1–2 days at most. Before cooking, remove husks and silks.

Preparation: To remove kernels, hold ear over a large bowl and slice kernels off with a sharp knife. **Sauté** kernels or **bake** in recipes. **Boil** whole ears in large pot 4–7 minutes. **Steam** ears in basket over boiling water, covered, 6–10 minutes. **Roast or grill** ears this way: pull back leaves, remove silk and wrap leaves back around corn, soak in water 10 minutes, place corn directly on hot grill 15–20 minutes. Or remove husks and silk, brush with melted butter, wrap in foil, and roast 20–30 minutes in oven or 15–20 minutes on grill. **Microwave** ears in a covered dish with a few tablespoons of water; 4 ears take 5–7 minutes.

Serving suggestions: Not usually eaten raw. Dress fresh corn with butter and salt. Mix kernels with cooked lima beans to make succotash, or add to pasta, salads, or soups (p. 120). Use discarded cobs to flavor soup stocks.

Nutrients (when boiled): Vitamin B6, niacin, thiamin, folate; antioxidants lutein and zeaxanthin (yellow varieties); protein.

1 dozen ears raw = 6 cups kernels
1 lb cooked = 6 cups

Cranberries

AUTUMN

Description: These tart, bright red berries are grown in huge, sandy bogs on low, trailing vines. They are usually at their peak in October or November.

Selection: Buy only richly colored berries; pale ones were picked too early and are likely to be sour. Avoid wet or mushy berries.

Storage and handling: Cranberries can be refrigerated, tightly wrapped, for at least 2 months or frozen up to a year. Before serving, place cranberries in a colander (or leave in box if it has holes) and rinse in cold water.

Preparation: Use raw as is, or chop and grind before mixing with a sweetener and other ingredients. **Cook** with sugar and water to make a simple cranberry sauce. Be sure to cook cranberries only until their skins pop or they will become bitter.

Serving suggestions: Cranberries are very tart and pair well with apples or oranges in salads (p. 231). They are often used like raisins in baked goods (p. 220). Dried cranberries make a delicious snack on their own or in granola (p. 354).

Nutrients: Vitamin **C**; anthocyanins antioxidants; **fiber**.

1 lb raw = 4 cups
1 lb cooked = n/a

Cucumbers

SUMMER

Description: Slicing cucumbers usually have smooth skins and are long, round cylinders with a sweet flavor. Long, slender English cucumbers (also called Dutch or Japanese) have thin skins and contain few seeds. Pickling cucumbers are best used for making sweet or dill pickles.

Selection: Select firm, crisp cucumbers with no blemishes or yellowing. Ones that feel heavy for their size are likely to be crisper. Small cucumbers generally have fewer seeds.

Storage and handling: Store in the refrigerator in a loosely sealed plastic bag for up to a week. Before eating, wash in cold water.

Preparation: Remove tough or waxed skin with a vegetable peeler. Remove large seeds by slicing the cucumber in half lengthwise, then scraping seeds out with a spoon. Salting cut cucumbers and letting them sit in a colander for about 1 hour will remove some of their water, which will keep them from diluting salad dressing. Dry them thoroughly before tossing with the dressing.

Serving suggestions: Not usually eaten cooked. Eat cucumbers plain or with a light sprinkling of salt or a flavorful dip. Slice and chop for use in tossed salads. For cucumber salad, slice and dress with a simple vinaigrette or yogurt (p. 123).

Nutrients: Vitamin K.

1 lb raw = 4 cups
1 lb cooked = n/a

Edamame

SUMMER

Description: Edamame (which means "beans on a branch" in Japanese) are green soybeans. They have long been popular in Japan. They have a nutty, sweet flavor and creamy yet slightly crunchy texture.

Selection: Select pods that are brightly colored, plump, smooth, and firm.

Storage and handling: Soybeans will last a week in a loosely sealed plastic bag in the refrigerator. Before eating, wash in cold water.

Preparation: Fresh soybeans may be shelled before cooking, but shelling will be easier after cooking. **Boil** whole 7–10 minutes, drain, and immediately cool in cold water. When sufficiently cool to handle, squeeze the pod until the beans pop out. **Steam** or **microwave** pods 4–5 minutes.

Serving suggestions: Not usually eaten raw. Toss steamed edamame pods with salt and pull the beans out as you eat them (with your hands or your teeth); discard the pod. Cooked shelled beans are delicious with a little butter or olive oil, salt, and pepper. Add cooked shelled beans to soups, casseroles, stir-fries, or salads (p. 130).

Nutrients (when boiled): Vitamin **C**, **folate**, **thiamin**, riboflavin, niacin; **iron**, **calcium**, **potassium**; **protein**; **fiber**.

1 lb raw = 3 cups shelled
1 lb cooked = 3 cups shelled

Edible flowers

Description: Among the more common edible flowers are violets, marigolds, nasturtiums, and chamomile. Other varieties include borage, chervil, chrysanthemums, clover, dandelions, daylilies, roses, hyacinths, gladiolas, hollyhocks, impatiens, lilacs, and pansies. The blossoms of chive, garlic, squash, and pea are also edible.

Selection: Learn which flowers and parts of flowers are edible—some flowers are poisonous, and some plants with edible blossoms have other poisonous parts. Use caution. Flowers from florists, nurseries, or garden centers have likely been treated with pesticides not approved for food crops. Flowers picked from beside a road may have been sprayed as well.

Storage and handling: Rinse flowers and remove undesired parts such as stems. Place between paper towels to dry, then refrigerate if needed. Some species will last a few days.

Preparation: Make tea with one tablespoon of petals per cup boiling water, steep 10 minutes.

Serving suggestions: Sprinkle on salads or use as garnishes. Steep petals in vinegar 3 weeks for a floral-infused vinegar for salad dressings. Stir chopped petals into softened butter for a colorful spread. Large squash blossoms can be dipped in a batter and fried, or stuffed and baked.

Nutrients: Vitamins A and C (some varieties).

1 lb raw = varies
1 lb cooked = varies

Eggplant

Description: Eggplant is a tear-shaped, usually purple-black vegetable. Its fleshy and substantive texture makes it a good replacement for meat. Asian eggplant, a more slender variety, is typically sweeter.

Selection: Choose eggplant with bright, shiny, taut skin and no soft spots. Larger eggplants are more likely to have lots of seeds and a bitter flavor.

Storage and handling: Eggplant can be kept on the countertop for several days.

Preparation: Trim the green caps and slice or dice the flesh. Remove skin with a vegetable peeler if desired. Salting older eggplant before cooking removes bitter flavors. Cut as desired, sprinkle with salt, leave in colander for 30 minutes, squeeze gently, and pat dry. **Sauté** salted, drained cubes in small amount of hot oil 6–8 minutes, stirring or shaking constantly, until browned and tender. **Broil** peeled slices, brushed with oil and placed on a broiler pan rack, 5 inches from heat source until browned on each side. **Microwave** cubed eggplant, covered, 3–4 minutes.

Serving suggestions: Not usually eaten raw. Sauté eggplant with other vegetables or with garlic and herbs (p. 152). Roasted eggplant can be topped with a thin layer of pesto or olive tapenade, or sprinkled with cheese, and then broiled (p. 144). Try eggplant burgers (p. 168).

Nutrients (when cooked): fiber.

1 lb raw = 6 cups
1 lb cooked = 2½ cups

Fennel

SUMMER, AUTUMN

Description: Much like a licorice-flavored celery, fennel is crisp and crunchy with a pronounced flavor when raw. Cooked fennel has a much milder anise flavor and a soft, not stringy texture.

Selection: Choose large, firm, crisp fennel with creamy white bulbs and bright green fronds.

Storage and handling: Fennel will keep in a plastic bag in the refrigerator for 3–4 days.

Preparation: Remove the fronds (reserve for use as an herb) and stalks (use to grill with fish or thinly slice to eat). Trim a thick slice from the root end and slice the bulb in half. Remove the core from each half. Slice or chop if desired. **Steam** whole fennel bulbs in a basket over boiling water, covered, 8–15 minutes if you'll finish cooking by some other method, or 20–35 minutes till tender if serving immediately. **Microwave** whole bulbs in a covered dish with a little water, 8–10 minutes.

Serving suggestions: Add chilled raw fennel to salads or vegetable trays. The bulb is often used in Mediterranean dishes (p. 151). Boil diced bulb and add to rice, pasta, or polenta. Use the fronds for garnishes.

Nutrients: Vitamin C; potassium; fiber.

1 lb raw = 2½–3 cups
1 lb cooked = 2¼ cups

Grapes

AUTUMN

Description: Grapes come in a variety of colors (red, white, and blue) and types (seedless or with seeds, table grapes, or wine grapes). Concord grapes are the most common in farmers' markets and home gardens.

Selection: Choose clusters of richly colored, fragrant, plump grapes. They should be firmly attached to pliable stems. Avoid fruits that are soft, wrinkled, moldy, or wet.

Storage and handling: Refrigerate in a loosely sealed plastic bag for up to a week. Rinse in cold water when ready to eat.

Preparation: Remove large seeds if desired.

Serving suggestions: Eat table grapes as is, include on a fruit or cheese plate, or halve and add to salads. Frozen grapes are a refreshing treat or can be added to smoothies. Concord-type grapes make great pies (p. 270), jelly, and juice. Make focaccia with Concord grape halves pressed into the dough and sprinkled with sugar before baking.

Nutrients: Vitamins **C** (with skin) and **K**; anthocyanins antioxidants (red varieties).

1 lb raw = 2 cups
1 lb cooked = n/a

Green beans

Description: Green beans (which may be other colors as well, and are also referred to as string beans) have long, edible pods and small inner beans. Thick Romano beans take longer to cook, and thin, tender haricots verts cook quickly.

Selection: Choose crisp, firm, brightly colored beans that snap easily. Thinner beans are usually more tender and sweeter.

Storage and handling: Refrigerate green beans no more than a few days in a loosely sealed plastic bag. Before using, wash well.

Preparation: Snap off ends of pods by hand or trim with a small knife. Some green beans have strings that need to be removed before cooking. Very fresh beans are best boiled or steamed to retain their color and flavor, but older beans are more flavorful when braised or roasted. **Steam** or **boil** beans about 5 minutes. **Roast** in the oven (p. 67). **Microwave** a half pound of green beans, 4–7 minutes.

Serving suggestions: Eat fresh raw green beans plain. Dress cooked beans with butter, lemon butter, sautéed onions or mushrooms, toasted almonds, Parmesan cheese, ham, or cooked bacon (p. 140). Add a gingery sauce to steamed green beans (p. 156).

Nutrients: Vitamins A, **C**, K, folate; fiber.

1 lb raw = 4 cups
1 lb cooked = 2½ cups

Kale

Description: Kale, a hardy green, can survive severe frost. It grows in individual stalks and appears in the market in bunches. Curly, black (dinosaur, Tuscan, lacinato), and red kale, and other varieties are generally interchangeable and can be used in place of collard greens.

Selection: Choose dark green, crisp leaves and thinner stalks. After a frost kale is sweeter.

Storage and handling: Remove excess moisture and refrigerate in a loosely sealed plastic bag for up to 4 days. Before eating, wash thoroughly.

Preparation: Remove the tough stalk and central vein by hand (by sliding from the base to tip) or with a knife, and chop or tear leaves for cooking. **Boil** or **steam** 4–8 minutes. **Sauté** onions in a frypan, then add raw chopped kale and a few tablespoons of water, cover, and cook till kale is tender, about 8 minutes; uncover for a few minutes to allow water to evaporate. **Microwave** in a covered dish with a little water, about 4 minutes.

Serving suggestions: Slice young kale leaves and add to salads. Mature kale is not typically eaten raw. Sauté with corn and sweet red pepper (p. 235). Sprinkle cooked kale with vinegar; serve with polenta (p. 394). Add raw kale to soups for the last few minutes of cooking time (p. 221). Mix leftovers with mashed potatoes to make the Irish dish colcannon.

Nutrients (when boiled): Vitamins **A**, **C**, K; cancer-preventing compounds sulforaphane, isothiocyanate, and indoles; fiber. Also significant amount of Vitamin B6 and calcium.

1 lb raw = 8 cups
1 lb cooked = 2–3 cups

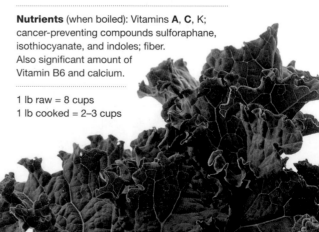

Kohlrabi

SUMMER, EARLY AUTUMN

Description: Kohlrabi consists of a long stalk and large leaves protruding from a spherical base. This base, a root, tastes like radishes when raw and broccoli when cooked. Varieties include purple and pale green.

Selection: Choose kohlrabi with fresh-looking leaves, bright, even color, and no soft spots or cracks. Bulbs the size of a peach or smaller yield best texture and flavor.

Storage and handling: Refrigerate in loosely sealed plastic bag for several days. If leaves show signs of decline, discard them before storing. Before eating, wash in cold water.

Preparation: Trim stalks and leaves. If eating raw, peel kohlrabi root to expose the white inner flesh, then cut as desired. If eating cooked, wait to peel until after cooking. **Bake** in a covered dish with a few tablespoons of liquid at 350° F / 180° C, 50–60 minutes. **Boil** covered, 30-35 minutes. **Microwave** whole trimmed kohlrabies in covered dish with a few tablespoons of liquid, 6–9 minutes. **Sauté** shredded peeled kohlrabi; first sprinkle with salt and let sit 30 minutes, then squeeze water out.

Serving suggestions: Raw kohlrabi slices or sticks make a tasty snack. Add slices to salads or grate and marinate in salad dressing. Season cooked kohlrabi with butter, cream sauce, cheese sauce, or fresh herbs. Try them in a sauté (p. 153). Cook leaves along with root or use as you would other hardy greens.

Nutrients (for bulb): Vitamins B6 and **C**; potassium; fiber.

1 lb raw = 1½ cup
1 lb cooked = 1 cup

Leeks

SPRING, SUMMER, AUTUMN

Description: This sweet, subtly flavored onion relative is often used for seasoning but can also be served as a vegetable on its own. Ramps are a wild variety of leek.

Selection: Choose firm, crisp leeks with dark green leaves. Thin or medium leeks (1½ inch in diameter at most) have the best flavor and texture; thicker leeks are fine for soup.

Storage and handling: Refrigerate loosely wrapped in plastic in the produce drawer for a week or more. Before eating, trim the dark green tops, tough outer leaves, and a very thin slice from the root end and reserve to flavor soup stocks. Halve leeks lengthwise and wash in a bowl of water, gently spreading the layers apart.

Preparation: Slice or cook whole. **Sauté** chopped leeks in several tablespoons of butter, 8–10 minutes. **Boil** in small amount of water, 12 minutes or until just tender. **Steam** in basket over boiling water, covered, about 15 minutes. Leeks don't **microwave** well.

Serving suggestions: Not typically eaten raw. Top cooked leeks with lemon butter, cream sauce, cheese sauce, marinara, or fresh tomato sauce. Or marinate in vinaigrette. Add leftovers to soups or mashed potatoes. Try them in a quiche (p. 78). Use in place of cooked onions in any recipe.

Nutrients: antitumor compound allicin; bioflavonoid antioxidants.

1 lb raw = 6 cups
1 lb cooked = n/a

Lettuce

SPRING, SUMMER, AUTUMN

Description: Lettuce varieties abound. Most head lettuces and looseleaf lettuces have relatively mild flavors, and vary in appearance, color, and texture. Other leafy greens used for salad include romaine, arugula, curly endive, frisée, chicory, and watercress; these are more intensely-flavored.

Selection: Choose crisp, fresh lettuce and salad greens. Because they are very perishable, they should be purchased only in excellent condition.

Storage and handling: Refrigerate crisper varieties up to 7 days, wrapped in slightly damp paper towels in a plastic bag from which the air has been removed. Before eating, separate leaves from the head and swish in a bowl of cold water until no grit is present. Dry in a salad spinner or make your own: place the greens in a clean pillowcase (one reserved for this purpose), take outside, and swing it around until the greens are dry.

Preparation: Be sure the greens are dry, as dry greens hold dressing better. Tear—do not cut—into pieces. Hardier, sharper-tasting greens like escarole and chicory can be **sautéed** in butter or oil.

Serving suggestions: Toss raw lettuce or greens with vinaigrette or your favorite dressing and chopped vegetables or fruit, toasted nuts, and/or dried fruit (p. 58); serve immediately. Leftover lettuce can be added to soup or quiche. The sharper tasting greens do well with a hot bacon dressing.

Nutrients: Vitamins A (dark green lettuces) and K; lutein and zeaxanthin antioxidants (green lettuce).

1 lb raw = 6–10 cups
1 lb cooked = n/a

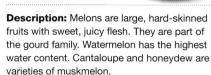

Melon

SUMMER

Description: Melons are large, hard-skinned fruits with sweet, juicy flesh. They are part of the gourd family. Watermelon has the highest water content. Cantaloupe and honeydew are varieties of muskmelon.

Selection: Melons should give to gentle pressure at the blossom end and smell sweet. Hard melons should sound hollow when knocked with a knuckle. Avoid any melons with lumps or soft spots and watermelons with a flat side. Choose cantaloupe that are heavy for their size, with a fruity aroma and thick, well-raised netting.

Storage and handling: Keep uncut melons at room temperature until fully ripened, then refrigerate for up to 5 days. Before cutting, wash the skin well. Cut melon can be refrigerated, wrapped tightly in plastic, up to 3 days.

Preparation: Cut honeydew and cantaloupe in half and scoop out the seeds. Remove skin if desired and cut into wedges, balls, or slices.

Serving suggestions: Eat melon plain or in fruit salads. Chill and drizzle with lime juice. Use in sherbets and sorbets.

Nutrients: Varies; most varieties are high in Vitamins A and C.

1 lb raw = 2 cups
1 lb cooked = n/a

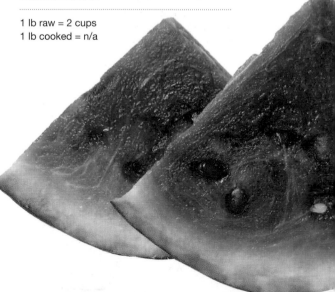

Mushrooms

Description: Edible varieties of this fungus include button, cremini, portobello, shiitake, oyster, morel, and chanterelle. Dried mushrooms are available year round.

Selection: Mushrooms should be dry and firm, never slimy. Specialty mushrooms should smell woodsy, not moldy or sharp.

Storage and handling: Blot excess moisture with paper towels. Place mushrooms in a paper bag (never plastic) and refrigerate several days. When ready to eat, use a damp paper towel to remove any dirt or brush gently with a vegetable brush. Wash only especially dirty mushrooms, since they absorb water and will become soft quickly.

Preparation: Halve, quarter, slice, or dice as desired. For shiitakes and portobellos, remove the stem. Mushrooms can be **broiled**, **grilled**, **roasted** or sautéed. **Sauté** by melting butter, adding halved or quartered mushrooms, increasing heat to medium-high, and cooking until juices have evaporated and mushrooms are browned, about 8 minutes. To use dried mushrooms, immerse them in boiling water and set aside for 20–30 minutes. Drain. Remove stems and chop as desired.

Serving suggestions: Add sliced raw mushrooms to tossed salads. Season cooked mushrooms with salt, pepper, and fresh herbs. Chop and add to soups and sauces (p. 76).

Nutrients: Vitamin D, riboflavin, niacin.

1 lb raw = 2–4 cups
1 lb cooked = 1¾ cup

Mesclun

Description: Mesclun is a blend of lettuces, herbs, and tender young greens usually used for salads. The flavor can vary from mild, if it's mostly lettuces, to peppery, if more arugula, chicory, cresses, frisée, radicchio, and mustard greens are included. The variation in colors and shapes makes for an attractive presentation.

Selection: Mesclun is very perishable, so buy it absolutely fresh—it should be richly colored and have no browning or wilting.

Storage and handling: Refrigerate up to 3 days wrapped in slightly damp towels in a plastic bag. Before using, swish in a bowl of cold water until no grit is present. Dry in a salad spinner or make your own: place the greens in a clean pillowcase (one reserved for this purpose), take it outside, and swing it around until the greens are dry.

Preparation: Make sure the mesclun is clean and dry, and then tear the leaves into desired sizes. The more peppery varieties can be cooked: remove any tough stems, tear into pieces, and **steam**, wilt, **stir-fry**, or **microwave**. Avoid overcooking.

Serving suggestions: Dress raw mesclun with a small amount of a light, mild dressing so as not to mask its delicate flavors. Especially delightful used in hummus sandwiches or pita pockets.

Nutrients: Varies.

1 lb raw = 6–10 cups
1 lb cooked = n/a

Okra

SUMMER

Description: Okra is a green, fuzzy, deeply ridged pod. Most common in warmer climates, it can also be grown in cooler areas if the proper variety and cultivation techniques are used.

Selection: Choose bright green pods about 3–4 inches long. They should be firm and moist, not spotted, moldy, limp, or dry.

Storage and handling: Store in a plastic bag in the refrigerator 2–3 days. When ready to use wash well in a bowl of cold water.

Preparation: Remove stem end and slice if desired. Prevent okra from becoming slimy by adding vinegar or other acidic ingredients such as tomatoes when **cooking**, or by breading okra with cornmeal before **frying**.

Serving suggestions: Okra can be fried (p. 144), pickled, or added to curries (p. 143), sautés, and soups. Okra is used in gumbo, a southern specialty soup, to help thicken it. Substitute okra for summer squash in ratatouille (p. 152). Dress cooked okra with butter and lemon juice, butter, and curry powder, or toss with a vinaigrette and chill.

Nutrients: Vitamins A, B6, **C**, **K**, thiamin, folate; calcium; fiber.

1 lb raw = 8 cups whole (4 c. sliced)
1 lb cooked = 2¼ cups

Onions

YEAR-ROUND

Description: Varieties of this bulb vegetable include yellow, red (milder and sweeter), white, pearl, Spanish (very mild), and sweet onions. Other members of the onion family include green onions, leeks, shallots, garlic, and garlic scapes.

Selection: Onions, garlic, and shallots should have dry, papery outer skins and be very hard. Green onions should have a bright color and firm texture.

Storage and handling: Store yellow and white onions somewhere cool and well-ventilated. Wrap green onions and sweet onions in plastic and store in the refrigerator.

Preparation: Cut off the stem and root end of the onion. Remove the papery outer layers of skin. Cut in half and lay each half flat side down to slice or chop. **Sauté** sliced or chopped onions in oil or butter till soft before adding to dishes. For a deeper, richer flavor, continue sautéeing until onions brown, or even longer until they become dark brown and caramelize, about 30 minutes over low heat. **Miorowave** peeled onions in a covered dish with a small amount of water, 5–6 minutes.

Serving suggestions: Use raw onions or green onions in salads (p. 65). Top sandwiches with sliced sweet onions. Serve cooked onions with melted butter and herbs or in a white cream sauce. Use the green stems from fresh onions for cooking or in salads if they are not too strong.

Nutrients: Vitamins B6 and C; antitumor compound allicin, bioflavonoid antioxidants; fiber.

1 lb raw = 4 cups sliced
1 lb cooked = 2 cups

Parsnips

AUTUMN, WINTER

Description: Parsnips, a root vegetable, look like creamy white carrots. They have a sweet, nutty flavor.

Selection: Choose firm, crisp parsnips; avoid any that bend or have soft spots. Smaller parsnips may be sweeter and creamier. If you buy large parsnips, taste the core—if it's tough or lacks flavor, you'll need to remove it before cooking.

Storage and handling: Refrigerate in a plastic bag for a week or more. Before eating, wash in cold water.

Preparation: Remove peel with a vegetable peeler and trim both ends. Cut as desired. **Boil** parsnip chunks, covered, about 15 minutes. **Steam** chunks in a basket over boiling water, covered, 8–10 minutes if you're eating as is, 12–15 minutes if you plan to purée. **Roast** in the oven (p. 307). **Microwave** chunks in a covered dish with a few tablespoons liquid, 4–6 minutes.

Serving suggestions: Cut raw fresh parsnips into sticks like carrots and eat with dip, or shred and add to salad. Season cooked parsnips with butter, salt, pepper, and herbs. Add sugar during sautéeing/braising for a glazed result. Also excellent paired with maple syrup in a cream soup (p. 288). Cooked parsnips can be puréed with or mashed instead of potatoes. Roasting enhances sweetness (p. 307).

Nutrients: Vitamins **C** and **K**, folate; potassium; **fiber**.

1 lb raw = 3 cups
1 lb cooked = 2 cups

Peaches

SUMMER

Description: Peaches are a round stone fruit with orange or white flesh and fuzzy skin. There are three main types: clingstone, with flesh that firmly adheres to the pit; semi-freestone; and freestone, with flesh that is easily separated from the pit. Other stone fruits include sweet or sour cherries, apricots, and plums.

Selection: Fruits should be fragrant and soft but not mushy. Skin near the stem should be yellow or cream colored; if it's green, the peach was picked too early.

Storage and handling: Store in a cool place. Do not refrigerate. Handle gently. Wash before eating.

Preparation: Slice around the seam and twist the two halves apart. Remove the pit by lifting or cutting it out. Pull skin off with a thin-bladed knife if desired. Slice or chop if desired. **Grill** peach halves brushed with melted butter over indirect heat 8–10 minutes, then drizzle with maple syrup. **Bake** whole unpeeled peaches, sprinkled with sugar, in a pan with a little water at 350° F / 180° C until soft.

Serving suggestions: Raw peaches, apricots, plums, and sweet cherries are delicious plain. Apricots combine well with chicken and pork in main dishes (p. 171). Use sour cherries and other stone fruits in baked desserts (p. 184).

Nutrients: Vitamins A and C; fiber.

1 lb raw = 2 cups
1 lb cooked = 2 cups or less

Pears

AUTUMN, WINTER

Description: The texture of pears ranges from very soft, creamy, and juicy to firm and crisp. Colors range from brown to gold to green to red.

Selection: Choose firm pears without bruises or soft spots.

Storage and handling: Pears will continue to ripen at room temperature. They are ripe when the flesh surrounding the stem yields slightly to gentle pressure. Store ripe pears in the refrigerator for up to 3 days. Wash in a bowl of cold water before eating.

Preparation: Halve or quarter lengthwise, remove stem and core with paring knife. Peel if desired; pear skins tend to toughen upon cooking. **Poach** by adding pears to hot flavorful liquid (fruit juice or water with citrus peel, sweetener, spices) and simmering, covered, until pears are transparent and just tender, basting occasionally. Halved pears can be poached in the microwave, 6–8 minutes. **Bake** like apples.

Serving suggestions: Eat fresh raw pears as is or add to salads (p. 229). Serve pears as part of a cheese, fruit, and nut plate. Use in baked desserts (p. 264).

Comments: Most pears discolor quickly after cutting, so use them quickly or toss with an acid source such as diluted lemon juice.

Nutrients: Vitamin C; antitumor compound allicin, bioflavonoid antioxidants, anthocyanin antioxidants (red-skinned varieties); fiber.

1 lb raw = 2¼ cups
1 lb cooked = 2 cups

Peas

SPRING, SUMMER

Description: Three main types are available. Shell peas need to be removed from a pod before eating. Sugar snap peas have sweet, edible pods and peas. Snow peas are an edible, young flat pod with immature peas inside.

Selection: Peas must be fresh. Look for bright green color and pods that feel crisp. Pods should snap, not bend. For snow peas, choose small flat pods.

Storage and handling: Use immediately, or refrigerate in a plastic bag for up to 4 days. Wash before eating.

Preparation: Shell peas: press your thumb into the pod seam until it pops open, then scrape the peas out with your thumb. Sugar snap or snow peas: remove the stem and pull down along the pod, removing any strings on the sides. **Boil** peas in small amount of water, 2–4 minutes, then drain and season or run under cold water to stop the cooking if serving cold. **Steam** in a basket over boiling water, covered, 4–5 minutes. **Microwave** in a covered dish with a little liquid, about 5 minutes.

Serving suggestions: Add raw peas to salads. Season boiled peas with butter and fresh herbs, sautéed onions, mushrooms, or toasted nuts. Add to stir-fries (p. 69) or make fresh pea soup (p. 55).

Nutrients: Vitamins **A**, B6, **C**, **K**, thiamin, riboflavin, niacin, folate; iron, potassium; lutein and zeaxanthin antioxidants; **fiber**.

1 lb raw = 4 cups unshelled (1 cup shelled)
1 lb cooked = 1 cup

Peppers

SUMMER, AUTUMN

Description: Peppers fall into two basic categories: sweet and hot. Sweet peppers can be green, red, orange, yellow, or purple. Green ones are actually unripe and have a stronger flavor. Hot peppers (chilies) range from relatively mild poblanos to astoundingly hot habañeros.

Selection: Look for firm, shiny, brightly colored peppers with no browning or mushy spots.

Storage and handling: Refrigerate 3–4 days in a plastic bag. Green peppers keep longer than ripe ones.

Preparation: For sweet peppers, cut around the stem, then pull on it to remove the core with seeds attached. Cut the pepper in half and trim any remaining membrane. For hot peppers, slice off the stem and halve the pepper. Remove the seeds and membrane if you wish to decrease the heat. **Sauté** sliced or chopped peppers in olive oil or butter, 3–10 minutes. **Roast** in the oven (p. 146). **Microwave** pepper pieces in a covered dish with a little water, 4–6 minutes for crisp-tender texture, 8–10 for very soft.

Serving suggestions: Add raw sweet peppers to vegetable platters or salads. Sauté peppers with other vegetables. Stuff whole sweet bell peppers (p. 157). Hot peppers are great in salsa (p. 195).

Nutrients: Vitamins A, B6, **C**, K; anthocyanin antioxidants (red and purple varieties), lutein and zeaxanthin antioxidants (green and yellow varieties); fiber.

1 lb raw = 2 cups
1 lb cooked = 2 cups or less

Persimmons

AUTUMN

Description: There are two commonly available types of these squat, orange fruits. Astringent, soft-ripe Hachiya persimmons are very tart unless fully ripe, when they turn sweet and gelatinous on the inside. Firm-ripe Fuyu persimmons are more like an apple, with a mild, sweet flavor.

Selection: Choose smooth, brightly colored persimmons that are plump and glossy. Ones with yellow patches are unripe.

Storage and handling: If not fully ripe, keep persimmons at room temperature until ripe, then eat right away or refrigerate a day or two.

Preparation: Wash soft-ripe persimmons gently, then cut in half. Cut out the core and discard the seeds. To make pulp, scoop out the flesh with a spoon, discard skins, and purée pulp or mash with a fork. Pulp freezes well. Crisp firm-ripe persimmons can be roasted, dried, or eaten raw; just remove the top green leaves and center core; there's no need to peel.

Serving suggestions: Dice or slice firm-ripe persimmons and add to fruit or vegetable salads. A soft-ripe persimmon is like a thin skin full of thick jelly. Use in smoothies or substitute persimmon pulp for zucchini in quick breads or cookies (p. 269).

Nutrients: Vitamins **A** and **C**; **fiber**.

1 lb raw = 2 cups
1 lb cooked = 2 cups or less

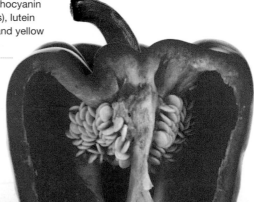

Potatoes

YEAR-ROUND

Description: These tubers come in three main types: baking potatoes, the most starchy, which become dry and fluffy when cooked; boiling potatoes, the least starchy; and all-purpose potatoes. Any variety harvested before it develops its full amount of starch is considered a new potato.

Selection: Choose smooth, firm potatoes with no mold, soft spots, sprouting, or green color.

Storage and handling: Store in a well-ventilated place away from apples or onions. New potatoes keep for only a week, but other types keep several weeks. Avoid sunlight, which causes potatoes to turn green. Before cooking, scrub potatoes with a brush in cold water or peel with a vegetable peeler and rinse.

Preparation: Boil chopped potatoes about 15 minutes. If desired, mash potatoes after draining well. **Bake** whole starchy potatoes at 400–450° F / 200–230° C, 45 minutes or longer. **Microwave** new or boiling potatoes in covered dish with ¼ cup water, 8–12 minutes. Microwave whole baking potatoes, pierced with a fork, 4–6 minutes for 1 potato.

Serving suggestions: Mix leftover mashed potatoes with a beaten egg and fry for potato pancakes. Try oven-roasted fries instead of french fries (p. 308). Use in soups (p. 285).

Nutrients (when baked with skin): Vitamins **B6** and **C**, thiamin, **niacin**, **folate**; iron, **potassium**; fiber.

1 lb raw = 3 cups sliced or chopped
1 lb cooked = 2¼ cups sliced or chopped
(1¾ cup mashed)

Pumpkins

AUTUMN, WINTER

Description: Pumpkins come in various sizes (traditionally round) and colors (traditionally orange). Some have been especially developed for pie making and seed roasting. Smaller pumpkins are generally better for cooking.

Selection: Make sure to buy the right pumpkin for your purpose. Pumpkins should be bright colored, firm, and have the stem attached.

Storage and handling: Store whole pumpkins 1-2 months in a dry, cool, well-ventilated spot. Once cut, pumpkin will keep refrigerated in a loosely sealed plastic bag for about a week. Wash outside of pumpkin before cutting.

Preparation: Bake unpeeled halves or wedges, seeds and pulp removed, flesh side down in a pan with a little water at 350° F / 180° C, 60–90 minutes. **Steam** chunks, covered, in a basket over boiling water, 15–20 minutes. **Boil** chunks 8–12 minutes or **microwave** in a covered dish, 8 minutes. Toss seeds with vegetable oil (1 tablespoon per cup of seeds) and salt (½–1 teaspoon per cup of seeds), spread on a cookie sheet, and bake at 250° F / 120° C until dry. Use seeds and fibers to flavor stock.

Serving suggestions: Not usually eaten raw. Use puréed cooked pumpkin in soups, bread (p. 216), pie, and cheesecake (p. 266).

Nutrients (when boiled): Vitamins **A** and C, riboflavin; potassium; alpha- and beta-carotene antioxidants; fiber.

1 lb raw = 2 cups chopped
1 lb cooked = 1 cup

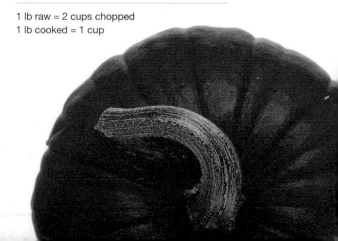

Raspberries

SUMMER, AUTUMN

Description: Raspberries and other brambleberries (blackberries, boysenberries, mulberries) are soft fruits with tart, intensely flavored juice. They come in a variety of colors—red, black, purple, and gold. They grow on canes with or without thorns. Their high liquid content and thin membranes make them fragile.

Selection: Look for firm, plump, richly colored berries with no soft spots or discolorations. All berries should be dry with no mold or signs of juice leaking on the container. They will not ripen after picking.

Storage and handling: Remove any berries that look overripe. Refrigerate up to 2 days. Do not wash berries until just before serving. Wash gently and drain well on paper towels.

Preparation: Use in recipes as desired.

Serving suggestions: Delicious plain or with yogurt. Blend into smoothies. Use in baked goods (p. 180), frozen desserts, jams (p. 208), and vinaigrettes (p. 135). Blackberries pair well with apples for pies (pp. 188–89).

Nutrients: Vitamins **C** and K; anthocyanins antioxidants (blackberries); **fiber**.

1 lb raw = 3 cups
1 lb cooked = n/a

Rhubarb

SPRING, SUMMER

Description: Rhubarb is a perennial that requires a winter dormancy. Only the thick red and green stalks are edible; the leaves and roots are toxic due to excessive oxalic acid. Rhubarb has a tart flavor, so is served sweetened and cooked.

Selection: Choose rhubarb that has a bright, vivid color and feels dry, firm, and crisp. Avoid stalks that are limp or wilted or have brown areas.

Storage and handling: Refrigerate in a plastic bag up to 1 week. Before using, wash well.

Preparation: Remove any leaves or root ends if still attached. Slice or chop as desired. Rhubarb is typically stewed or added to recipes for baked goods. It should be cooked only in nonaluminum pots because it will react with the metal.

Serving suggestions: Not eaten raw. Serve paired with sweeteners in sauces, baked goods, and desserts (p. 95). Strawberries and rhubarb are frequently used together since they ripen in the same season (p. 99).

Nutrients (when cooked): Vitamins C and **K**; **calcium**; fiber.

1 lb raw = 4 cups
1 lb cooked = 2 cups

Rutabagas

AUTUMN, WINTER

Description: Although rutabagas, a root vegetable, are often compared to turnips, they have a sweeter flavor and are not peppery, as turnips can be. They also have a lower moisture content than turnips and so keep better.

Selection: Choose rutabagas that are firm, smooth-skinned, and feel heavy for their size; avoid any with cracks or bruises.

Storage and handling: Refrigerate in a plastic bag up to 3 weeks. Before cooking, wash in a bowl of cold water.

Preparation: Pare the skin as well as a thin outer layer of the flesh. **Boil** chopped rutabaga 20–25 minutes. **Microwave** diced rutabaga, covered, for about 12 minutes. **Roast** in the oven (p. 307).

Serving suggestions: Shred young, tender rutabagas for use in salads. Mash and serve cooked rutabagas like or with mashed potatoes. Add diced rutabagas to chicken potpie or lamb stew (p. 321). As with other winter root vegetables, roasting brings out the sweetness (p. 307).

Nutrients: Vitamin **C**; potassium; fiber.

1 lb raw = 3½ cups
1 lb cooked = 2 cups

Spinach

SPRING, SUMMER, AUTUMN

Description: Spinach is a leafy green. Curly spinach requires cooking. Flat-leaf spinach is sweeter and more tender, so it can be used for cooking or salads. Tatsoi, an Asian vegetable, may substitute for spinach in cooking. Baby spinach is very tender and is ideal for salads.

Selection: Choose dark green spinach with a fresh smell.

Storage and handling: Refrigerate up to 3 days wrapped in slightly damp paper towels in a plastic bag. Before using, swish in a bowl of cold water until no grit is present. Dry in a salad spinner or make your own: place the greens in a clean pillowcase (one reserved for this purpose), take it outside, and swing it around until the greens are dry.

Preparation: If the stems seem tough, remove them by hand or with a knife. Cut or tear leaves as desired. **Steam**, covered, in a basket over boiling water, 5 minutes. **Microwave** in a covered dish with a little liquid, about 5 minutes. Fresh spinach decreases dramatically in volume when cooked: 2 pounds will cook down to 2 cups.

Serving suggestions: Use raw young tender leaves in salads (p. 61). Add chopped spinach to soups during the final cooking minutes. Season steamed spinach with butter, salt, and pepper. Sauté with garlic and blend with cream cheese and seasonings to make a dip (p. 99).

Nutrients: Vitamins **A**, C, **K**, folate; lutein and zeaxanthin antioxidants.

1 lb raw = 3–6 cups
1 lb cooked = 1 cup

Strawberries

SPRING, SUMMER

Description: The first berry of the season, strawberries are plump, sweet red fruits with tiny seeds dotting their exterior. There are two types: the traditional June-bearing and the day-neutral, which bear all summer long.

Selection: Choose plump, bright red berries with fresh green caps attached. Avoid limp, wilted, moldy, or bruised berries as well as those that have white or green parts. They will not ripen after picking.

Storage and handling: Ripe strawberries don't keep well, but they can be refrigerated for 1–2 days. Handle gently as they bruise easily. Immediately before serving, swish in a bowl of cold water. Do not soak.

Preparation: Remove caps and slice as desired. While strawberries are usually eaten raw, they can be cooked in desserts or jams. To obtain the most flavor, mash or crush the berries.

Serving suggestions: Halve, quarter, or slice fresh berries and sprinkle with a little sugar (not necessary if berries are very sweet), let stand 5–10 minutes to allow juices to form, and serve as is or over shortcake (p. 379). Add sliced fresh strawberries to salads of fresh greens (p. 61). Try them in a chilled fruit soup (p. 57).

Nutrients: Vitamin **C**; anthocyanin antioxidants; fiber.

1 lb raw = 2⅔ cups
1 lb cooked = n/a

Summer squash

SUMMER

Description: Three main kinds of summer squash are available: zucchini, yellow, and pattypan. They range in color from a white, light green through yellow to almost black. In shape, they range from round with scalloped edge to crookneck to long.

Selection: Choose young tender squash, small to medium in size, with shiny, taut skin. Avoid any with soft spots or scarring.

Storage and handling: Refrigerate in a plastic bag for up to a week. When ready to use, wash and trim the ends. No need to peel if young and tender. Use squash blossoms the day they are picked or store in a plastic bag for a day or two.

Preparation: **Sauté** thin half-moons of zucchini and yellow squash in olive oil and garlic, and serve as a side dish or toss with pasta. **Steam** peeled squash chunks in a basket, covered, over boiling water, 15–20 minutes. **Boil** unpeeled chunks of squash until soft, about 20 minutes.

Serving suggestions: Use young squash raw in salads (p. 126) or on vegetable trays. Since squash are rather bland in themselves they are usually paired with other foods such as tomatoes or herbs (p. 138). Larger squash can be stuffed. Shred and use in baked goods—muffins, brownies (p. 192), or cakes (p. 327). Stuff and fry squash blossoms or slice them into other dishes.

Nutrients: Vitamins B6 and **C**, riboflavin.

1 lb raw = 4 cups
1 lb cooked = 2½–3 cups

Sweet potatoes

AUTUMN, WINTER

Description: In addition to the commonly seen orange, these tubers can have yellow, white, or even purple flesh. Although sweet potatoes are sometimes referred to as yams, true yams are quite different, with very thick skin and starchy flesh.

Selection: Choose firm, unblemished sweet potatoes.

Storage and handling: Store in a dark, cool (55–58° F / 13–15° C), well-ventilated place, wrapped individually in newspaper, for a month or more. Before cooking, scrub sweet potatoes with a brush in a bowl of cold water and peel if desired.

Preparation: Boil whole unpeeled sweet potatoes 35–45 minutes. To preserve nutrients, peel, if desired, after cooking. **Microwave** whole sweet potatoes, pricked with a fork, about 8 minutes. Microwave chunks, covered, about 5 minutes. **Bake** whole unpeeled sweet potatoes, rubbed with a little oil if desired, at 350° F / 180° C, 45–50 minutes.

Serving suggestions: Cooked sweet potatoes take well to sweet spices like cinnamon, ginger, nutmeg. Mash cooked sweet potatoes and serve seasoned with butter, salt, and pepper; or mixed with applesauce, butter, and sweet spices; or topped with chopped nuts and baked. Great paired with black beans (p. 312).

Nutrients (when cooked): Vitamins **A**, **B6**, **C**, thiamin, niacin, riboflavin; **potassium**; alpha- and beta-carotene antioxidants; fiber.

1 lb raw = 3 cups sliced or chopped
1 lb cooked = 1–1¼ cup puréed

Swiss chard

SUMMER, AUTUMN

Description: Swiss chard's dark green, ruffled leaves are similar to spinach but chewier. Chard stems come in many colors—all have similar flavor and cooking properties.

Selection: Choose bunches with dark green leaves and vividly colored stems. Leaves and stems should feel crisp and smell fresh and earthy.

Storage and handling: Store in a loosely sealed plastic bag in the refrigerator, excess moisture removed, for 3–5 days. Before using, cut leaves away from the stems. Wash leaves in a series of bowls of cold water. Rinse stems and trim blemishes.

Preparation: Swiss chard stems are tougher than the leaves and require longer cooking time. **Boil** stems, cut into 1- to 2-inch lengths, about 8 minutes. Add leaves after the stems have cooked 5 minutes.

Serving suggestions: Very tender young chard leaves may be added to green salads. Cooked chard leaves may be chilled and dressed with vinaigrette. Add raw sliced stems or leaves to soups; allow 10 minutes to cook stems, 4–5 minutes for leaves. Marinate blanched stems in a vinaigrette and serve at room temperature. Combine cooked greens with eggs, milk, bread, and cheese and bake (p. 243).

Nutrients (when boiled): Vitamins **A**, **C**, E, **K**; calcium, **iron**, **potassium**; lutein and zeaxanthin antioxidants; fiber.

1 lb raw = 5–6 cups
1 lb cooked = 2–3 cups

Tomatillos

Description: Tomatillos, also called Mexican green tomatoes, are a tomato relative. These small (1- to 2-inch diameter), tart green vegetables grow encased in papery husks that split and become purplish when ripe. Tomatillos can ripen to yellow but are better used green. Another husk tomato is the ground cherry, which is similar in size and shape to a cherry tomato but is orange in color.

Selection: Choose tomatillos that are firm, green, shiny, and firmly attached to their husks. Avoid those that have yellowed or feel sticky.

Storage and handling: Store in a paper bag in the refrigerator up to 1 month. Pull off papery husks by hand, then wash by swishing in a bowl of cold water.

Preparation: Boil 15–20 minutes or until soft. **Roast** unhusked tomatillos at 450° F / 230° C for 10–15 minutes or until soft.

Serving suggestions: Add chopped raw tomatillos to guacamole. Boil tomatillos with chilies, onions, and garlic in broth till soft, then purée in blender with cilantro and lime juice for salsa verde (green salsa). Try them in enchiladas (p. 174). Ground cherries can be eaten raw, used in salads, desserts (p. 186), and jams and jellies. They are also excellent dipped in chocolate.

Nutrients: Vitamins **C** and K, niacin; potassium; fiber.

1 lb raw = 2 cups
1 lb cooked = 1½ cup

Tomatoes

Description: Tomatoes come in several colors (red, orange, yellow, and green) and shapes (round, plum, and cherry). Yellow and orange ones are often lower in acid content than the more common red.

Selection: Look for vivid colors and smooth skins. Ripe tomatoes will give slightly when squeezed gently.

Storage and handling: Store tomatoes on the counter, never in the refrigerator. Ripe tomatoes will last several days this way, and not quite ripe ones will continue to ripen.

Preparation: Remove the core by cutting around the stem end with a small serrated knife. If desired, remove the skin by dipping tomatoes in boiling water for 10–30 seconds, until the skins crack; then dip quickly in cold water. Cut off stem ends and slip off skins. To remove seeds: cut off top and bottom of tomato, reserve. Squeeze middle section gently. For cherry or grape tomatoes, remove any green stems. **Bake**, **broil**, **grill**, or **sauté** tomatoes. **Microwave**, covered, 3–4 minutes.

Serving suggestions: Eat fresh tomatoes sliced or in sandwiches. Cherry tomatoes are a tasty snack, with or without dip. Add chopped tomatoes or halved cherry tomatoes to salad or pasta (p. 149). Plum tomatoes are well suited to cooking; use in cooked salsa and Italian dishes (p. 160).

Nutrients: Vitamins A and **C**; potassium; antioxidant lycopene (highest in cooked tomato products).

1 lb raw = 2 cups
1 lb cooked = 1½ cup

Turnips

AUTUMN, WINTER

Description: When young and fresh, these half-white, half-purple root vegetables range in flavor from very sweet to a little peppery; older ones can be hot and bitter.

Selection: Choose smooth, unblemished turnips. They should feel firm and heavy for their size. Greens should look fresh. Turnips 2 inches or less in diameter are usually more tender.

Storage and handling: Refrigerate in a plastic bag up to a week. Wash in a bowl of cold water.

Preparation: Baby turnips need not be peeled, but tough skins of other turnips can be removed with a peeler or knife. **Blanch** large or old turnips in boiling water 4–5 minutes to get rid of a strong or bitter flavor. **Boil** whole or chopped turnips; pieces will take 5–8 minutes, small whole turnips 15–20 minutes. **Roast** in the oven (p. 307). **Microwave** small whole turnips in a little water, covered, 4 minutes. Drain and finish cooking as desired. Turnip greens may be boiled or steamed.

Serving suggestions: Slice or julienne young turnips and eat raw with a dip or peanut butter. Add shredded raw turnips to salads. Bake turnips with sweeter root vegetables like carrots and parsnips. When boiled and then puréed with a potato, turnips make a delicious, low-starch alternative to mashed potatoes.

Nutrients: Vitamin C.

1 lb raw = 3½ cups
1 lb cooked = 2 cups

Wild greens

LATE WINTER, EARLY SPRING

Description: Edible wild greens include dandelion greens, purslane, ramps, sorrel, lamb's-quarters, chickweed, chicory, garlic mustard, shepherd's purse, fiddleheads, wild prickly lettuce, mache, and onion grass. Native varieties vary according to geography and climate.

Selection: Use caution! In many cases, poisonous plants closely resemble—and grow near—the edible ones. Pick wild greens only if you're certain they have not been sprayed with pesticides or herbicides. Most edible wild greens are best when picked very early in spring, when they are young and tender.

Storage and handling: Refrigerate up to 3 days wrapped in slightly damp paper towels in a plastic bag. Wash by swishing in a bowl of cold water until no grit is present. Dry in a salad spinner or make your own: place the greens in a clean pillowcase (one reserved for this purpose), take it outside, and swing it around until the greens are dry.

Preparation: Most greens can be **sautéed, boiled,** or wilted by adding to a hot dressing.

Serving suggestions: Use raw in salads if tender. Chop dandelion greens and stir into a warm bacon dressing (p. 63). Add fresh greens to soups. Try sorrel with rhubarb in a crisp dessert (p. 93).

Nutrients: Varies; some varieties are high in Vitamins A, C, K.

1 lb raw = varies
1 lb cooked = varies

Winter squash

Description: Most have yellow or orange flesh. Butternut and acorn are two popular varieties. Spaghetti squash becomes like long strands of spaghetti upon cooking. Delicata are a smaller cylindrical squash that cook quickly and have a thin skin. Sugar loaf is a shorter and sweeter version of delicata.

Selection: Choose hard winter squash that feels heavy for its size and has an intact stem.

Storage and handling: Store in a cool, dry place for several weeks. Wash before cutting.

Preparation: Cut squash in half and remove seeds. (To make this easier, pierce squash and microwave 1–2 minutes.) Use seeds and fibers to flavor stock. Butternut squash can be peeled before cooking. **Bake** with cut sides down in a pan with a little water, at 400° F / 200° C for 30 minutes. Bake spaghetti squash whole, pricking with a fork first, 40–90 minutes at 350° F / 180° C. **Steam** peeled squash chunks in a basket, covered, over boiling water, 15–20 minutes. **Boil** unpeeled chunks of squash until soft, about 20 minutes. **Microwave** in a covered dish; halved squash takes 12–13 minutes, squash chunks about 8 minutes. Microwave spaghetti squash whole (poke a few holes in the skin first), 15 minutes, then scrape flesh from peel with a fork, separating into strands.

Serving suggestions: Flavor cooked squash with brown sugar or maple syrup and butter, or olive oil and herbs. Cooked spaghetti squash can be used like pasta. Squash halves can be stuffed (p. 253).

Nutrients (when cooked): Varies; most varieties are high in Vitamins A and C, potassium, alpha- and beta-carotene antioxidants, fiber.

1 lb raw = 2 cups diced
1 lb cooked = 1 cup

Herbs

Description: Fresh herbs, a natural complement to fresh produce, are varied: annuals, biennials, and perennials; strong or mild, sweet or sour. They can be grown year-round in mild climates or in a pot on your windowsill.

Selection: Choose herbs that look like a living plant, fresh and green. Avoid those that are shriveled or have dark spots.

Storage and handling: Once picked, herbs do not keep long. Store them upright in a glass of water in the refrigerator, first removing any damaged leaves and slightly trimming the stalks. Or wrap them in a damp paper towel and store in a plastic bag in the refrigerator produce drawer.

Preparation: When ready to use, swish in a bowl of cold water, wrap in paper towels (or a clean dish towel), and shake dry. Chop and use in recipes; or tear or snip fresh herbs for better flavor. To dry herbs, tie together bunches and hang them upside down in a cool, dark place. When dry, crumble the leaves and store in small airtight jars. Dried herbs are more pungent in flavor than fresh, so use only 1 teaspoon of the dried herb where you would use 2–3 teaspoons of the fresh.

HOW TO USE FRESH HERBS:

BASIL: An indispensable ingredient of Italian cooking. Tear leaves to sprinkle over salads and sliced tomatoes or add to pasta sauces and Mediterranean cooked dishes at the last minute. Make pesto (p. 193).

BAY LEAF: Use in stews, soups, and sauces. Add to marinades and stock; boil in milk for custard or rice pudding. Always remove before serving.

CHIVES: A versatile flavoring and garnish. Finely snipped chives go well with eggs, salads, soft cheeses, potatoes, and fish (p. 90). When cooking with chives, add at the last minute to retain their delicate flavor.

CILANTRO / CORIANDER: Prized for its fresh, clean fragrance and flavor, cilantro (fresh coriander) is widely used in Middle Eastern, Asian, and Mexican cooking. Add fresh leaves to salad, salsa, dip (p. 397), curry, and chili; it is best included at the end of cooking time. Cook chopped stems with beans and soups. Add coriander seeds, which have a distinctly different, sweeter taste, to soups, sauces, and vegetable dishes.

DILL: The mellow flavor of dill leaves, or dill weed, combines well with potato dishes (p. 303), yogurt dips, cucumber salads, dressings, autumn and winter stews, green beans, and fish dishes. Use the flowering tops or seed in egg, seafood, and potato dishes, or for pickling.

MARJORAM: A taste reminiscent of oregano, but with a sweeter flavor. Can be used in soups, stews, bean dishes, dressings, and sauces, and in marinades for vegetables, fish, or lamb (p. 88).

MINT: Mints can refresh, cool, and enliven. Infuse for an invigorating tea (p. 100). Add fresh spearmint or applemint to new potatoes, peas, fruit salads, and drinks.

OREGANO: Indispensable in Mediterranean cooking, it is particularly well-suited to tomato-based sauces. Try rubbing on roasting meat or using in meatballs (p. 373).

PARSLEY: Flat-leaf parsley has the most flavor and is best for cooking (p. 360). Sauté finely chopped leaves with garlic and add at the last minute to steak, fried fish, or vegetables. Sprinkle finely chopped curly parsley over boiled potatoes.

ROSEMARY: Add sparingly to meat dishes, particularly lamb and pork. Infuse slow-cooking dishes with sprigs; remove before serving. Sprinkle over focaccia (p. 112–13). Makes a delicious herb butter for vegetables.

SAGE: This strong-flavored herb combines well with other strong flavors. Mix leaves with onion for poultry stuffing. Cook with rich, fatty meats such as pork and duck or with vegetables (p. 240). Blend into cheeses or butter.

SAVORY: Its peppery spiciness improves the flavor of legumes and all kinds of beans, even frozen or canned. Use in sauces (p. 70). Adds flavor to salt-free diets.

THYME: Fresh thyme is very pungent—use sparingly. Add to stocks, marinades, stuffings, sauces, and soups. Sprinkle over roasted vegetables (p. 72). Also suits poultry, shellfish, and game. Lemon thyme is a wild variety with a more pronounced lemon aroma. Great in bread (p. 108).

Yahweh, what variety you have created
arranging everything so wisely:
Earth is completely full of things you have made.
(Psalm 104:24 JB)

Snow turns to mud. Mud turns to humus. And we leave our cocoons of artificial light and heat to breathe the fresh air, feel the sun's warmth, and plunge our hands into the soil. All around us the gray of winter recedes as bright shades of green burst forth. Spring invites us to connect with the land on which we live and recognize that eating locally and seasonally is healthy for the earth and our environment.

spring

Breads and Breakfast

Soups

Salads

Sides

Main Dishes

Desserts

Extras

asparagus

garlic scapes

green onions

leeks

lettuce

maple syrup

mint

mushrooms

new potatoes

peas

radishes

rhubarb

spinach

strawberries

wild greens

Invitations to Action

Visit a farmers' market to see what is in season where you live.

Grow something edible—even if it is only an herb in a flower pot.

Choose sustainably grown or organic foods.

If eating seasonally is new to you, start with a goal of eating two to three seasonal meals a week.

Learn to be adventuresome at your farmers' market and try new foods. Small local farmers play an important role in preserving crop genetic diversity.

Choose fish and seafood based on what is locally available, abundant, and well-managed.

connect with the land

Vegetarian Menu

Weeknight Menu

. . . .

86 **Chicken or Tofu Stir-Fry**
    Rice or Pasta of choice
92 **Rhubarb Sauce over ice cream**

. . . .

61 **Strawberry Spinach Salad**
46 **Maple Walnut Scones**

Weekend Menu

. . . .

90 **Baked Trout with Lemon Garlic**
    or Asian Grilled Salmon
72 **Herb Roasted New Potatoes**
67 **Roasted Asparagus**
95 **Rhubarb Almond Flake**

**Convert some of
your lawn into a
vegetable garden.**

**Use drip irrigation
or use a soaker
hose to apply
water slowly to
the base of plants.
Large amounts of
water are lost by
sprinklers that spray
water into the air.**

**Plant fruit or nut
trees.**

Maple Walnut Scones

Good for breakfast, dessert, or with a fresh salad for supper.

. . . .

3½ cups / 875 ml flour
1 cup / 250 ml walnuts or other nuts, finely chopped
4 teaspoons baking powder
1 teaspoon salt
Combine thoroughly.

⅔ cup / 150 ml butter, chilled
Cut in until mixture resembles coarse crumbs.

1 cup / 250 ml milk
½ cup / 125 ml maple syrup
Stir in and work into soft dough; knead 5–6 times. Roll out ½ inch /
1 cm thick, about a 7-inch / 18-cm round. Cut into 10–12 wedges;
place on greased baking sheet. Bake in preheated oven at 425° F /
220° C until golden, 15–18 minutes. Serve immediately.

Yields 10–12 scones
. . . .

JOANNE BOWMAN, BROOKLINE, MASSACHUSETTS

Today the air feels pregnant with spring. Oh, I admit it doesn't look real spring-like with eight inches of snow on the ground. But the air—ah, just take a breath! In the sunshine it's warm, fresh, expectant.

Yes, today's the day. Get out the brace and bit, the hammer, the old milk jugs and the spouts. Put on your boots and coat. It's maple-sugaring time.

Life is surging up the trees. Of course, it still looks like winter. The trees are still naked; the ground is still covered with snow. But here's a maple tree. You drill the first hole. Press hard and turn. Slowly the wood shavings fall to the ground. Ah, they're damp. Remove the bit. Clean the hole. Look! A drop—two, three. The sap is running!
—MBL

Sustainable agriculture is concerned with ways of farming that can go on indefinitely—producing enough safe, healthy food for all of us. This means caring for the land, the soil: the source of our food. It means caring for the broader ecological system: water supplies, the air, and wildlife whose lives are tied to ours.

Sustained agriculture is also concerned with money. In addition to biological balance, if the system is not economically viable, it won't last.

Finally, sustainable agriculture is concerned with quality of life—for those who produce our food as well as society as a whole.
—CHW

Rhubarb Muffins

. . . .

1½ cup / 375 ml flour (may use all whole wheat flour)
1 cup / 250 ml whole wheat flour
1 teaspoon baking soda
1 teaspoon baking powder
½ teaspoon salt
Combine thoroughly.

1 cup / 250 ml buttermilk, sour milk, or plain yogurt
¾ cup / 175 ml brown sugar
½ cup / 125 ml oil
1 egg, beaten
2 teaspoons vanilla
In a separate bowl, mix well. Stir in dry ingredients until just moistened.

1½ cup / 375 ml rhubarb, diced
½ cup / 125 ml nuts, toasted and chopped (optional)
Stir in. Fill greased muffin tins two-thirds full.

¼ cup / 60 ml sugar
1 tablespoon butter, melted
1 teaspoon ground cinnamon
1 teaspoon flour
Combine and sprinkle on top of batter. Bake in preheated oven at 375° F / 190° C until toothpick inserted in center comes out clean, 20 minutes. Remove from pans and cool on wire racks.

Yields 12 muffins

. . . .

MARILYN SWARTZENTRUBER, GOSHEN, INDIANA
CATHERINE KLASSEN, LANDMARK, MANITOBA

Strawberry Bread

"A coworker gave me this recipe when she heard about all the strawberries I was getting from our little backyard patch," says contributor Mary Ann Weber.

. . . .

1 cup / 250 ml flour
½ cup / 125 ml whole wheat flour
2 teaspoons ground cinnamon
½ teaspoon salt
½ teaspoon baking soda
Combine in a medium bowl. Set aside.

1¼ cup / 300 ml strawberries, mashed
¾ cup / 175 ml sugar
⅔ cup / 150 ml oil
2 eggs
Mix together in a large bowl. Stir in dry ingredients until just combined. Pour into greased 8-inch / 1.5-L loaf pan and bake in preheated oven at 350° F / 180° C until toothpick inserted in center comes out clean, 1 hour.

Yields 1 loaf Ⓥ
. . . .

Summer variation: Replace strawberries with peeled, finely chopped peaches, blueberries, or a combination.

. . . .

MARY ANN WEBER, GOSHEN, INDIANA
SARAH MYERS, MOUNT JOY, PENNSYLVANIA
MARY KEITH, SEFFNER, FLORIDA

Fields and fields of corn. Or acres and acres of soybeans. This is the picture of the typical large corporate farm of modern agriculture. In 2007 the average U.S. farm was 421 acres, and monoculture—planting one crop—and heavy, sophisticated machinery make it possible for just a few people to farm so much land. But monoculture depletes the quality and resiliency of the soil. Erosion occurs more frequently, washing away precious topsoil.
—CHW

"Yahweh, what variety you have created arranging everything so wisely: Earth is completely full of things you have made." (Psalm 104:24, Jerusalem Bible)

On the hillside between my house and garden I've identified over twenty varieties of spring flowers—from the common dandelion to the less common jack-in-the-pulpit. I'm sure there are more that I haven't identified. Indeed God has created variety and arranged things so wisely. It makes me wonder if humanity's use of monoculture is not so wise. —MBL

Strawberry Brunch Soufflé

Don't let the "soufflé" title mislead you; this dish is super simple to make. It must be served straight from the oven, so have your fruit and toppings (and hungry guests) ready at the table. In summer, try juicy berries or sliced peaches.

. . . .

3 cups / 750 ml strawberries or other fresh fruit, sliced
2 tablespoons sugar
Sprinkle sugar on fruit, toss gently, and set aside.

2 tablespoons butter
Preheat oven to 375° F / 190° C. While oven heats, place butter in 9-inch / 1-L pie pan and place in oven to melt. Swirl pan to grease bottom and sides.

3 eggs
1½ cup / 375 ml milk
Beat together with mixer or in blender.

¾ cup / 175 ml flour
⅓ cup / 75 ml sugar
¼ teaspoon salt
¼ teaspoon vanilla
Add and beat until smooth. Pour batter into pie pan and bake until edges are golden brown and center is set, 25–30 minutes. Spoon berries on top and serve immediately, cut into wedges. Pass sour cream or plain yogurt and brown sugar to sprinkle on top.

Serves 4 Ⓥ
. . . .

SHERYL SHENK, HARRISONBURG, VIRGINIA

Spring Celebration Soup

An excellent meal starter. Serve with a hearty bread such as Whole Wheat Flax Bread (p. 347).

. . . .

2 cloves garlic, minced
In soup pot sauté in 1 tablespoon olive oil until golden, 1 minute.

⅓ cup / 75 ml green onions, chopped
1 cup / 250 ml carrots, thinly sliced
Add and sauté 5–7 minutes.

1 cup / 250 ml asparagus, chopped
2 cups / 500 ml chicken or light vegetable broth
2–3 tablespoons lemon juice (fresh preferred)
⅛ teaspoon salt
Add and cook gently until asparagus is just barely tender (do not overcook).

½ cup / 125 ml watercress or spinach, torn
2–4 tablespoons fresh parsley, chopped
Stir in and heat through, 1–2 minutes. Garnish with chopped fresh basil and grated Swiss or Parmesan cheese. Serve immediately.

Serves 2–4
. . . .

KELLI BURKHOLDER KING, GOSHEN, INDIANA

The pasture, bleached and cold two weeks ago,
Begins to grow in the spring light and rain;
The new grass trembles under the wind's flow.
The flock, barn-weary, comes to it again,
New to the lambs, a place their mothers know,
Welcoming, bright, and savory in its green,
So fully does the time recover it.
Nibbles of pleasure go all over it.
—Wendell Berry, author and farmer[1]

Velvety Vegetable Soup

. . . .

1 medium onion, chopped
4 cups / 1 L leeks, diced, white part and 1 inch / 2.5 cm
  of green
1 cup / 250 ml celery, diced
Sauté in ¼ cup / 60 ml olive oil over medium-low heat until wilted,
15 minutes.

2 tablespoons fresh tarragon, chopped; or 2 teaspoons dried
1 tablespoon fresh thyme, chopped; or 1 teaspoon dried
1 teaspoon salt, or to taste
½ teaspoon pepper
Add and stir well.

4 cups / 1 L chicken or vegetable broth
3 cups / 750 ml potatoes, diced
Add, cover, and simmer until potatoes are tender, 15 minutes.

1 bunch spinach, chopped
Add and simmer for 5 minutes. Remove from heat. Purée with
immersion blender in pot or in small batches in regular blender or
food processor. Return soup to pot and place over low heat.

½ cup / 125 ml milk (optional)
Add, if using, and heat through. Add additional water or broth if
thinner consistency is preferred. Adjust seasonings and serve.
Optional garnish: a swirl of plain yogurt and/or sprigs of fresh
herbs, such as parsley, thyme, or a celery leaf. Purple chive
blossoms are beautiful over the pale green soup.

Serves 4–6
. . . .

LISA LOEWEN EBERSOLE, CORVALLIS, OREGON

Just as the overuse of antibiotics in the human body makes diseases resistant to them, pesticides used on farms become less effective the more they're used. Statistics from the U.S. Department of Agriculture show that in 2000, U.S. farms used ten times the amount and toxicity of insecticides as was used on farms in 1945, but the damage by pests had increased rather than fallen.[2]
—CHW

Sausage and Greens Soup

"The soup used to be referred to as 'weed soup' because of all the greens,"
says contributor Alison Froese-Stoddard. The green onions or chives, dill, and
sorrel—well worth seeking out for this soup—may be frozen together in recipe
portions for quick use in wintertime, notes contributor Anna Ens.

. . . .

8 ounces / 250 g bulk sausage
Brown in soup pot and drain all but a spoonful of fat.
Remove meat.

1 cup / 250 ml onion, green onions, or chives, chopped
garlic scapes to taste, minced (optional)
Sauté in reserved fat until soft. Return sausage to soup pot.

4 cups / 1 L chicken or vegetable broth
1 cup / 250 ml potatoes, diced
salt and pepper to taste
Add, bring to boil, reduce heat, and simmer until potatoes are soft,
10–15 minutes.

1½ cup / 375 ml evaporated milk
1–3 cups / 250–750 ml fresh spinach, kale, dandelion,
    lamb's-quarters, purslane, burdock, watercress, or
    other tender young greens, chopped
parsley to taste, chopped (optional)
Add and cook until tender (just 1 minute for spinach, a few extra
minutes for greens such as kale or dandelion). Garnish each bowl
with freshly grated Parmesan cheese.

Serves 4
. . . .

Somma Borscht variation: Substitute chopped cooked ham and
ham broth. Reduce milk to ¼ cup / 60 ml. Use tangy fresh sorrel if
available, but if not, add 1 tablespoon vinegar with the greens, plus
2–4 tablespoons chopped fresh dill. Optional: Carefully break an
egg or two into the hot soup and cook without stirring until eggs
are cooked. Or serve with chopped hard-cooked eggs.

. . . .

ALISON FROESE-STODDARD, WINNIPEG, MANITOBA
ANNA ENS, WINNIPEG, MANITOBA
SARAH BEACHY, HARRISONBURG, VIRGINIA

Asparagus Soup

Using nonfat dry milk powder allows you to increase the nutrients and "creamy-ness" without the fat, notes contributor Mary Beth Lind. "Most of my old cream soup recipes call for real cream. Now I seldom cook with cream but I still like a 'fuller' taste, so I use extra dry milk power."

. . . .

1 pound / 500 g asparagus
Cut off tip ends and blanch them until just tender, 3–5 minutes. Drain (saving water for some of the broth) and set aside asparagus tips. Chop the spears, peeling the tough ends first if needed.

2 cups / 500 ml water, or chicken or vegetable broth
1 medium potato, peeled and chopped
1 small onion, chopped (optional)
1 stalk celery or celery leaves, chopped (optional)
Cook with chopped asparagus spears until soft, 15–20 minutes. Remove from heat, cool slightly, and purée until smooth. Return to heat.

2 cups / 500 ml chicken or vegetable broth
1 cup / 250 ml dry milk powder
2 tablespoons flour
salt and pepper to taste
Blend separately. Add to soup and cook over medium heat, stirring constantly until mixture thickens slightly.

½ cup / 125 ml plain yogurt
Drain yogurt slightly through a fine mesh strainer or cheesecloth. Place a dab of yogurt in each bowl and pour hot soup over it. Garnish with the reserved asparagus tips.

Serves 4
. . . .

Summer/autumn options: Substitute broccoli, cauliflower, or leeks (not in combination) for the asparagus spears, lengthening cooking time of vegetables as needed.

. . . .

MARY BETH LIND, HARMAN, WEST VIRGINIA
JILL HEATWOLE, PITTSVILLE, MARYLAND

Fresh Pea Soup

The green of spring in a bowl. Use frozen peas in winter for a delicious reminder that spring is coming soon.

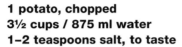

....

1 onion, chopped
In large saucepan sauté in 1 tablespoon olive oil until golden, 7–10 minutes.

1 potato, chopped
3½ cups / 875 ml water
1–2 teaspoons salt, to taste
Add and cook over medium heat until soft, 10–15 minutes.

3 cups / 750 ml peas
Add and cook until bright green. Purée in blender or food processor or with immersion blender. Taste and adjust seasoning. Serve warm. Optional garnish: a dollop of sour cream or plain yogurt in each bowl, or a sprinkle of chopped fresh dill or parsley.

Serves 4 (V) (Gf)
....

Variation: Add 1 cup / 250 ml cooked, chopped ham after pureeing.

....

KANDACE HELMUTH, AKRON, PENNSYLVANIA

Rivers that once poured into the ocean are trickling away to nothing as the global demand for water increases. One-fifth of the world population didn't have enough water in 2009.[3] In North America, the Ogallala Aquifer—a huge underground water supply, lying beneath 225,000 square miles in the "breadbasket" of the U.S. central plains—is steadily depleting. Improvements in conventional irrigation techniques have slowed this process, yet much more of this "fossil" water is being pumped out of the aquifer than naturally comes back in.

The drip irrigation methods possible on small farms—in which water seeps slowly into the ground at the precise points where it's needed—use much less water than sprinkler systems. Practices commonly used on small farms like cover crop rotations and leaving crop residue on the fields also help retain moisture by building soil organic matter.
—CHW

Nova Scotia Hodgepodge

"Hodgepodge is traditionally made from the thinning of carrots early in the season, when the first peas are on the vine and new one-inch potatoes can be harvested without pulling up the whole plant," says contributor Brenda Leenders. "I have never seen this recipe written down anywhere. Whenever I asked I was told there was no need for one."

. . . .

2 tablespoons butter
Melt over medium heat in soup pot.

1 onion or handful of fresh onion tops or green onions
Add and sauté until soft.

2 cups / 500 ml vegetable broth
1 cup / 250 ml green beans
10–12 small new potatoes
4–6 medium carrots or handful of baby carrot thinnings
Add and gently simmer until vegetables are just tender.

½ cup / 125 ml peas
Stir in and cook until bright green, another minute.

2 cups / 500 ml milk
Add and gently heat until hot. Season to taste with salt and pepper and serve immediately with a sprinkle of chopped fresh herbs such as oregano, thyme, lovage (sparingly), chives, or garlic.

Serves 6 Ⓥ
. . . .

BRENDA LEENDERS, TRURO, NOVA SCOTIA

The water ran slowly; but it was "running water." The old mountaineer was proud of the clear spring water that with the help of gravity flowed into his home. However, washing dishes for the older couple, I often got impatient with the slow water. In my house, I had a pressurized tank so my water flowed fast and freely from my spigots. Unfortunately it also flowed fast and freely down the drain. Using the slower gravity-fed spring water, I used less and reflected more. Now, at home, that reflection guides my water usage. —MBL

We make it a priority to eat organic foods when they're available in our small town. What I think is key, though, is buying as close to the source as possible. There are several reasons for this: Building personal relationships with the grower helps strengthen the community and creates new friendships. It's also easier to ask questions then, like, "Is this organic?" and "When did you last spray the strawberries?" so you know what you are eating—and you also let the grower know that you do care about how food is produced.

I recently heard someone say, "Eat the view," and I think that's really good advice. I want my children to grow up knowing what healthy farms look like, ones where animals have good lives and chemical usage is minimal. Buying food from local producers equals good food and a healthier environment.
—Beth McMahon, Sackville, New Brunswick

Chilled Strawberry Soup

"I'm a soup 'dunker'—I like to dunk hot homemade bread in a bowl of hot soup. I've discovered that chilled fruit soups take well to dunking also," says contributor Sarah Myers. "Strawberry bread (p. 49) is delightful dunked in this strawberry soup!"

1 cup / 250 ml apple juice
¾ cup / 175 ml water
⅔ cup / 150 ml sugar
½ teaspoon ground cinnamon
⅛ teaspoon ground cloves
Combine in saucepan and bring to boil over medium heat. (Or mIcrowave in glass bowl until boiling.) Remove from heat; cool.

3 cups / 750 ml strawberries
¼ cup / 60 ml water
Purée until smooth in blender. Pour into a large bowl.

2 cups / 500 ml plain yogurt
1 teaspoon vanilla
Add to puréed strawberries with apple juice mixture. Cover and refrigerate until well chilled. Garnish with additional strawberry halves (optional). The soup freezes well and is especially good with small ice crystals left in.

Serves 6 Ⓥ Ⓖⓕ

SARAH MYERS, MOUNT JOY, PENNSYLVANIA

Spring Greens Salad

Choose one of these variations to use on those first fresh greens in the spring.

....

**8 cups / 2 L leaf lettuce, baby spinach, mesclun or other
  mixed greens, stems removed, torn into bite-sized pieces**
Combine with selected toppings from the options listed below.
Pour half of selected dressing over salad just before serving, then
more as needed. Refrigerate leftover dressing.

Serves 4 ⓥ
....

Topping options:

**2 green onions, chopped
1 small red onion, cut into thin rings
1 cup / 250 ml bean sprouts or radishes
1 cup / 250 ml celery, chopped
2 cups / 500 ml mushrooms, sliced
½ cup / 125 ml bacon pieces, cooked and crumbled
2–3 hard-cooked eggs, sliced
½ cup / 125 ml walnuts or slivered almonds, toasted
chive blossoms**

....

Basic vinaigrette dressing:

**2 tablespoons Dijon mustard
2 tablespoons red wine vinegar
3 tablespoons olive oil or nut oil
1 tablespoon fresh lemon juice (optional)
salt and pepper to taste**
Combine in jar with tight-fitting lid. Shake well. (Especially
recommended with walnuts.)

....

Celery seed dressing:

**¼ cup / 60 ml sugar
½ teaspoon each dry mustard and salt
1½ teaspoon onion, chopped
3 tablespoons vinegar
⅓ cup + 1 tablespoon / 90 ml oil
1 teaspoon celery seed**
Blend first 6 ingredients in blender or with immersion blender until
slightly thickened. Stir in celery seed.

....

. . . .

Strawberry vinaigrette:

1 cup / 250 ml strawberries, sliced
4 teaspoons rice vinegar
4 teaspoons lemon juice
1 tablespoon sugar
1½ teaspoon honey
¼ teaspoon salt
⅛ teaspoon each powder, onion powder, dried basil leaves,
    dried parsley flakes, pepper
¼ cup / 60 ml olive oil

Purée strawberries in blender or with immersion blender. Add
remaining ingredients except oil. Blend, then gradually add oil
while blending on low speed.

. . . .

Ginger dressing:

6 tablespoons olive oil
3 tablespoons balsamic vinegar
2 tablespoons brown sugar
2 tablespoons soy sauce
1 teaspoon paprika
1 teaspoon Dijon mustard
2–3 cloves garlic, minced
2–3 inches / 5–7 cm ginger root, peeled and minced
freshly ground pepper to taste

Combine in jar with tight-fitting lid. Shake well. (Especially
recommended with green onlons, raisins, nuts, and chopped
spring apple.)

. . . .

Creamy dressing:

⅓ cup / 75 ml mayonnaise
¼ cup / 60 ml plain yogurt
½ tablespoon sugar
½ teaspoon salt

Mix until smooth. (Especially recommended with spinach, onions,
and hard-cooked egg.)

. . . .

BASIC VINAIGRETTE: JOANNE BOWMAN, BROOKLINE, MASSACHUSETTS
CELERY SEED DRESSING: VIRGINIA HARTSOUGH, GOSHEN, INDIANA
STRAWBERRY VINAIGRETTE: KATIE MEYER, FRESNO, OHIO
GINGER DRESSING: MITZY ZAHM, EUGENE, OREGON
CREAMY DRESSING: MARY BETH LIND, HARMAN, WEST VIRGINIA

Strawberry Spinach Salad

One of the most frequently contributed recipes, this salad has endless variations. The only givens are spinach and strawberries. And even they can be varied.

. . . .

4 cups / 1 L spinach or other mixed greens, stems removed and torn
1 cup / 250 ml fresh strawberries, peaches, blueberries, kiwi fruit, or combination, sliced
Combine with selected toppings. Pour half of selected dressing over salad just before serving, then more as needed. Refrigerate leftover dressing.

Serves 4 ⓥ
. . . .

Topping options:

2 green onions, chopped
1 small red onion, cut into thin rings
1 clove garlic, minced
½ cup / 125 ml asparagus, cut into 1-inch / 2.5-cm pieces, blanched and chilled
2 tablespoons sunflower seeds, toasted
½ cup / 125 ml bacon pieces, cooked and crumbled
½ cup / 125 ml walnuts or slivered almonds, toasted
½ cup / 125 ml salted peanuts
½ cup / 125 ml cheese, shredded
1 teaspoon lemon or orange peel, grated
1 cup / 250 ml cooked turkey, chopped

. . . .

Two-seed dressing:

¼ cup / 60 ml sugar or honey
2 tablespoons sesame seeds
1 tablespoon poppy seeds
¼ cup / 60 ml cider vinegar or balsamic vinegar
¼ cup / 60 ml olive oil
⅛ teaspoon Worcestershire sauce
¼ teaspoon paprika (optional)
salt and pepper to taste
Combine in jar with tight-fitting lid. Shake well. (For basic vinaigrette, omit seeds.)

>>>

>>>

. . . .

Pineapple dressing:

½ cup / 125 ml pineapple juice concentrate, thawed
2 tablespoons vinegar
1 tablespoon oil
1½ teaspoon lemon juice
1½ teaspoon poppy seeds
¼ teaspoon dried basil
Combine in jar with tight-fitting lid. Shake well.

. . . .

Peanut dressing:

½ cup / 125 ml oil
¼ cup / 60 ml water
¼ cup / 60 ml salted peanuts
3 tablespoons honey
2 tablespoons cider vinegar
Blend until smooth.

. . . .

Rhubarb dressing:

2 cups / 500 ml rhubarb, chopped
½ cup / 125 ml sugar
¼ cup / 60 ml vinegar
¾ cup / 175 ml oil
2–3 tablespoons onion, grated
1½ teaspoon Worcestershire sauce
¼ teaspoon salt
Cook rhubarb, sugar, and vinegar over medium heat until soft.
Drain in sieve. Discard pulp. To 6 tablespoons of this juice, add
remaining ingredients. Shake in jar or whisk together. Chill at least
1 hour before serving.

. . . .

RUTH BOWMAN, SALEM, OHIO
SARAH BULLER FENTON, TREMONT, ILLINOIS
JUDY HILDEBRAND, CRYSTAL CITY, MANITOBA
TWO-SEED DRESSING: DORIS SHOEMAKER, DAKOTA, ILLINOIS
PINEAPPLE DRESSING: GLORIA SNIDER, RICHMOND, VIRGINIA
PEANUT DRESSING: SHERYL SHENK, HARRISONBURG, VIRGINIA
RHUBARB DRESSING: ANNIE LIND, PORTLAND, OREGON

Dandelion Bacon Salad

Dandelion greens are available at many farmers' markets. If you gather wild ones, just make sure they haven't been sprayed with pesticides.

. . . .

¼ cup / 60 ml lemon juice or vinegar
¼ cup / 60 ml honey or sugar, more or less to taste
⅛ teaspoon salt
Blend in a small bowl.

½ cup / 125 ml evaporated milk
Stir in.

4 slices bacon
Fry in a Dutch oven or very large frypan and drain on paper towel. Remove all but 1 tablespoon bacon fat from pan. Crumble bacon and set aside.

1 tablespoon flour
Add to reserved bacon fat in frypan, heat, and stir until smooth. Slowly stir in the lemon mixture. Heat and stir until thickened. Turn off heat but leave pan on the burner.

8 cups / 2 L tender dandelion greens, chopped
Add to warm dressing and stir gently to coat. Garnish with bacon.

Serves 4–6
. . . .

Variation: Substitute escarole, endive, or Boston lettuce. Other optional garnishes include chopped hard-cooked egg, red onion, mushrooms, or dried cherries.

. . . .

RHODA LEHMAN, SARASOTA, FLORIDA
MILDRED METZLER STEINER, GOSHEN, INDIANA
MARY MEYER, FRESNO, OHIO

My dad, who loves a manicured lawn, hates dandelion in his yard. He sprays, fertilizes, rolls, and mows trying to get rid of the dandelion. I just eat it. I love the deep, earthy taste of spring in a dandelion salad.
—MBL

Marinated Radish Salad

"Refreshing!" said one tester. Another added: "Creative, beautiful, and yummy even for someone who still has an uneasy relationship with radishes."

....

8 large bunches radishes, sliced, diced, or julienned
8 green onions, sliced
¼ cup / 60 ml fresh dill, chopped; or 1 tablespoon dill seed
Combine.

½ cup / 125 ml olive oil
¼ cup / 60 ml lemon juice
1 teaspoon sugar
1 teaspoon Dijon mustard
½ teaspoon salt
pepper to taste
Stir together, pour over radish mixture, and toss lightly. Cover and refrigerate at least 2 hours but no longer than 4. Remove 30 minutes before serving. Stir.

1½ cup / 375 ml Swiss cheese, shredded
Sprinkle on top and serve.

Serves 6–8 Ⓥ
....

GLORIA SNIDER, RICHMOND, VIRGINIA

"Spring: The Cruelest Months." This is the title of a chapter in the book *Coming Home to Eat* by Gary Paul Nabhan. And it's true. Spring offers such hope for new life. On the first warm day I'm ready for fresh lettuce but I have to wait; and waiting is so hard, so cruel. Lettuce and radishes, the quickest growing seeds, take forty-plus days to mature. And so I sit, still eating root cellared foods while I watch and wait for the lettuce and radishes to grow. —MBL

The world is losing its genetic crop diversity. Of the thousands of varieties of potatoes once grown in the Andean highlands, for example, Russet potatoes account for about two-thirds of the U.S. crop. But so what? Why does it matter?

• Don't put all your potatoes in one basket. In the 1840s some 2.5 million Irish people were killed or displaced after a blight killed their potato crop: a single "lumper" species upon which their very lives depended. Other potato varieties have demonstrated resistance to that disease. Imagine what could happen—worldwide—when we all start relying on a very narrow range of species for our food.

• Got a headache? Aspirin originally was extracted from the bark of willow trees and is just one example of importance of plants for medicines. What's called a weed today may be a lifesaver—or dinner—tomorrow.

• Now take a deep breath. We live in a closed system, our biosphere. Everything is related to everything else: plants, animals, water, weather, landscape, the air we breathe. When one part is fouled or destroyed, we can't know how that will impact other parts.

• The earth is the Lord's. Across religions of the world is an understanding that nature is created and sustained by God; we are accountable for our behavior among these other creatures of God.

—CHW

Garlic Potato Salad

As one tester put it, "A very pleasing and light-tasting potato salad with a Mediterranean flavor." Garlic scapes are the curly flowers/stalks from the plant, picked before it blooms. What used to be discarded is now gourmet.

. . . .

6 cups / 1.5 L new potatoes, cubed
Boil in water until tender, about 5 minutes. Drain and set aside.

6 garlic scapes or 3 cloves garlic, minced
1 cup / 250 ml green onions, minced
¼ cup / 60 ml olive oil
2 tablespoons balsamic vinegar
2 teaspoons fresh rosemary, chopped; or 1 teaspoon dried
salt and pepper to taste
Combine in a large bowl. Add cooked potatoes and stir to coat. Chill about 3 hours before serving.

Serves 6–8 (V) (Gf)
. . . .

JESSICA SEEM, BROOKTONDALE, NEW YORK

Sesame Chicken Couscous Salad

. . . .

1½ cup / 375 ml chicken broth
1 teaspoon soy sauce
1 teaspoon sesame oil or olive oil
Combine and bring to boil.

1 cup / 250 ml uncooked couscous
Place in large bowl and stir in boiling broth. Cover and let stand
5–8 minutes. Fluff with fork.

2 green onions, sliced
1 large red sweet pepper, chopped (optional)
Stir in. Cover and refrigerate until chilled.

1½ cup / 375 ml sugar snap peas or snow peas
¾ cup / 175 ml broccoli florets
Steam peas 1 minute. Add broccoli and steam 2 more minutes or
until crisp-tender. Rinse in cold water and drain.

1 cup / 250 ml cooked chicken, chopped
Add to couscous with broccoli and peas.

¼ cup / 60 ml lemon juice
2 tablespoons olive oil
2 teaspoons soy sauce
¼ teaspoon pepper
1 teaspoon sesame oil (optional)
Combine and mix into couscous mixture.

¼ cup / 60 ml slivered almonds, toasted
1 tablespoon sesame seeds, toasted
Mix in immediately before serving. Serve chilled or at room
temperature.

Serves 4
. . . .

Variation: Substitute bulgur for couscous. Allow to stand in the
boiling liquid, covered, for 30 minutes.

. . . .

JILL HEATWOLE, PITTSVILLE, MARYLAND

Roasted Asparagus

"My mother introduced me to asparagus when I was a child," writes contributor Paula Spurr. "We had moved to a new home in Alberta, and one spring morning she came dancing into the kitchen, saying, 'There is an asparagus patch growing in the garden! Yippee!' I figured any vegetable that could make my mom dance must taste good."

. . . .

1 pound / 500 g asparagus
Break off woody ends. Lay spears in single layer on baking sheet.

3–4 cloves garlic, minced
olive oil
Sprinkle with garlic then drizzle with oil. Bake in preheated 400° F / 200° C oven or grill, shaking the pan or partially turning every few minutes. When asparagus starts to look wrinkled and brown in some spots, about 5 minutes on the grill, a bit longer in the oven, remove from heat. Season to taste with salt and pepper. If desired, drizzle with balsamic vinegar or lemon juice immediately before serving. Serve hot or at room temperature.

Serves 2–4 Ⓥ Ⓖⓕ
. . . .

Cheese topping variation: Combine 1 ounce / 30 g crumbled goat cheese, ½ teaspoon chopped fresh rosemary, ½ teaspoon chopped fresh chives, and ¼ cup / 60 ml chopped walnuts; it will have a crumbly texture. Spoon over cooked asparagus.

. . . .

Summer variation: Substitute raw green beans for asparagus. May add a thinly sliced yellow or red onion.

. . . .

PAULA SPURR, THREE HILLS, ALBERTA
HAROLD MACY, COURTENAY, BRITISH COLUMBIA
BERNITA BOYTS, SHAWNEE MISSION, KANSAS

In India, organic agriculture is referred to as *ahimsic krishi*, or "nonviolent agriculture." This is because it is based on compassion for all species.
—Vandana Shiva, director of the Research Science Foundation for Science, Technology and Natural Resource Policy[4]

Sugared Asparagus

Delicious, super easy, and a nice change from the more savory asparagus dishes. A classic-to-be.

. . . .

2 tablespoons butter
2 tablespoons brown sugar
Melt together in large frypan over medium high heat until dissolved.

2 pounds / 1 kg asparagus, cut in 2-inch / 5-cm pieces
Add and sauté 2 minutes.

½ cup / 125 ml chicken or vegetable broth
Stir in, bring to boil, cover, and simmer until just tender, 6–8 minutes. Remove asparagus to a warm dish. Return liquid to a boil and simmer uncovered until sauce is reduced by half, about 5 minutes. Pour over asparagus, sprinkle with 1–2 tablespoons toasted sesame seeds (optional) and serve.

Serves 4–6
. . . .

JILL HEATWOLE, PITTSVILLE, MARYLAND

Three Pea Stir-Fry

Simple and elegant. Try this basic stir-fry method with other vegetable combinations.

. . . .

1 large clove garlic, minced
1 tablespoon ginger root, minced
⅛–¼ teaspoon crushed hot chilies
Heat 1 tablespoon oil in large frypan over moderately high heat until hot but not smoking. Add ingredients and stir-fry until fragrant, about 1 minute.

1½ cup / 375 ml sugar snap peas, cut in 1-inch / 2.5-cm pieces
1½ cup / 375 ml snow peas, cut in 1-inch / 2.5-cm pieces
Add and cook until crisp-tender, about 3 minutes.

1 cup / 250 ml peas
Add and stir-fry until hot, about 2 minutes. Remove from heat.

1 teaspoon soy sauce
1 teaspoon sesame seed oil
Stir in. Sprinkle with toasted sesame seeds and salt to taste. Serve immediately.

Serves 4 (V)

. . . .

Fresh greens variation: Spinach, Swiss chard, kale, arugula, dandelion greens, baby bok choy, and other tender young greens may be prepared using this stir-fry method. Instead of the three kinds of peas, handful by handful add 12–16 loosely packed cups / 3–4 L stemmed and chopped fresh greens and stir to coat with oil and garlic. Stir in crushed hot chilies, cover, and cook until just wilted and heated through, about 5 minutes. Add water if necessary. Season with salt and pepper to taste. Drizzle with balsamic vinegar immediately before serving.

. . . .

Citrus variation: Omit garlic, crushed dried chilies, soy sauce, sesame seed oil, and sesame seeds. Add ½ teaspoon grated orange peel with the sugar snap and snow peas.

. . . .

REGINA CHRISTMAN MARTIN, BROWNSTOWN, PENNSYLVANIA
JOCELE MEYER, FRESNO, OHIO
KELLI BURKHOLDER KING, GOSHEN, INDIANA

Wild Mushroom Sauce

Lucky enough to find wild mushrooms at your farmers' market or the woods? First make sure you've accurately identified them, then try this intensely flavored sauce, delicious over rice, pasta, potatoes, meats, or polenta, as shown (recipe on p. 394). In autumn, when wild chanterelles appear in Northwest evergreen forests, this sauce is marvelous over baked winter squash.

. . . .

¼ cup / 60 ml onion, chopped
Sauté in 1 tablespoon olive oil over medium heat until slightly browned, 2–3 minutes.

1 heaping cup / 250 ml fresh mushrooms such as shiitake, morels, or chanterelles, chopped
½ cup / 125 ml water
Add, cover, and simmer for 15 minutes.

½–1 teaspoon soy sauce
½–1 teaspoon fresh savory or thyme; or ½ teaspoon dried
⅛ teaspoon pepper
Add and bring to boil.

4 teaspoons cornstarch dissolved in ¼ cup / 60 ml water
Stir in and heat, stirring occasionally, until thickened, 2 minutes. Add salt if needed. Garnish with chopped fresh parsley (optional).

Serves 2–3 Ⓥ
. . . .

Soup variation: Add 1–2 cups / 250–500 ml broth (or half evaporated milk) at the end. Cook another 2–4 minutes, stirring occasionally, until thickened.

. . . .

MARLIN BURKHOLDER, HARRISONBURG, VIRGINIA
CATHLEEN HOCKMAN-WERT, CORVALLIS, OREGON

"O taste and see that the Lord is good." (Psalm 34:8a)

In the spring, most of my neighbors hunt for morels, a wild mushroom. While I like morels, I've never been good at finding them. So early yesterday morning as I took a walk through the misty woods, I was surprised by, as Julian of Norwich called it, a "showing of God." I wasn't even looking for morels, I was just walking through the woods enjoying the mystical spring morning, and there right in my path was a morel.
—MBL

Herb Roasted New Potatoes

. . . .

1 large shallot, coarsely chopped
1 large clove garlic, minced
1 bay leaf, crumbled
1 tablespoon fresh thyme, chopped
1 tablespoon fresh sage, chopped
1 tablespoon fresh oregano, chopped
¾ teaspoon salt
½ teaspoon pepper
Blend together in a food processor or blender.

½ cup / 125 ml olive oil
Add and blend until shallot is finely chopped. Transfer ⅓ cup / 75 ml of herb mixture to a large bowl.

16 small red or white new potatoes, scrubbed and patted dry
Add to bowl with the herb mixture. Toss potatoes to coat well. Transfer potatoes to large oiled baking sheet. Bake in preheated oven at 375° F / 190° C, turning occasionally for even browning, until tender when pierced with a small knife and crusty brown, about 45 minutes. Transfer potatoes to a shallow bowl. Drizzle with the remaining herb mixture and serve immediately.

Serves 3–4 Ⓥ ⓖf
. . . .

MEGAN GOOSSEN, DINUBA, CALIFORNIA

Sausage Asparagus Skillet

. . . .

1 pound / 500 g bulk sausage
1 medium onion, chopped (optional)
Fry together until lightly browned. Drain fat.

4–5 medium potatoes, chopped
½ cup / 125 ml water
salt and pepper to taste
Add, cover, and simmer 10 minutes.

1 pound / 500 g asparagus, cut in 1-inch / 2.5-cm lengths
Add and simmer an additional 10 minutes or until potatoes are
tender. Add extra water if needed.

½ cup / 125 ml cheese, shredded
Sprinkle on top.

Serves 4–5

. . . .

DONNA GOCKLEY, PHILADELPHIA, NEW YORK
DOROTHY SEBES, HANSTON, KANSAS

In genetically modified foods, genes with desirable traits are inserted into seeds. Many farmers have eagerly purchased seeds with improved insect resistance, for example, because it reduces their need to handle toxic pesticides. Roundup Ready crops can be sprayed with the herbicide of the same name, leaving the soybeans or corn healthy but killing the weeds.

What's not to like? Questions remain about the long-term safety of genetically modified foods, for human consumers and for ecosystems. But one thing is clear: the modified seeds are created and patented by transnational companies such as Monsanto. When a farmer buys them, he may plant them just once; the resulting grain may not be planted as seed. He'll need to buy seeds again instead.

Losing control of something as basic for survival as seeds for staple crops is of grave concern for people in developing countries. Research conducted by agribusinesses is aimed at making profits, and their advances in biotechnology benefit those who can pay for them.

In *Harvest in the Balance* (Mennonite Central Committee, 2002) Andrew Hough notes concerns, expressed most strongly in Mexico and Brazil, that "the multinational corporations producing biotechnology are able to exercise more control over their governments than large sectors of those populations. . . . Many in India," he says, "view biotechnology as another form of colonization."
—CHW

Lemon Asparagus Pasta

. . . .

8 ounces / 250 g angel hair pasta
2½ cups / 625 ml asparagus, cut into 1-inch / 2.5-cm pieces
Cook pasta in boiling water 4 minutes. Add asparagus and cook
2 minutes longer or until tender. Drain.

1 tablespoon butter
½ cup / 125 ml green onions, chopped
1½ teaspoon lemon peel, grated
3 tablespoons lemon juice
While pasta cooks, melt butter in large frypan over medium heat.
Add green onions and lemon peel and sauté 1 minute. Add lemon
juice and cook until liquid is almost evaporated.

¾ cup / 175 ml milk
2 eggs
Beat together. Add with pasta and asparagus to pan with green
onions. Cook over low heat until milk mixture is slightly thick, about
4 minutes. Do not boil.

1 tablespoon fresh dill, chopped; or 1 teaspoon dried
¼ teaspoon salt
⅛ teaspoon ground nutmeg
Stir in. Serve immediately.

Serves 4–6 Ⓥ

. . . .

MARY BETH LIND, HARMAN, WEST VIRGINIA

In preparation for tilling, a
common practice by many Native
American tribal groups was to
sing a song before the earth was
broken, a custom valued because
tilling the earth is a God-ordained
task. Too often we think of tilling
as laborious and mistakenly
accept the notion that it is a
consequence of disobedience.
We must remember that tilling
the earth was God-given before
the fall (Genesis 2:15). . . . If we
view the earth as a sacred gift
of God and treat it accordingly,
we, too, will sing a song with
beautiful lyrics. "The earth is
the Lord's." And the earth is a
beautiful song God made visible.
—Lawrence Hart, Cheyenne
peace chief and Mennonite
pastor[5]

Shiitake Mushroom Pasta

Perfect to celebrate the first mushrooms of spring.

. . . .

3 tablespoons butter
2½ cups / 625 ml shiitake or other mushrooms, chopped
1 cup / 250 ml onion, minced
1 teaspoon salt
Melt butter in frypan over medium heat. Add mushrooms, onion, and salt. Cook uncovered for 10 minutes.

7 tablespoons dry sherry or vegetable broth
2 tablespoons flour
Stir in sherry, then turn heat to low and slowly sprinkle in flour. Keep stirring for a minute or two after all the flour is in.

1 large clove garlic, minced
pepper to taste, freshly ground
Add and continue to cook and stir over low heat 5–10 minutes.

⅔ cup / 150 ml water or additional broth
1 cup / 250 ml sour cream or plain yogurt, room
    temperature
Stir into sauce, mixing well until it is completely incorporated and heated throughout. Serve over hot cooked pasta and top with freshly grated Parmesan cheese.

Serves 4–6 Ⓥ
. . . .

Autumn variation: Serve over sweet potatoes or on toast.

. . . .

SARAH MYERS, MOUNT JOY, PENNSYLVANIA

Creamed Asparagus or Spinach

. . . .

1 pound / 500 g asparagus, cut in ¾-inch / 2-cm pieces;
  or 3 cups / 750 ml fresh spinach, loosely packed
Cook asparagus in small amount of water until just tender, 10–12
minutes. Drain and set aside. Steam spinach and set aside.

1 tablespoon butter
1 tablespoon flour
2 cups / 500 ml milk
Melt butter in frypan over medium heat. Stir in flour until smooth.
Gradually add milk, stirring constantly until smooth. Cook over
medium heat, stirring occasionally, until mixture thickens. Stir in
asparagus or spinach; season with salt and pepper to taste. Serve
over buttered toast or in omelets or popovers.

Serves 2 (main dish), 3–4 (side dish) Ⓥ
. . . .

Omelet for one: Whisk together 2 eggs and 1 tablespoon milk.
Place a nonstick frypan over medium heat. Pour in beaten eggs.
As they set, lift edges, letting uncooked portion flow underneath.
When eggs are set, spread creamed spinach or asparagus over
half the omelet. Fold over and serve.

. . . .

Popovers for two: Combine ½ cup / 125 ml whole wheat pastry
flour, ½ cup / 125 ml milk, 2 eggs, ½ teaspoon sugar, ¼ teaspoon
dried thyme, and ¼ teaspoon salt. Beat with an electric mixer or
in blender until smooth. Set aside for 15 minutes. Preheat oven to
400° F / 200° C. While oven heats, dab a little butter in six muffin
cups and place in oven to melt. Brush melted butter on bottom and
sides of muffin cups. Stir batter and divide evenly among muffin
cups. Bake without opening the oven door until puffed, firm, and
starting to brown, 25 minutes. Immediately pierce with a knife to
release steam. Fill with creamed spinach or asparagus and serve.

. . . .

MILDRED METZLER STEINER, GOSHEN, INDIANA
CHERYL HOCHSTETLER SHIRK, HYATTSVILLE, MARYLAND
PEARL HOOVER, FAIRFAX, VIRGINIA

Spring Quiche Trio

....

3 eggs
1 cup / 250 ml evaporated milk
¼ teaspoon salt
¼ teaspoon pepper
Beat together and set aside.

9-inch / 1-L unbaked pie crust (p. 380) or crumb or potato
 crust (see right)
Prepare selected filling (below) and pour into crust topped by egg-milk mixture and ending with a sprinkle of reserved cheese. Bake in preheated oven at 425° F / 220° C for 15 minutes. Reduce heat to 350° F / 180° C and bake until browned on top and set in the middle, another 25–30 minutes. Cool for 10 minutes before serving.

Serves 4–6
....

Asparagus filling:

1–1½ cup / 250–375 ml asparagus, cooked and chopped
1 cup / 250 ml Swiss cheese, shredded
½ cup / 125 ml bacon, fried and crumbled; or cooked ham, diced
¼ cup / 60 ml green onion or onion, chopped
1 tablespoon fresh rosemary, chopped; or 1 teaspoon dried
 or ¼ cup / 60 ml fresh dill, chopped
Mix together, adding herbs to egg-milk mixture.

....

Leek-spinach-broccoli filling:

1 cup / 250 ml leeks, thinly sliced
1 cup / 250 ml broccoli, chopped
2 cups / 500 ml spinach, chopped
1 cup / 250 ml Swiss cheese, shredded
½ cup / 125 ml bacon, fried and crumbled (optional)
Sauté leeks and broccoli together in a greased frypan 5–10 minutes. Add spinach and cook until wilted. Place bacon and cheese in bottom of crust, then top with vegetable mixture.

....

Leek filling: Ⓥ (recommended with the potato crust)

1½ cup / 375 ml ramps (wild leeks) or leeks, chopped
1 cup / 250 ml cheese, shredded
Layer into crust.

....

· ·

Potato crust: Ⓖⓕ

3 cups / 750 ml uncooked potatoes, coarsely grated
3 tablespoons oil
Mix together. Press into bottom and sides of a 9-inch / 1-L pie pan. Bake in preheated oven at 425° F / 220° C until just starting to brown, about 15 minutes. Add filling and bake as directed.

· ·

Crumb crust:

⅓ cup / 75 ml flour
⅓ cup / 75 ml whole wheat pastry flour
⅓ cup / 75 ml cornmeal
½ teaspoon salt
¼ teaspoon baking powder
⅓ cup / 75 ml butter
fresh or dried herbs, to taste (optional)
Lightly mix together dry ingredients. Cut in butter until crumbly. Pat firmly into bottom and sides of a 9-inch / 1-L pie pan, adding a little water if needed to stick together.

· ·

ASPARAGUS FILLING: MARGARET HIGH, LANCASTER, PENNSYLVANIA
LEEK-SPINACH-BROCCOLI FILLING: HEATHER MCFARLAND, SHERWOOD, OREGON
LEEK FILLING: MARY BETH LIND, HARMAN, WEST VIRGINIA

Weather seems to be the topic of choice among us gardeners. We complain about too much rain or too dry or too hot or too cold. To avoid this complaining cycle, I've decided to do something each day that will like it hot, or cool, or wet, or dry. For example, I'll transplant something and hope it rains, but I'll also hoe something and hope for hot dry weather to kill the weeds. I'll plant tomatoes hoping for hot weather, and I'll plant broccoli hoping for cool weather. I guess this is called diversified farming, but I call it joyful farming because whatever happens I have something (of course, not everything) about which to be happy and grateful.
—MBL

Heirloom Beans with Leeks

Any midsized dried bean will work, but this rustic, satisfying dish is an especially good way to show off pretty heirloom beans such as Yellow-Eye, Etna, Anasazi, or Yin Yang. Just don't let the beans get mushy. Serve with cornbread or a crusty loaf and a leafy salad.

. . . .

2 cups / 500 ml dried Great Northern beans or other medium dried beans, sorted and rinsed
Rinse and soak in water overnight or by using quick method (p. 404). Drain.

1 bay leaf
1 teaspoon salt
Add with fresh water to cover beans. Cover and bring to a boil. Simmer, covered, until just tender, 20–45 minutes or longer, depending on the beans used. Drain beans and remove bay leaf.

2–4 slices thick-cut bacon
In Dutch oven or very large frypan, fry until crisp and drain on paper towel. Remove drippings from pan.

6 cups / 1.5 L leeks, thinly sliced (white part and tender greens)
Add 2 tablespoons olive oil to pan and sauté leeks 10 minutes. Crumble bacon and add to beans with leeks.

2 tablespoons rice vinegar or white vinegar
Add and mix well.

Serves 8 Gf

. . . .

JACKIE SWARTZENDRUBER, CORVALLIS, OREGON

"Come to the waters . . . why do you spend your money . . ." (Isaiah 55:1-2)

Of course, Isaiah is not talking about bottled water, but on reading this verse my mind jumps to the rows—actually aisles—of bottled water in supermarkets. Our free water supply seems less secure all the time—decreasing in both quantity and quality; while bottled water is steadily increasing in amount and variety. What would happen if we took care of God's gift of water instead of marketing it?
—MBL

Indonesian Leek Pie

"I created this recipe when we were looking for some satisfying dairy-free ideas for our family," writes Elizabeth Kerle, who operates Denison Farms in Corvallis, Oregon, with husband Tom Denison. "Friends from Indonesia said it reminded them of a recipe from their homeland."

. . . .

2 tablespoons butter
Melt in Dutch oven or large frypan.

3 large leeks, thinly sliced
½ teaspoon salt
Add and sauté 30 minutes.

1 cup / 250 ml coconut milk
1 egg, beaten
juice and grated rind of 1 large lemon or 2 limes
Add and mix well.

9-inch / 1-L unbaked pie crust (p. 380)
Pour into pie crust. Bake in preheated oven at 350° F / 180° C for 35–40 minutes, until filling is set.

Serves 4–6 Ⓥ

. . . .

ELIZABETH KERLE, CORVALLIS, OREGON

The newsletter from our community farm starts the same way this year as it has the past five: "Produce from the ground will have dirt on it." I chuckle, but it's not supposed to be funny. The organic vegetable farm that I have been a member of for almost a decade has lost more members due to the fact that excited newbies, who are eager to support a farm and eat locally grown produce, quickly lose their revolutionary zeal when they have to wash their weekly distribution of earth-caked food. The natural world is anything but natural to us urban dwellers.
—Marla Kiley, Denver, Colorado[6]

Vegetable or Fruit Oven Pancake

Oven pancakes take some time to bake but they're a snap to throw together.
Serve with soup or salad for a light lunch, brunch, or supper.

. . . .

1 tablespoon butter
Preheat oven to 400° F / 200° C. While oven heats, place butter in
9-inch / 1-L pie pan and place in oven to melt. Swirl pan to grease
bottom and sides.

⅔ cup / 175 ml asparagus, cut in 1-inch / 2.5-cm pieces
Steam lightly on stovetop or in microwave (or use leftover roasted
asparagus, p. 67). Place in bottom of pie pan.

¾ cup / 175 ml milk
⅔ cup / 150 ml flour
2 eggs
¼ teaspoon salt
Mix in blender until smooth (or whisk smooth in bowl). Pour over
asparagus. Bake until puffed and golden brown, 20–25 minutes.

½ cup / 125 ml cheese, shredded
Sprinkle on top, cut into wedges, and serve immediately.

Serves 1–3 Ⓥ

. . . .

Vegetable variation: Try other seasonal vegetables (alone or in
combination), such as broccoli or thinly sliced leeks. Mushrooms
may be lightly sautéed in butter and added. Coarsely shredded
summer squash and thinly sliced peppers may be used without
cooking before baking (pass the salsa with this combination).
Chopped fresh (or dried) herbs, such as parsley, savory, or thyme
are also good additions.

. . . .

Fruit variation: Peel and thinly slice 1 large apple or pear and
place on top of melted butter in pie pan. Return to oven and bake
until soft, about 10 minutes. Sprinkle with 2 teaspoons brown
sugar and a dash of ground cinnamon. Prepare pancake batter
as directed, adding 2 teaspoons sugar, ½ teaspoon vanilla, and
¼ teaspoon ground cinnamon. Pour over soft fruit and bake as
directed. Sprinkle with powdered sugar and serve immediately.

. . . .

JOANNE BOWMAN, BROOKLINE, MASSACHUSETTS
ELAINE JANTZEN, HILLSBORO, KANSAS

Spinach Squares

. . . .

3 eggs
1 cup / 250 ml milk
½ cup / 125 ml whole wheat pastry flour
½ cup / 125 ml flour
1 teaspoon baking powder
Mix together.

2–2½ cups / 500–625 ml cheese, shredded
8 ounces / 250 g fresh spinach or sorrel, chopped
Mix in and press into greased square baking pan. Bake in preheated oven at 350° F / 180° C until knife comes out clean, 30–35 minutes.

Serves 4 Ⓥ

. . . .

CHERYL HOCHSTETLER SHIRK, HYATTSVILLE, MARYLAND

"One-stop shopping" takes on a new look at farms like Glen Valley Organic Farm outside of Vancouver, British Columbia. This cooperatively owned farm produces vegetables, orchard fruit, cut flowers, medicinal herbs, berries, and chickens for eggs and meat, all on fifty acres.

This kind of integrated, managed biodiversity benefits the farm in many ways. One operation can support another: composted chicken manure fertilizes the vegetables, while the trimmed vegetable tops feed the chickens.

Frequent rotation of what's planted where enriches the soil, because each crop extracts and deposits different nutrients. (Chemical fertilizers, in contrast, may feed a particular crop but leave the soil biologically depleted.) Crop rotation helps to control pests, too; a bug that loves cornstalks, for instance, can't survive if grains are planted there. Flowering plants like dill and fennel also attract beneficial insects that eat things like aphids.

Planting cover crops and plowing them under as "green manure," leaving crop residue on fields, no-till methods (a way of planting that disturbs the soil as little as possible), and biotill practices (letting an established live crop prepare the soil for planting the following crop) are other ways that small farmers build healthy soil and prevent erosion.
—CHW

Veggie Burrito Bake

. . . .

1 large clove garlic, minced
1 medium onion, minced
¾ cup / 175 ml uncooked rice
¾ teaspoon ground turmeric
Sauté in saucepan in 1 tablespoon oil until onion is tender. Stir often.

1½ cup / 375 ml chicken or vegetable broth
Add and mix well. Simmer, covered, until liquid is absorbed, about
15 minutes for white rice, 40 minutes for brown rice. Remove from
heat, let stand 5 minutes, fluff with fork.

16 cups / 4 L fresh spinach, loosely packed
1½ teaspoon garlic, minced
salt and pepper to taste
While rice cooks, heat 1 tablespoon oil in frypan on high heat. Add
garlic and spinach, one handful at a time as it wilts, adding a little
water as needed to prevent sticking. Spinach should be moist, with
loose leaves, not clumped together.

2 cups / 500 ml cooked black beans
1 tablespoon chili powder
Mix in a bowl. Layer ingredients as follows in 2-quart / 2-L
casserole: half the spinach, all the rice, all the beans, remaining
spinach.

1 cup / 250 ml Monterey Jack cheese, shredded
Sprinkle on top. (At this point, casserole may be tightly covered
and refrigerated.) Cover and bake at 375° F / 190° C until sizzling,
45 minutes. Or heat in microwave about 10 minutes then let stand
5 minutes. Serve by spooning into warm flour tortillas. Optional
garnishes: salsa, avocados, guacamole, sour cream, Tabasco
pepper sauce, chopped fresh cilantro, lime wedges.

Serves 4
. . . .

LEANN AUGSBURGER, CLAREMONT, CALIFORNIA

Chicken or Tofu Stir-Fry

The best stir-fries are made with the freshest vegetables—which makes this recipe a great choice as a celebratory "market-day" (or CSA-delivery day) meal.

. . . .

¾ cup / 175 ml chicken or vegetable broth
3 tablespoons light soy sauce
2 tablespoons brown sugar
1 tablespoon sesame oil
1 tablespoon sesame seeds
1 tablespoon cornstarch
2 teaspoons ginger root, peeled and minced
1½ teaspoon garlic, minced
½ teaspoon crushed dried chilies or Tabasco sauce (optional)
Whisk together in a small bowl. Set aside.

**1 pound / 500 g boneless chicken, cut in cubes or thin
    strips; or 1 block firm tofu, cubed**
In large frypan over medium-high heat sauté in a small amount of olive oil until meat is cooked through or tofu is lightly browned. Remove tofu.

**1 cup / 250 ml snow peas or sugar snap peas, cut in
    1-inch / 2.5-cm pieces**
Add to frypan. Add soy sauce mixture and bring to a boil, stirring. Reduce heat and simmer until sauce thickens, 3 minutes.

**12 ounces / 350 g fettuccine, spaghetti, buckwheat soba
    noodles, or rice noodles, cooked**
½ cup / 125 ml green onions, chopped
Mix in. Top with browned tofu if using and serve immediately.

Serves 4–6
. . . .

Variation: Add other vegetables according to the length of time needed to cook until crisp-tender. Add first: thinly sliced carrots. Next: sliced, peeled broccoli stems, onions, bell pepper strips, asparagus, chopped Swiss chard stems, cabbage. Next: broccoli florets, along with the soy sauce mixture. Next: sliced mushrooms and summer squash. Last: fresh greens like spinach or tatsoi.

. . . .

KIM BURKHOLDER, SANTA FE, NEW MEXICO
JUDY LEATHERMAN, PHILADELPHIA, PENNSYLVANIA

Grilled Maple Barbecue Chicken

Leftovers make extra special chicken salad.

. . . .

¾ cup / 175 ml maple syrup
3 tablespoons cider vinegar
2 tablespoons oil
1 tablespoon onion, minced; or ¼ teaspoon onion powder
½ teaspoon salt
¼ teaspoon pepper
Combine in a tight-sealing container and shake until blended.

6 boneless chicken breasts or thighs, or chicken legs
Add to container and marinate, refrigerated, at least 1 hour. Place
everything in a microwavable dish and microwave together for 5
minutes. Remove chicken. Pour marinade into a small saucepan;
bring to a boil and boil 3–5 minutes. Place chicken on gas grill over
medium heat, cover, and grill 5 minutes. Turn chicken, brush with
marinade, and grill another 5 minutes. Continue to turn, baste, and
grill until tender. If any marinade is left, boil it and serve separately
with the chicken.

To bake: Place chicken skin side up in a greased pan. Pour
marinade on top and bake at 350° F / 180° C, basting every
15–20 minutes, until done (about 1 hour with bone in, less if using
boneless meat).

To panfry: Remove chicken from marinade and cook in oiled
frypan. When nearly cooked, pour in some marinade, which will
caramelize. Add about 3 tablespoons of water to the pan, stir, and
serve glaze over the meat.

Serves 6 Ⓖⓕ
. . . .
SHERYL SHENK, HARRISONBURG, VIRGINIA

Herb Roasted Lamb

. . . .

1½ tablespoon soy sauce
1 tablespoon oil
2½ teaspoons fresh thyme, chopped; or ¾ teaspoon dried
1½ teaspoon fresh marjoram, chopped; or ½ teaspoon dried
1 teaspoon salt
½ teaspoon pepper
½ teaspoon ground ginger
1 bay leaf, crumbled
Combine and set aside.

1 leg of lamb, trimmed of excess fat
½ teaspoon garlic, chopped in slivers
Cut small slits in the meat and insert garlic slivers with tip of knife.
Rub spice mixture thoroughly over and into the meat. Place on
a rack in a roasting pan and roast uncovered at 350° F / 180° C.
Roast 20–25 minutes per pound. Let stand 20 minutes before
carving.

Serves 6–8
. . . .

Variation: Serve leftovers, sliced, in pita bread with yogurt sauce:
Combine ¾ cup / 175 ml plain yogurt, 3 tablespoons chopped
fresh mint, 1½ tablespoon lemon juice and ½ cup / 125 ml
chopped cucumbers (optional).

. . . .

GARY GUTHRIE, NEVADA, IOWA
MARSHALL KING, GOSHEN INDIANA

I love to walk slowly through the fields on our farm. This ritual is primarily a time of planning, but it is also an important time of prayer and meditation.

Dear God, show me how to walk on this good land.

After fifteen years of farming, I feel as though I know so little. Oh, I know a few of the nearly three hundred beetle species here. I know most of the common weeds and the birds that nest on these acres. I know the toads, the salamanders, and the fireflies that land in our children's hands. But what about the rest? How small would this farm have to be in order to know all the life-forms that share it? How can I learn to let go of my own narrow design for this landscape?

Creator God, teach me how to understand my place within this cycle of life that I am so privileged to be part of. Teach me to walk slower in the hopes of knowing and caring more deeply for this piece of your good earth that has been entrusted to me.
—Dan Guenthner, Common Harvest Farm, Osceola, Wisconsin

Marinated Lamb Chops

"I have used this recipe several times now and each time I've gotten wonderful compliments about the flavor," one tester reported. "This is one I will use over and over."

. . . .

**8 loin lamb chops, 1 inch / 2.5 cm thick, trimmed of
    excess fat**
Place in a deep ceramic or glass bowl.

1 small onion, sliced
1 clove garlic, minced
3 tablespoons olive oil
2 tablespoons wine vinegar
1 tablespoon lemon juice
**1 tablespoon fresh rosemary, chopped;
    or 1 teaspoon dried, crushed**
2 teaspoons prepared mustard
¼ teaspoon ground ginger
¼ teaspoon salt
Combine and pour over meat. Cover and marinate in the refrigerator for 4–5 hours. Broil over a hot charcoal fire or under an oven broiler for 5–10 minutes per side for medium rare.

Serves 4
. . . .

GARY GUTHRIE, NEVADA, IOWA

Baked Trout with Lemon Garlic

. . . .

4 whole trout or trout fillets or other mild fish
4 cloves garlic, minced
2 lemons, sliced
If using whole trout put garlic and lemon slices inside the cavity and on top of fish or fillets.

2 tablespoons oil or butter, melted
Brush over top. Bake in preheated oven at 450° F / 230° C until fish flakes easily with fork, 5–15 minutes (time will depend on thickness). Fish also may be wrapped in foil and grilled.

Serves 4 (Gf)
. . . .

MARY BETH LIND, HARMAN, WEST VIRGINIA

Several of the world's major fishing areas—including the northwest Atlantic Ocean—have reached or exceeded their natural limits; fish are being taken faster than they can reproduce themselves. Pollution and habitat destruction further reduce fish populations.

To help consumers as they consider dinner options, Monterey Bay Aquarium and Environmental Defense Fund publish lists of best seafood choices to the worst, based on which are most abundant and well-managed (check online for apps and wallet-sized cards). Recommendations vary by region, but most North American conservationists currently agree on these:

Best picks: clams, mussels, scallops, and oysters; wild Alaskan salmon and halibut; farmed arctic char, catfish, and rainbow trout; sablefish/black cod; Pacific sardines; tilapia; albacore tuna.

Worst: farmed or Atlantic salmon; mahimahi; orange roughy; imported swordfish; bluefin tuna; red king crab; most shrimp and prawns.
—CHW

Asian Grilled Salmon

Easy to prepare, easy to clean up, and marvelous flavor.

. . . .

1½ pound / 750 g wild salmon fillets
Place in the middle of a large piece of aluminum foil and turn up sides to make a boat.

½ cup / 125 ml green onions or chives, chopped
Sprinkle evenly over salmon.

2 tablespoons soy sauce
1 tablespoon garlic, minced
1 tablespoon sesame oil
1 tablespoon ginger root, peeled and minced
Whisk together in bowl and pour evenly over salmon. Bring sides of foil together and seal edges. Put the closed foil package on a gas or charcoal grill and cook at medium heat until the fish flakes, about 20 minutes.

Serves 4
. . . .

HEATHER MCFARLAND, SHERWOOD, OREGON

Barbecued Salmon

Wild salmon is available locally off the Pacific Coast. Those in other regions may want to try these recipes with different local fish.

. . . .

½ cup / 125 ml cider vinegar
¼ cup / 60 ml butter
2 tablespoons brown sugar
2 tablespoons ketchup
2 teaspoons salt
1 teaspoon garlic salt
1 teaspoon onion salt
1 teaspoon Worcestershire sauce
Combine in saucepan. Heat and stir until butter is melted and salt dissolved.

3 pounds / 1.5 kg wild salmon fillets
Remove the skin and cut into serving-sized pieces not more than 1 inch / 2.5 cm thick. Place in baking dish and pour sauce over fish. Let stand 10 minutes. Remove from marinade, place on foil, and grill over medium hot flame, basting often with sauce, until well-browned and fish flakes. Do not overcook. Serve immediately.

Serves 8–9

. . . .

FLOYD AND CLAUDIA LAPP, MOLALLA, OREGON
CYNTHIA HOCKMAN-CHUPP, CANBY, OREGON

The farmed salmon industry has grown enormously in recent years, sharply bringing down prices. One might think this would decrease pressure on wild salmon and other fish, but this proves not to be the case.

Salmon farms are like large-scale animal farms in that they generate great amounts of waste in densely stocked netpens. Unlike on land, where manure can be collected and managed, in salmon farming fish waste is released directly into the ocean. The sheer amount threatens other marine life.

Salmon are carnivores, and the pellets fed to domesticated salmon are made of fish meal and fish oil. Two to three pounds of wild fish caught elsewhere in the world are needed to produce each pound of farmed Atlantic salmon.
—CHW

Rhubarb Sauce

"Rhubarb isn't hard to grow even in a small space," notes contributor Laurie Longenecker. "I transplanted a rhubarb plant from my grandma's country garden into my small city backyard flower bed and it is doing just fine."

....

4 cups / 1 L rhubarb, chopped
½ cup / 125 ml honey; or 1 cup / 250 ml sugar
1 tablespoon tapioca
1 teaspoon ground cinnamon (optional)
Combine. Let stand for 10 minutes or until some juice forms. Heat slowly to boiling. Cool and serve over ice cream. Or try stirring in sliced strawberries or raisins and serve for breakfast or as a side dish, in place of applesauce.

Serves 4 Ⓥ Ⓖⓕ
....

LAURIE LONGENECKER, LANCASTER, PENNSYLVANIA
HELEN GLICK, MILLERSBURG, OHIO
IDA HUEBERT, GALVA, KANSAS

No sane bird befouls its own nest. As a youth hiking through the mountains, I carefully and joyfully drank from the many mountain springs. The fresh water gurgling from the rocks seemed to be holy, as if Moses had walked through there and struck the rocks, making water flow from them. Now, I carry a water bottle and drink from a bottle instead of a mountain spring because I've been told the water has pollutants making it unsafe to drink. I have learned that these pollutants, which limit my joy of drinking from mountain springs, are caused by the sulfur- and mercury-spuming power plant, which provides energy for my home. How sane am I?
—MBL

Rhubarb Sorrel Crisp

"Fabulous!" reported one tester. "A wonderfully creative use of rhubarb and sorrel, and the perfect sweetness—allowing the tartness of the rhubarb and the bite of the sorrel to come through."

. . . .

4 cups / 1 L rhubarb, finely chopped
2 cups / 500 ml sorrel, finely chopped; or strawberries, sliced
1 cup / 250 ml sugar
1 tablespoon orange peel, grated
1 teaspoon vanilla
Combine in a large saucepan. Bring to a boil over medium-high heat, then reduce to medium and cook 4 minutes, stirring frequently.

¼ cup / 60 ml water
3 tablespoons cornstarch
Dissolve cornstarch in water. Add to rhubarb mixture and cook until thickened, stirring constantly. Set aside.

1½ cup / 375 ml flour (may substitute part oat bran)
1½ cup / 375 ml rolled oats
¾ cup / 175 ml brown sugar
¾ cup / 175 ml butter
½ teaspoon salt
½ teaspoon ground cinnamon
½ cup / 125 ml walnuts or other nuts, chopped (optional)
Mix together until crumbly. Place about 3½ cups / 875 ml of crumb mixture into greased 9 x 13-inch / 3.5-L baking pan and press to make an even layer. Pour in rhubarb/sorrel mixture and spread evenly. Sprinkle remaining crumb mixture over top. Bake in preheated oven at 350° F / 180° C for 30–40 minutes. Cut into squares.

Serves 12 Ⓥ
. . . .

ANGELIKA DAWSON, ABBOTSFORD, BRITISH COLUMBIA

Rhubarb Almond Flake

A very special spring treat. Worth the effort!

....

3 cups / 750 ml flour
1 cup / 250 ml shortening
1 tablespoon baking powder
1 teaspoon salt
Cut together with a pastry cutter or two forks until shortening is the size of small peas.

2 eggs
milk
In a measuring cup, beat eggs. Add enough milk to make 1 cup / 250 ml liquid. Add this to flour mixture and form into a ball, using additional milk if needed. Grease a baking sheet or jelly roll pan. Divide dough in half. Roll one half out and fit in pan.

1½ cup / 375 ml sugar
4 teaspoons quick-cooking tapioca
6–8 cups / 1.5–2 L rhubarb, chopped
Mix together sugar and tapioca. Sprinkle half of mixture over dough. Spread rhubarb on top. Sprinkle with remaining sugar and tapioca. Roll out remaining dough and place over top (dough pictured is cut into strips). Seal edges.

1½ cup / 375 ml slivered almonds
6 tablespoons butter
½ cup / 125 ml sugar
2 tablespoons milk
1 teaspoon vanilla
Combine in saucepan and bring to a boil, 2–3 minutes. Spread over pastry. Bake in preheated oven at 400° F / 200° C for 20 minutes; place an extra baking sheet on a lower rack to catch any drips. (If it seems to be browning too quickly, cover lightly with foil.) Reduce temperature to 300° F / 150° C and bake until golden, another 35–40 minutes. Cool completely.

Serves 12–15

....

LORI BOHN, WINNIPEG, MANITOBA

Rhubarb Pie

. . . .

2 eggs
Separate yolks from the egg whites. Beat egg whites into stiff peaks. Beat egg yolks separately.

1 cup / 250 ml sugar
3 tablespoons flour
¼ teaspoon salt
Mix with egg yolks.

3 cups / 750 ml rhubarb, chopped
Add to egg mixture. Fold in the beaten egg whites.

9-inch / 1-L unbaked pie crust (p. 380)
Pour mixture into pie crust and bake in preheated oven at 425° F / 220° C for 10 minutes. Reduce heat to 350° F / 180° C and continue baking for 30 minutes or until set.

Yields 1 pie Ⓥ
. . . .

Filling variation: Instead of separating the egg whites and yolks, add the whole eggs to the flour, sugar, and salt. Flavor with 1 teaspoon vanilla and/or ½ teaspoon ground nutmeg or the grated grind of one orange. Mix well. Fold in rhubarb. Pour mixture into pie crust.

. . . .

Berry variation: Substitute fresh or frozen blueberries or strawberries for part of the rhubarb; decrease sugar.

. . . .

Crumb topping variation: Combine ½ cup / 125 ml flour or rolled oats with ¼ cup / 60 ml sugar or brown sugar. Cut in 2 tablespoons butter until mixture is crumbly. Sprinkle over rhubarb mixture then bake as above.

. . . .

Tart variation: Instead of pie crust, bake rhubarb mixture on an unbaked Shortbread Tart Crust (p. 381).

. . . .

ANDI KUENNING, MINNEAPOLIS, MINNESOTA
RHONDA HAIGHT, WINNIPEG, MANITOBA
SARAH GLICK, BELLEVILLE, PENNSYLVANIA

"They look on the outward appearance, but the Lord looks on the heart." (1 Samuel 16:7b)

When we grew strawberries for market, most of our customers initially chose the biggest and brightest berries. And these were good berries. But over time and with experience, our customers began choosing the smaller darker berries. Taste won over appearances.
—MBL

Strawberry Pie

If you have lots of strawberries, omit the juice or water and use an additional cup of mashed berries. Wonderful!

. . . .

1 cup / 250 ml sugar
3 tablespoons cornstarch
Blend in a saucepan.

1 cup / 250 ml strawberries, mashed
½ cup / 125 ml orange juice or water
Add and cook over medium heat, stirring constantly, until the mixture thickens and boils. Boil and stir for 1 minute. Remove from heat.

2 tablespoons lemon juice
Stir in and cool.

4–6 cups / 1–1.5 L whole strawberries
9-inch / 1-L unbaked pie crust (p. 380), graham cracker crust, or Shortbread Tart Crust (p. 381)
When cooked fruit is cool, gently fold in additional strawberries and pour into crust. Chill for 3 hours.

Yields 1 pie Ⓥ
. . . .

Summer variation: Substitute blueberries or peaches for the strawberries.

. . . .

TANYA HERSHBERGER, CANTON, OHIO
NANCY MUCKLOW, KINGSTON, ONTARIO
ELEANOR BEACHY, HESSTON, KANSAS

Strawberry Ice Cream

. . . .

2–3 cups / 500–750 ml strawberries, mashed
2 cups / 500 ml whipping cream, whipped to soft peaks
1¼ cup / 300 ml sweetened condensed milk (p. 385)
1 cup / 250 ml cold water
6 tablespoons sugar
½ teaspoon vanilla
¼ teaspoon salt

Chill all ingredients. In mixing bowl, beat all ingredients together with an electric mixer. Pour into a 9 x 13-inch / 3.5-L pan and freeze 3–4 hours, or until mushy. Remove from freezer and return to mixing bowl. Beat until smooth but not melted. Return to pan and freeze another 3 hours.

Yields about 2 quarts / 2 L Ⓥ Ⓖⓕ
. . . .

Summer variation: Substitute 6 peeled and crushed fresh peaches for the strawberries (or try blueberries) and almond extract for the vanilla.

. . . .

AMY DUECKMAN, ABBOTSFORD, BRITISH COLUMBIA
SHERYL SHENK, HARRISONBURG, VIRGINIA

In my experience, the shorter the food chain, the greater the pleasure in a meal.

When I chat with the farmer who raised the food or know the food's story, it's more enjoyable to partake.

Gardening makes the food chain even shorter. When seeds dumped in our compost heap sprouted and yielded seventy-two butternut squash, I just had to laugh. When we harvested ten quarts of strawberries in our patch's first true season, I was even happier.

Our four brussels sprout plants have produced golf ball–sized miniature cabbages, delightful when eaten a half hour after picking. That's when the food chain is almost short enough to jump rope with.
—Marshall V. King, Elkhart, Indiana

Rhubarb Strawberry Jam

. . . .

6 cups / 1.5 L rhubarb, diced
2 cups / 500 ml strawberries, mashed lightly
Bring to boil in large saucepan with heavy bottom.

3–4 cups / 750 ml–1 L sugar
Add and boil uncovered 20 minutes, stirring frequently to prevent
scorching. Pour into hot, sterile jars to within ½ inch / 1 cm of top.
Seal with sterile lids and process in boiling water bath 10 minutes.

Yields 7–8 half-pints / 1.6–1.8 L (V) (Gf)
. . . .
CARL EPP, WINNIPEG, MANITOBA

Garlic Spinach Dip

. . . .

2 tablespoons garlic, minced
Sauté in 1 teaspoon oil until soft.

8 cups / 2 L fresh spinach
Chop, then add to frypan one handful at a time as it wilts, adding
a little water as needed to prevent sticking. Place cooked spinach
and garlic in blender or food processor.

8 ounces / 300 g light cream cheese, softened
¼ cup / 60 ml milk
⅛ teaspoon salt
dash Tabasco pepper sauce
Add to blender, cover, and blend until smooth. May serve as is or
heat through. Garnish with chopped tomato or shredded Monterey
Jack cheese (optional). Serve with tortilla chips or toasted pita
wedges.

Yields 2 cups / 500 ml (V) (Gf)
. . . .
VIRGINIA HARTSOUGH, GOSHEN, INDIANA

Orange Mint Tea

A light, refreshing beverage inspired by the tea served at the café at the Ten Thousand Villages store in Ephrata, Pennsylvania.

. . . .

3 cups / 750 ml water
5–6 sprigs fresh mint (each about 6 inches / 15 cm, well rinsed)

Bring water to boil in a saucepan. Add mint, cover, remove from heat, and steep 15 minutes or longer. Remove mint.

⅓ cup / 75 ml sugar, or to taste

Add and stir until dissolved. The resulting concentrate may be cooled and frozen for later use.

2 cups / 500 ml orange juice
½ cup / 125 ml lemon juice
water and ice

Combine juices in a ½-gallon / 2-L serving pitcher. Add mint concentrate plus water and ice to fill the pitcher. Chill completely and serve garnished with mint sprigs and thin slices of oranges or lemons (optional).

Yields 2 quarts / 2 L Ⓥ ⒼⒻ

. . . .

CATHLEEN HOCKMAN-WERT, CORVALLIS, OREGON
RICHARD SARKER, EPHRATA, PENNSYLVANIA

Aromatic Creator God,

I smell your glory in the just-plowed earth
    awaiting spring planting.
I smell your glory in the air after the rain.
I smell your glory in bruised mint leaves
      being prepared for tea.
I smell your glory on my fingertips
        after cleaning strawberries
          for my family to eat.
Your glory pervades the air
    in fragrant blooms
      of hyacinth, lilac, and rose,
    in freshly baked bread
        and Sunday-dinner roast,
    in the fishy smell of the pier
        and the musky smell of the barnyard,
    in the sweet bury-your-nose-in-it
      scent of a newborn babe.
For the odors of your glory
      and the sense of smell,
I give you thanks.

—DONNA MAST, SCOTTDALE, PENNSYLVANIA

The earth brought forth vegetation . . .
    trees of every kind bearing fruit
  with the seed on it.
  And God saw that it was good.
       (Genesis 1:12)

Summer comes and our toes feel the earth
beneath. We dance between the sun and shade.
Our dinner tables move outdoors. Our gardens
and markets overflow with gifts from God.
Summer invites us to find balance in the midst
of abundance and to nourish our bodies by
making healthy choices about the quantity
and quality of food we enjoy.

s u m m e r

Main Dishes

basil	kohlrabi
berries	melon
cherries	okra
cilantro	peaches
corn	peppers
cucumbers	plums
eggplant	summer squash
fennel	tomatoes
green beans	

Extras

Desserts

Canning

nourish the body

Create no-food zones in your home.

Aim to eat nine (not just five) fruits and vegetables per day.

Try to eat your colors every day: eat something red, green, orange/ yellow, white, and blue/purple.

Connect exercise and eating: try gardening instead of going to the gym for your exercise.

Invitations to Action

Try one new food per week. It may take ten to fifteen tries for a child to accept a new food.

Sweeten foods with honey instead of refined sugar or corn syrup.

Vegetarian Menu

Weeknight Menu

Weekend Menu

Know what you are eating: read labels.

Start or take part in a community garden—a place where many people can grow some food of their own.

Plant marigolds, chrysanthemums, chives, onions, garlic, basil, savory, horseradish, mint or thyme among your garden plants. Their natural odors and root secretions repel some insects.

Lemon Thyme Bread

While lemon thyme may be hard to find, it's worth seeking out for this bread.
And don't skip the lemon glaze!

. . . .

2 cups / 500 ml flour
2 teaspoons baking powder
¼ teaspoon salt
Sift together. Set aside.

6 tablespoons butter, softened
1 cup / 250 ml sugar
2 eggs
2 tablespoons lemon juice
2 tablespoons fresh lemon thyme, finely chopped
1 tablespoon lemon peel, grated
In a separate bowl beat butter until creamy with an electric beater.
Gradually add sugar, beating until fluffy. Add eggs one at a time,
beating well after each addition. Mix in remaining ingredients.

⅔ cup / 150 ml milk
Add to bowl alternately with dry ingredients, mixing until smooth.
Pour batter into greased and floured 8 x 4-inch / 1.5-L loaf pan.
Bake in preheated oven at 325° F / 160° C for 55–60 minutes. Let
stand in pan for 5 minutes. Remove to wire rack.

½ cup / 125 ml powdered sugar
1 tablespoon lemon juice
Mix together in a small bowl. Slowly pour glaze over the warm loaf.

Yields 1 loaf Ⓥ

. . . .

CATHY BOSHART, LEBANON, PENNSYLVANIA

Summer days as a child often found me sitting on the back porch with Mom and siblings shelling peas, peeling apples, or doing what we called BORING jobs. We would try to liven up the time by holding contests: who could shell the most peas in a minute or who could cut an apple into exact quarters. We tried anything to break the monotony of the job.

Now I crave times like those. I love to sit on the porch and do "mindless" tasks. It is as I sit shelling peas or stand picking blueberries that my soul makes the long journey from my head to my heart and I come home to myself.
—MBL

Berry Muffins

Delicious versatility! Try a variety of flours and berries or even zucchini.
Tester says, "I divide the batter in half and add different fruits based on what
the family likes."

. . . .

1½ cup / 375 ml whole wheat flour
1 cup / 250 ml rolled oats
1 tablespoon baking powder
½ teaspoon salt
1 teaspoon ground cinnamon (optional)
Combine in a bowl.

1 egg
1 cup / 250 ml milk
¼ cup / 60 ml oil
¼ cup / 60 ml honey
In another bowl combine and mix well. Add wet ingredients to the
dry ingredients and stir until just moistened.

1½ cup / 375 ml fresh or frozen berries: saskatoons,
mulberries, raspberries, blueberries, wineberries,
blackberries, marionberries
Fold in berries. Fill well-greased muffin tins two-thirds full. Sprinkle
top with cinnamon sugar. Bake in preheated oven at 400° F /
200° C for 15–20 minutes.

Yields 12 muffins (V)
. . . .

Wheat germ or flaxseed variation: Replace rolled oats with
½ cup / 125 ml additional whole wheat flour and ½ cup / 125 ml
raw wheat germ. Or use ¾ cup / 175 ml additional whole wheat
flour and ¼ cup / 60 ml flaxseed meal.

. . . .

Summer squash variation: Replace berries with an equal
amount of shredded summer squash.

. . . .

DIANE JONSON, CARSTAIRS, ALBERTA
JUDY HILDEBRAND, CRYSTAL CITY, MANITOBA
TAMARA BRUBAKER, MOUNT JOY, PENNSYLVANIA

Corny Cornbread

Excellent with chili or with butter and honey. The corn helps keep the bread moist and delicious.

. . . .

2 cups / 500 ml cornmeal
¼ cup / 60 ml honey or brown sugar
1 teaspoon salt
1 teaspoon baking soda
Combine.

2 cups / 500 ml milk, yogurt, or combination
3 eggs, beaten
Mix in.

2 cups / 500 ml corn
1 teaspoon hot or mild green chilies, minced (optional)
Mix in. Pour into greased 2½-quart / 2.5-L casserole or ovenproof frypan. Bake in preheated oven at 350° F / 180° C until toothpick inserted in center comes out clean, 40 minutes.

Serves 9 Ⓥ ⒼⒻ
. . . .

AUDREY HESS, GETTYSBURG, PENNSYLVANIA

Zucchini Yeast Rolls

A combination of different summer squashes, coarsely shredded, result in lovely soft rolls flecked with yellow and green. Shape bigger portions to make sandwich rolls, which are perfect for tomato sandwiches, or use this dough in Veggie Bread Ring (p. 114).

. . . .

2–3 cups / 500–750 ml summer squash, shredded
1 cup / 250 ml water
½ cup / 125 ml sugar
3 tablespoons oil
2 teaspoons salt
Combine in a saucepan and heat slowly until warm, stirring to blend. Or warm in microwave.

1 cup / 250 ml bread flour
1 cup / 250 ml whole wheat bread flour
⅓ cup / 75 ml dry milk powder
2 tablespoons active dry yeast
½ teaspoon ground mace (optional)
Combine in a mixing bowl. Add liquid ingredients and beat well until smooth.

1¾–2½ cups / 425–625 ml bread flour
Stir in enough additional flour to make a soft dough. Knead 8–10 minutes until smooth and elastic. Place in greased bowl, turn to grease both sides, cover with a damp cloth and let rise until doubled in bulk. Punch down and let rise 10 minutes. Shape rolls and place on a greased baking sheet. Cover and let rise until doubled. Bake in preheated oven at 350° F / 180° C until golden brown, 25–35 minutes. Brush with milk for a soft crust and let stand for 5–10 minutes before removing to a wire rack.

Yields 24 rolls Ⓥ
. . . .

Tip: Shredded uncooked zucchini may be frozen in freezer boxes for this bread. Squash may also be cooked and mashed, then frozen in 1½-cup / 375-ml portions.

. . . .

NAOMI ZIMMERMAN, IRWIN, OHIO

Focaccia

Serve with a green salad for a light summer meal. Try other toppings: pesto, sun-dried tomatoes, olives, mushrooms. "I find it easiest to cut flatbreads and pizzas with heavy kitchen scissors," says contributor Kirsten Beachy Alderfer.

. . . .

1 cup / 250 ml warm water
1 tablespoon active dry yeast
Combine in a large bowl, stirring until yeast dissolves.

1 cup / 250 ml whole wheat bread flour
2 tablespoons olive oil
1 tablespoon sugar
1½ teaspoon salt
Mix in, stirring until smooth.

1¾–2¼ cups / 425–560 ml bread flour
Add enough additional flour to make a stiff dough. Knead 8–10 minutes until elastic. Place in greased bowl, turn to grease both sides, cover with a damp cloth, and allow to rise until doubled in bulk, 45 minutes.

handful fresh basil leaves, snipped fine
Fold into dough, kneading only as much as needed to distribute evenly. Cover and let dough rest 10 minutes. Pat and stretch to fill a greased 10 x 15-inch / 25 x 40-cm jelly roll pan. Lightly rub top of dough with olive oil. Cover lightly with a damp cloth. Let rise 10 minutes. Top with one of the following toppings and bake in preheated oven at 450° F / 220° C until the crust is lightly browned, 12–20 minutes. If bottom gets brown before top is done, finish under the broiler. Serve immediately.

Serves 6 Ⓥ
. . . .

Tomato topping:

2 cups / 500 ml cherry tomatoes, halved
3 cloves garlic, minced
½ cup goat cheese, feta cheese, or mozzarella, shredded
coarse salt and freshly ground pepper
2 tablespoons olive oil
Gently press tomatoes and garlic into surface of the dough, cut side up for cherry tomatoes. Sprinkle with cheese, then salt and pepper. Drizzle with olive oil.

. . . .

. . . .

Pepper feta topping:

2–3 cups / 500–750 ml yellow, orange, and red sweet
    peppers, thinly sliced
1 cup / 250 ml sweet or red onion, thinly sliced into rings
3 cloves garlic, minced
2 tablespoons olive oil
fresh oregano and thyme, to taste, or dried Italian herbs
salt and crushed hot chilies (optional)
¾ cup / 175 ml feta cheese or goat cheese, crumbled

Combine everything except cheese and spread over dough.
Top with cheese.

. . . .

Garlic Parmesan topping:

2 tablespoons olive oil
3–4 cloves garlic, minced
¼ cup / 60 ml Parmesan cheese, freshly grated
2 tablespoons fresh basil, chopped; or 2 teaspoons dried
coarse salt and freshly ground pepper

In a small saucepan warm olive oil with garlic. Drizzle over dough.
Sprinkle with cheese and seasonings.

. . . .

Rosemary sandwich bread variation: Work into the dough
2 tablespoons chopped fresh rosemary instead of basil. Pat evenly
into a greased 9 x 13-inch / 3.5-L baking pan. Drizzle 1 teaspoon
olive oil over dough and smooth it over entire surface. Scatter
on top of dough 1 tablespoon chopped fresh rosemary, minced
garlic to taste, salt, freshly ground pepper, and 2 tablespoons
freshly grated Parmesan cheese. Let rise 15 minutes and bake
as directed. Remove from pan and cool on wire rack. Slice into
6 large pieces; split each in half and use for sandwiches.

. . . .

KIRSTEN BEACHY ALDERFER, MORGANTOWN, WEST VIRGINIA
GWEN PEACHEY, CORVALLIS, OREGON

I give several pints of cherry tomatoes to family, friends, and neighbors. We are getting lots, and it is hard to market them all. It's easy to be generous in the midst of excess. But to give the "firstfruits," to give away that first ripe tomato that I've fussed over and checked daily for the last month—that would be hard. —MBL

Veggie Bread Ring

An impressive addition to any potluck. Use vegetables in a variety of colors for the most attractive ring.

. . . .

2–4 cloves garlic, minced
2 cups / 500 ml fresh vegetables, minced, such as sweet
peppers, green onions, red onion, summer squash,
broccoli, spinach, purple cabbage, cauliflower,
shredded carrots
1 cup / 250 ml large curd cottage cheese, drained 5 minutes
through a sieve, or use dry curd cottage cheese
2 cups / 500 ml cheese, shredded
2–3 tablespoons fresh herbs, chopped; or 2 teaspoons dried
½ teaspoon salt
½ teaspoon ground red pepper, or to taste
8 ounces / 250 g tofu, diced as small as possible (optional)
¼ cup / 60 ml sunflower seeds (optional)
Mix well.

½ recipe Zucchini Yeast Rolls (p. 111); or whole wheat
bread dough for 1 loaf
Prepare dough according to directions through first rising. Punch down. On a lightly floured surface roll into an 18 x 24-inch / 45 x 60-cm rectangle. Cover with vegetable-cheese mixture, pressing down lightly. Roll dough into a long log, as for cinnamon buns. Bring ends of the log together and pinch shut. Transfer ring to a greased baking sheet. Using kitchen scissors or a sharp knife, slice into ring at 1-inch / 2.5-cm intervals, going about three-fourths of the way into the log. After making cuts all the way around, twist each piece slightly so the rolls fan out from center of the ring.

Cover with a damp cloth and let rise in a warm place 25 minutes. Bake in preheated oven at 350° F / 180° C for 20 minutes. Eat immediately or cool on wire rack and store in refrigerator.

Yields 1 large ring or 18 rolls Ⓥ
. . . .

To make rolls: Prepare as above except after rolling dough into a log, take a piece of thread or dental floss, put it around the log, and pull the ends together, pinching off one roll (1 inch / 2.5 cm thick) at a time. Place on a greased baking pan, allowing a little space between rolls. Continue as directed above.

. . . .

CATHLEEN HOCKMAN-WERT, CORVALLIS, OREGON

Dill Yeast Bread

Especially delicious warm or toasted.

. . . .

1 tablespoon dry active yeast
¼ cup / 60 ml warm water
Stir together to dissolve yeast. Set aside.

1 cup / 250 ml cottage cheese
In small microwavable bowl heat until warm (not hot); place in large mixing bowl.

2–4 tablespoons fresh dill, chopped; or 2 teaspoons dried
2 tablespoons sugar
1 tablespoon butter, melted, or oil
1 tablespoon onion, minced
2 teaspoons salt
¼ teaspoon baking soda
1 egg
Add to cottage cheese and mix together. Stir in yeast mixture.

1 cup / 250 ml whole wheat bread flour
½ cup / 125 ml cornmeal
1–1½ cup / 250–375 ml bread flour
Add, using enough white flour to handle easily. Knead 8–10 minutes until smooth and elastic. Place in greased bowl, turn to grease both sides, cover with a damp cloth, and let rise until doubled in bulk. Punch down and place into a well-greased 9 x 5-inch / 2-L loaf pan (or use a 1-quart / 1-L round casserole dish to make a round loaf). Cover and let rise again until doubled, about 45 minutes. Bake in preheated oven at 350° F / 180° C for 30–35 minutes (casserole dish may take longer). Remove from pan and brush with milk for a soft crust.

Yields 1 loaf Ⓥ
. . . .

ANDI KUENNING, MINNEAPOLIS, MINNESOTA

Blueberry Coffee Cake

Try it warm with milk poured on top.

. . . .

1 cup / 250 ml flour
½ cup / 125 ml whole wheat flour
½ cup / 125 ml sugar
1 tablespoon baking powder
1 teaspoon ground cinnamon
½ teaspoon salt
Combine in a large mixing bowl.

1½ cup / 375 ml blueberries
1 teaspoon lemon peel, grated (optional)
Gently fold in.

1 egg
½ cup / 125 ml milk
¼ cup / 60 ml butter, melted, or oil
Whisk together in a small bowl. Add to flour mixture and stir
carefully. Batter will be very stiff. Spread into greased 8 x 8-inch /
2-L baking pan.

⅓ cup / 75 ml sugar
⅓ cup / 75 ml whole wheat flour
⅓ cup / 75 ml walnuts or other nuts, chopped
2 tablespoons butter
1 teaspoon ground cinnamon (optional)
Mix together until crumbly and sprinkle over batter.

Bake in preheated oven at 425° F / 220° C until top is light golden
brown, 20–25 minutes. Serve warm or at room temperature.

Serves 9 Ⓥ

. . . .

LORRAINE PFLEDERER, GOSHEN, INDIANA
VALERIE BAER, BAINBRIDGE, PENNSYLVANIA

Zucchini Garden Chowder

"My friend served this at a playgroup and I loved it because it tasted good and was full of vegetables, which I am always trying to get into my children," says contributor Kerry Stutzman.

. . . .

2 tablespoons butter
Melt in soup pot over medium heat.

2 medium zucchini, chopped
1 medium onion, chopped
2 tablespoons fresh parsley, chopped
1 tablespoon fresh basil, chopped; or 1 teaspoon dried
Add and sauté until tender.

⅓ cup / 75 ml flour
¾ teaspoon salt
½ teaspoon pepper
3 cups / 750 ml water
Stir flour and seasonings into vegetables. Gradually stir in water to make a smooth stock.

3 chicken or vegetable bouillon cubes
1 teaspoon lemon juice
Add and mix well. Bring to a boil; reduce heat and cook, stirring often, for 2 minutes.

2 cups / 500 ml tomatoes, chopped
1½ cup / 375 ml evaporated milk
2 cups / 500 ml corn
Add and return to boil. Reduce heat; cover and simmer for 5 minutes until corn is tender.

2 cups / 500 ml cheddar cheese, shredded
¼ cup / 60 ml Parmesan cheese, freshly grated
Just before serving add and stir until melted. Add pinch of sugar to taste and garnish with chopped fresh parsley (optional).

Serves 6–8
. . . .

KERRY STUTZMAN, GREENWOOD VILLAGE, COLORADO

Fennel Leek Soup

. . . .

3 tablespoons butter or olive oil
6 cups / 1.5 L fennel bulb, chopped
4 cups / 1 L leeks, chopped
Melt butter or heat oil in soup pot. Add fennel and leeks and cook
15 minutes, stirring often.

2 cups / 500 ml chicken or vegetable broth
Add, cover, and simmer 20 minutes. Let cool slightly. Purée in
batches in food processor or blender.

⅔ cup / 150 ml fresh spinach, packed
Add to blender or food processor with some of the fennel-leek
mixture and process until smooth. Return mixture to the soup pot.

4 cups / 1 L chicken or vegetable broth
salt and pepper to taste
1 teaspoon ground cumin or celery salt (optional)
Stir into the soup pot and heat. Taste to adjust seasonings and
serve.

Serves 6
. . . .

KERRY STUTZMAN, GREENWOOD VILLAGE, COLORADO

Southwestern Corn Chowder

. . . .

½ cup / 125 ml sweet onion, chopped
Sauté in 1 tablespoon olive oil in a soup pot until soft.

2½ cups / 625 ml corn
3 cups / 750 ml chicken or vegetable broth
Add and cook 10 minutes. Remove 1 cup / 250 ml of solids with about ⅓ cup / 75 ml broth and place in blender or food processor; blend until smooth. Return this purée to the soup pot and heat until nearly boiling.

1 medium red sweet pepper, chopped
1 small tomato, peeled and seeded (if desired) and chopped
Stir in and heat another minute.

½ fresh lime
3 tablespoons fresh cilantro, finely chopped
Squeeze lime into soup and top with cilantro immediately before serving. Garnish individual bowls with Tabasco pepper sauce, lime wedges, and/or a dollop of plain yogurt or sour cream (optional).

Serves 4
. . . .

Variation: For a heartier soup add cooked black beans, lima beans, and/or chunks of cooked chicken or turkey. Using grilled corn, cut off the cob, imparts a delicious smoky flavor.

. . . .

KELLI BURKHOLDER KING, GOSHEN, INDIANA

Job Ebenezer headed a project that placed thirty-eight cheap plastic wading pools on the roof of the Evangelical Lutheran Church of America denominational offices in Chicago. Intensively planted, one pool could produce twenty-two pounds of vegetables per year—far more than commercial yields. Container gardens conserve soil and water while providing an inexpensive way for city-dwellers to participate in food production. "Growing food and caring for God's creation is a spiritual activity," Ebenezer stresses. "We do it because of God's commandment to till and to keep the earth in Genesis 2:15." —CHW

Fresh Tomato Soup

A soup with wonderful fresh tomato flavor. If you're making salsa or canning pasta sauce, use the last few cups of peeled tomatoes for this super easy soup.

. . . .

8 medium tomatoes, peeled and seeded (if desired)
  and chopped
4 or more cloves garlic, minced
Combine in saucepan and cook over medium heat, stirring occasionally, until tomatoes are soft.

3 cups / 750 ml water or vegetable juice
2 chicken or vegetable bouillon cubes
1 teaspoon sugar
2 sprigs of fresh basil, chopped
Add, bring to boil, simmer for 5 minutes, and serve.

Serves 4
. . . .

ELEANORE AND JOHN REMPEL-WOOLLARD, EDMONTON, ALBERTA

Chilled Gazpacho

Float cucumber croutons—cucumbers cut into crouton-sized pieces—on top.

. . . .

4 cups / 1 L tomatoes, chopped
2 cups / 500 ml beef or vegetable broth
1 cup / 250 ml cucumber, diced
1 cup / 250 ml green or red sweet pepper, diced
1 cup / 250 ml celery, diced
½ cup / 125 ml yellow or red onion, diced
2 tablespoons sugar
1 tablespoon lemon juice
1 teaspoon salt
several dashes Worcestershire sauce
10–12 drops Tabasco pepper sauce
6 ice cubes
green onions or chives, chopped (optional)
Mix together. Allow soup to stand for 30 minutes to let the ice cubes chill the soup and for the flavors to mingle.

Serves 4
. . . .

White gazpacho variation: Omit the broth and decrease the tomatoes to 1 cup / 250 ml. Add 3 cups / 750 ml chilled buttermilk.

. . . .

KATHY PROCTER, BELGRAVE, ONTARIO
CAROL SCHWEITZER, ALBANY, OREGON

For sixteen years, Marlin Burkholder operated a family dairy farm in Virginia. But chronic illness forced him to put the business on the auction block. His body could no longer tolerate the conventional farm's airborne molds, odors, and tractor diesel fumes. "The five-year struggle with this illness literally brought me to my knees," he says as he describes planting tomatoes or lettuce on the new CSA farm he founded on principles of sustainability.

"Whenever I work on my knees, my thoughts go back to the small rural Mennonite church of my childhood. There, when a call was made for prayer, the congregants would turn around in the pews and kneel on the floor, facing toward the back. In a sense I had to do something similar when I made the transition from dairy farming to the kind of farming I do today. God brought circumstances into my life that made it necessary for me to turn around and to face a different direction, not only for the restoration of my health but also for the healing of my farm." —CHW

Cucumber Salad Trio

Simple options for celebrating the humble cucumber.

· ·

3 cups / 750 ml cucumbers, thinly sliced
½ cup / 125 ml onion, thinly sliced
Use in a salad option below.

Serves 4 Ⓥ ⒼⒻ
· ·

Salad 1:

Place cucumbers and onion in a large bowl and sprinkle with
1 teaspoon salt. Let stand 1 hour. Drain.

⅓ cup / 75 ml sugar
¼ cup / 60 ml vinegar
½ teaspoon celery seed
Mix together in a saucepan. Bring to a boil, cook, and stir until
sugar is dissolved. Pour over cucumbers. Cover and marinate in
refrigerator for several hours or overnight. Keeps several days.

· ·

Salad 2:

¼ cup / 60 ml vinegar or lemon juice
2 tablespoons oil
½ teaspoon salt
1 tablespoon sugar (optional)
Mix together and add to the cucumbers and onions.

· ·

Salad 3:

Place cucumbers and onion in a large bowl and sprinkle with
1 teaspoon salt. Let stand 1 hour. Drain.

¾ cup / 175 ml plain yogurt
1 tablespoon fresh mint or dill weed, chopped
Add to the cucumbers and onions.

· ·

KAY SHUE, DALTON, OHIO
SHARON GARBER, MAHWAH, NEW JERSEY
RUTH STAUFFER, NICHOLVILLE, NEW YORK

Cucumber Tomato Relish

"We regularly had this relish (we called it goulash) with green beans when I was a kid," says contributor Karin Shank. *"It is a wonderful combination of sweet, sour, and crunchy!"* This colorful relish is also delicious with grilled meats.

. . . .

1 cucumber or 2 small zucchini, diced
1 pound / 500 g tomatoes, peeled and diced
½ cup / 125 ml sweet onion, thinly sliced
Combine in a medium bowl. Add dressing of choice, starting with half and adding more to taste.

Serves 6 (V) (Gf)
. . . .

Dressing 1:

¼ cup / 60 ml oil
2 tablespoons apple cider vinegar or red wine vinegar
2 tablespoons sugar
½ teaspoon salt
¼ teaspoon pepper
seasoning of choice: ⅛ teaspoon celery seed; ¼ cup / 60 ml fresh parsley, chopped; 1 tablespoon fresh oregano, chopped, and ¼ teaspoon dry mustard; or 1 tablespoon fresh basil, chopped
Whisk together until sugar is dissolved and dressing begins to thicken. Salad will keep, refrigerated, up to 3 days.

. . . .

Dressing 2:

½ cup / 125 ml sour cream
2 tablespoons fresh parsley, chopped
2 tablespoons fresh dill, chopped
2 tablespoons cider vinegar
1 tablespoon milk
½ teaspoon salt
¼ teaspoon prepared mustard
¼ teaspoon pepper
Stir together and combine with vegetables. Chill 1 hour. Salad will get watery with time.

. . . .

KARIN SHANK, RALEIGH, NORTH CAROLINA
KAREN BYLER, MONTROSE, COLORADO
GRETCHEN AND MARLYS WEAVER, GOSHEN, INDIANA

Greek Tomato Salad

A popular recipe among contributors and testers. Always rated "a keeper!"

. . . .

8 medium tomatoes, peeled and sliced
1 medium onion, thinly sliced
1 green pepper, chopped (optional)
1 cucumber, chopped (optional)
Combine in a dish.

2 tablespoons fresh basil, mint, or parsley, chopped
1 tablespoon olive oil
1 tablespoon wine vinegar or balsamic vinegar
1 clove garlic, minced (optional)
Mix and pour over the vegetables; toss lightly. Salt and pepper to taste. Garnish with ½ cup / 125 ml freshly shredded mozzarella or crumbled feta cheese, Kalamata olives, or sprigs of fresh herbs.

Serves 6 Ⓥ Ⓖⓕ
. . . .

RHODA BLOUGH, LOUISVILLE, OHIO
BETTY BRUNK, HARRISONBURG, VIRGINIA
JOANNE ROTH, WASHINGTON, IOWA

I'm just one of countless migrants who's wasted years in the fields. . . . I feel like [farmworkers will] never be noticed. I would be thrilled if someday the newspaper would say, "We would like to thank the farmworkers, the pickers. We appreciate the hours, the days, the weeks, they've spent harvesting our produce."

Migrants need to be recognized. Maybe I could be the one that makes everyone realize, "Lord, have mercy, those tomatoes I ate yesterday? Somebody picked them with their own hands."
—Dora Medina, restaurant owner in Faison, North Carolina, who spent most of her life as a farmworker[1]

Squash and Basil Salad

Summer squash grown without pesticides don't need to be peeled. Using a mix of colors adds visual appeal to this salad. Garlic scapes are the curly stalks from the plant, picked before it blooms.

. . . .

3–4 medium summer squash, julienned
2–3 tablespoons fresh basil, chopped
3–4 tablespoons Parmesan cheese, freshly grated
1–2 tablespoons garlic scapes, chopped;
      or add minced garlic to the dressing below
Toss together.

¼ cup / 60 ml red wine vinegar
¼ cup / 60 ml olive oil
½ teaspoon salt
¼ teaspoon pepper
¼ teaspoon sugar
Combine and pour over the salad. Mix, chill 1 hour, and serve. Best eaten the same day. May be served with lettuce and chopped green onions.

Serves 4–6 Ⓥ Ⓖⓕ

. . . .

KAREN BRANDES, STATE COLLEGE, PENNSYLVANIA
STEVE MININGER, SOD, WEST VIRGINIA

Our oldest child, Neil, was midway through college the summer he and a lifelong friend, Nick Hurst, presented their parents with an intriguing proposal: they invited us to pay for CSA shares at the Scarecrow Hill Community Farm near our home. The young men would volunteer time on the farm and—this was the clincher—cook once a week. How could we lose?

One day each week Neil and Nick would gather their share of produce and plan the evening meal on the foods available. What feasts they were: the inaugural meal featured baked zucchini, Harvard beets, salad greens, and homemade whole wheat bread. The boys always invited friends, and they would gather in the kitchen, helping to prepare the meal in progress. Whenever possible, we ate outside, beginning with a three-part round of "Dona Nobis Pacem." After eating we again joined our voices in song. I will never forget our zucchini summer!
—Norma Stauffer, Akron, Pennsylvania

Hot German Green Bean Salad

The taste of German potato salad—with green beans! Try leftovers cold.

. . . .

1½ pound / 750 g green beans, cut in 1-inch / 2.5-cm pieces
Cook, covered, in boiling water until barely tender. Drain, reserving
¼ cup / 60 ml cooking liquid.

3 slices bacon
Fry until crisp; remove all but 2 tablespoons drippings from frypan.
Drain bacon and crumble. Set aside.

2 tablespoons sugar
1 tablespoon lemon juice or white vinegar
½ teaspoon salt
1 small onion, sliced into rings
Add to bacon drippings along with reserved cooking liquid.

¼ cup / 60 ml cold water
2 teaspoons cornstarch
Mix together separately, stirring until dissolved. Stir into frypan.
Cook until thick and clear, stirring constantly. Add cooked beans
and heat through. Sprinkle with bacon and serve.

Serves 4–6 (Gf)
. . . .

ROBERTA SCHWINKE, MORRISON, MISSOURI

Stoplight Salad

The name refers to the colors in this tasty salad. Using grilled corn is optional but offers a lovely smoky flavor. Try this salad alongside grilled meats or as a light main dish.

. . . .

2 cups / 500 ml tomatoes, chopped and drained
2 cups / 500 ml corn
1 medium green pepper, diced
1 medium red sweet pepper, diced
¼ cup / 60 ml fresh cilantro, parsley, or basil, chopped
2 cups / 500 ml cooked black beans (optional)
Combine in a bowl.

3 tablespoons olive oil
3 tablespoons balsamic vinegar or lime juice
1 clove garlic, minced
Whisk together in a separate bowl. Pour over salad. Salt and pepper to taste. Toss gently and serve.

Yields 6–8 cups / 1.5–2 L Ⓥ Ⓖⓕ
. . . .

Southwest variation: Omit the tomatoes and add to the dressing 1½ tablespoon chopped fresh oregano, 1½ teaspoon ground cumin, ¾ teaspoon chili powder, and ¼ teaspoon cayenne pepper.

. . . .

Quinoa variation: Add 2 cups / 500 ml cooked quinoa. Serve with warm flour tortillas.

. . . .

CATHI BAER, ARCHBOLD, OHIO
LAURA TIESSEN, TORONTO, ONTARIO
KRISTEN BURKHOLDER, NORMAN, OKLAHOMA
MARJORIE LIECHTY, GOSHEN, INDIANA

Four Bean Salad

. . . .

¼ cup / 60 ml apple cider vinegar
¼ cup / 60 ml red wine vinegar
3 tablespoons olive oil
1 tablespoon sugar
1 teaspoon salt
¼ teaspoon pepper
Mix in a large bowl until blended.

1 pound / 500 g green beans, cut in 1½-inch / 3.5-cm
    pieces and blanched
1½ cup / 375 ml green soybeans (edamame)
2 cups / 500 ml cooked black soybeans or black beans
2 cups / 500 ml cooked pink beans
1 small red onion, diced
1 cup / 250 ml green pepper, diced
1 tablespoon each fresh basil, parsley, oregano, thyme,
    chopped; or 1 teaspoon each, dried
Add and toss to combine. Refrigerate at least 1 hour before
serving.

Serves 12 Ⓥ Ⓖⓕ
. . . .

LOIS BECK, ELKHART, INDIANA

War destroys life. It also destroys food systems for the living.

In northern Uganda, which has suffered the effects of one of Africa's longest running conflicts, dairy products, safe meat, and most fruit and vegetables disappeared from the market. As a result, "we watched general health decline among our neighbors, especially nursing mothers," say Dan and Kathryn Smith Derksen of their years with Mennonite Central Committee in Uganda. "The Acholi are a healthy, vibrant, hard-working people, but as they lost their cattle they lost many things: their main source of protein, their milk, and their way of farming produce, which all severely affected their nutrition."
—CHW

Whole Grain Tabouleh

This is a great dish for creatively using whatever is in season since the recipe really is just a base.

. . . .

1 cup / 250 ml uncooked bulgur, quinoa, or couscous
Prepare, fluff lightly with fork, and cool.

For bulgur: Rinse and drain. Add 2 cups / 500 ml boiling water, cover, and simmer about 10–15 minutes until water is absorbed.

For quinoa: Rinse and drain. Add 2 cups / 500 ml boiling water, cover, and let stand 10–20 minutes until water is absorbed. Ⓖⓕ

For couscous: Add 1 cup / 250 ml boiling water or broth, cover, and let stand 5–10 minutes until water is absorbed.

¼ cup / 60 ml green onions or onion, chopped
2 red or yellow tomatoes, seeded and chopped
½ cup / 125 ml fresh cilantro, parsley, or mint, chopped
1 cup / 250 ml fresh vegetables, diced:
    cucumbers, green or red sweet peppers, hot peppers,
    carrots, summer squash
1 cup / 250 ml cooked chickpeas (optional)
Add to cooled grains.

2 tablespoons lemon or lime juice
2 tablespoons olive oil
salt and freshly ground pepper to taste
Mix and pour over salad. Toss gently.

Yields 6 cups / 1.5 L Ⓥ
. . . .

BETHANY SPICHER, WASHINGTON, DISTRICT OF COLUMBIA
CAROL PEACHEY, AKRON, PENNSYLVANIA
RICHARD KULP, WILLISTON, VERMONT
PAT LEAMAN, LANCASTER, PENNSYLVANIA

Vegetable Pasta Salad

A great do-ahead recipe, as the salad tastes better the next day after the flavors blend.

. . . .

¼ cup / 60 ml red wine vinegar
½ teaspoon salt
⅛ teaspoon pepper
1 clove garlic, minced
1 tablespoon Dijon mustard (optional)
In a small bowl whisk together.

¼ cup / 60 ml olive oil
¼ cup / 60 ml fresh basil, cut in very thin strips
Whisk in oil gradually. Stir in basil and set aside.

4 ounces / 125 g uncooked whole wheat pasta such as
 rotini, bow tie, shells, or penne
Cook pasta. Drain and rinse with cold water. Place in large bowl and toss with one-third of the dressing.

2 cups / 500 ml fresh vegetables: green peppers, summer
 squash, cucumbers, broccoli florets, chopped
3 medium tomatoes, cut in thin wedges
½ cup / 125 ml olives, sliced
Layer ingredients on top of the pasta in the following order: vegetables, tomatoes, and olives. Top with remaining dressing.

¼–½ cup / 60–125 ml fresh basil leaves, loosely packed
2 tablespoons fresh parsley, chopped
Sprinkle on top. Cover and chill 4–24 hours.

½ cup / 125 ml Parmesan cheese, freshly grated, or feta
 cheese, crumbled
Sprinkle on top and toss lightly before serving.

Serves 6–8 Ⓥ
. . . .

Variation: Use a small pasta or orzo. Omit the cheese and olives. Add 2 cups / 500 ml cooked chickpeas along with the herbs.

. . . .

KAY SHUE, DALTON, OHIO
KATRINE ROSE, WOODBRIDGE, VIRGINIA
DEENA DYCK, WINNIPEG, MANITOBA

Greek Salad with Grilled Chicken

This is a terrific, low-fat main dish salad. Serve it with warm bread for a complete meal.

. . . .

¼ cup / 60 ml chicken broth
2 tablespoons red wine vinegar
1 tablespoon fresh oregano, chopped; or 1 teaspoon dried
2 teaspoons olive oil
1 teaspoon sugar
½ teaspoon salt
½ teaspoon pepper
1 clove garlic, minced
Combine in a small bowl. Set aside all but 2 tablespoons of this dressing. Preheat grill or broiler.

1 pound / 500 g skinless, boneless chicken breasts
Brush with the 2 tablespoons of dressing. Place on grill rack or broiler pan coated with cooking spray. Cook for 5 minutes on a side or until chicken is done. Cut into slices ¼-inch / 5 mm thick.

8 cups / 2 L lettuce or mixed salad greens, torn
1 cup / 250 ml cucumbers, sliced
1 cup / 250 ml tomatoes, coarsely chopped
2 slices red onion, separated into rings
Combine in a large bowl and toss with reserved salad dressing. Divide salad among 4 plates. Top with chicken.

¼ cup / 60 ml feta cheese, crumbled
8 pitted Kalamata olives, halved (optional)
Sprinkle over salad and serve.

Serves 4
. . . .

KIM BURKHOLDER, SANTA FE, NEW MEXICO

**I enjoy gardening for exercise; it's better than going to a gym!
—Gabija Zaikauskaite-Enns, Abbotsford, British Columbia**

Inspired by the success of community agriculture initiatives that link farmers and consumers, the Midcoast Fishermen's Cooperative in Maine started the first community-supported fishery in the United States, Port Clyde Fresh Catch. In similar ventures up and down the East and West Coasts, members pay a lump sum at the beginning of the season and then receive a weekly or monthly supply of fresh seafood. In addition to fish, some locations offer crabmeat, scallops, shrimp, lobster, oysters, mussels, clams, calamari, and kelp.
—CHW

Niçoise Salad

Briefly cooked, squeaky green beans are typically included in niçoise (nee-SWAHS) salad, but if fresh ones aren't in season, it's fine to leave them out. Substitute grilled tuna to make this main dish salad extra special.

. . . .

4 cups / 1 L lettuce or mixed salad greens, torn into bite-sized pieces
Toss with dressing then divide onto two plates. Add toppings (divided) and serve with freshly ground pepper.

Serves 2
. . . .

Dressing:

1½ tablespoon olive oil
1 tablespoon balsamic vinegar
½–1 tablespoon Dijon mustard
½ tablespoon lemon juice
½ teaspoon anchovy paste (optional)
Combine in jar with tight-fitting lid. Shake well.

. . . .

Toppings:

1 (5-ounce / 141-g) can tuna, drained
3 small potatoes, cooked and cut in quarters
2 hard-cooked eggs, cut in wedges
1 medium tomato, cut in wedges
⅔ cup / 150 ml green beans, lightly steamed, rinsed with cold water, and patted dry
10 niçoise olives or other olives

. . . .

MARGE BEKKER, GRAND FORKS, BRITISH COLUMBIA
DORIS YODER, NEWTON, KANSAS

Raspberry Vinaigrette Dressing

. . . .

½ cup / 125 ml maple syrup
½ cup / 125 ml oil
⅓ cup / 75 ml lemon juice
⅓ cup / 75 ml raspberries
1 teaspoon dry mustard
¼ teaspoon salt
¼ teaspoon pepper
Place in blender and blend until smooth.

1 tablespoon red onion, minced
2 tablespoons poppy seeds (optional)
Add to blender and pulse briefly.

Yields 1⅓ cup / 325 ml

. . . .

AUDREY METZ, WASHINGTON, DISTRICT OF COLUMBIA

Green Tomato Salsa Verde

"A fabulously bright green condiment—we really loved this recipe!" one tester exclaimed. Adjust the quantity of chili peppers to make this versatile dressing as hot as you like.

. . . .

1 cup / 250 ml green tomatoes, coarsely chopped
½–1 fresh jalapeño pepper or other chili pepper
2 cloves garlic, minced
2 green onions, white and green parts cut in 1-inch /
    2.5-cm pieces
⅓ cup / 75 ml water
Combine in a small microwavable bowl. Cover tightly. Microwave on high for 2–3 minutes. Let stand 1 minute. Carefully remove cover. Place cooked vegetables in blender or food processor.

¼ cup / 60 ml olive oil
2 tablespoons fresh cilantro, chopped
1 tablespoon lime juice
1 teaspoon salt
Add and blend until smooth. Use as a salsa over beans and rice or as a dressing on salads.

Yields 1½ cup / 375 ml

. . . .

GLORIA SNIDER, RICHMOND, VIRGINIA

Ten Nutrition Tips

As a dietitian, I frequently review what my clients have been eating. The client is asked to keep a record of everything she or he eats or drinks for twenty-four hours. People frequently fill out the forms in a hurry, so I get some interesting notes. My favorites are "hot gods" for hot dogs and "snakes" for snacks. So as I give nutritional advice, I am aware that I am perhaps questioning the "hot gods"—the sacred cows of our food culture—and exposing the potentially poisonous "snakes" on which we often snack: highly processed, high-fat, and sugary foods. —MBL

1. Make lifestyle choices—there is no magic pill. As a feature article in *Time* magazine reported, we are still trying to buy health and "perfect" weight by spending $1 billion a year on weight-loss drugs. For health or religious reasons, many of us frown on smoking. How many of us, for the same reasons, follow healthy eating patterns and get physical exercise?

2. Balance energy. Very simply, for weight maintenance, calories "in" must equal calories "out." Or the amount of energy expended must equal the amount of energy ingested. Similarly, to lose weight, calories out must be greater than calories in. To achieve this you must exercise more and/or eat less.

3. Eat a variety of whole foods in moderation. A whole food is a food that has not had any of its natural features taken away or any artificial substances added. It seems strange that we refine foods and then turn around and "enrich" them; why not just eat whole grains or whole wheat flour rather than enriched flour?

4. Drink water. Research shows that part of the obesity problem is caused by all the calories we are drinking. (The average teen gets 10–15 percent of daily calories from soda.) So instead of drinking beverages sweetened with high-fructose corn syrup or concentrated fruit juice, try drinking water. Water is the nutrient our bodies need in the greatest amount.

5. Eat lots of colorful vegetables and fruits—at least 4½ cups a day. As a general rule, the more colorful and darker the vegetable, the more nutrients it contains. And since no one vegetable or fruit has all the necessary nutrients, it is important to select a variety of colors: green (spinach, kale), yellow/orange (carrots, squash), white (cauliflower, garlic), red (tomatoes, strawberries), and purple (blueberries, plums).

6. Eat breakfast. Breakfast is the meal that most easily supplies fiber and calcium—in whole grain cereals and bread and milk. Fiber and calcium are both important nutrients for a multitude of reasons, including weight control. People who regularly eat breakfast are less likely to be obese.

7. Sit down to eat. We have become a society that eats on the run. Eating is seen as a consumption of calories rather than a time of communion with others. However, experts say that children from families who eat together usually have improved academic performance, higher self-esteem, are less obese, and are more likely to avoid drugs.

8. Eat mindfully. Pay attention to yourself, to your own body, and listen for the cues of both hunger and satiety. Don't eat when you're not hungry, and stop eating when you are full. It sounds simple but when bombarded with food or food advertising all around us, it is hard to resist.

9. Take it with just a grain of salt. Too much sodium (salt) intake is associated with high blood pressure. The best way to limit it is to eat fewer processed foods, which account for about 85 percent of our salt intake.

10. Cut the fat. While all fats have basically the same calories, not all fats are created equal. Unsaturated fats—found in oils—are considered desirable, especially the monounsaturated fats found in olive and canola oil. Saturated fats—found in butter, meat, whole milk, cheese—are less desirable because they contribute to heart problems. Trans fats—found in margarine and processed foods—are considered unsafe in any amount.

Summer Squash Skillet

Let the variety available from your garden or farmers' market, along with your tastes, determine the option you use.

∙∙∙

4 cups / 1 L summer squash: zucchini, yellow, or pattypan, sliced, diced, or shredded
½ cup / 125 ml onion, sliced or diced
½ teaspoon salt
¼ teaspoon pepper
Sauté together in 1 tablespoon oil until tender (time will depend on the size of the pieces). Add one of the options below.

Serves 4
∙∙∙

Option 1: Ⓥ Ⓖⓕ

½ green pepper or chili pepper, diced
2 tablespoons fresh parsley, chopped
1 tablespoon fresh basil, chopped
1 bay leaf
½ cup / 125 ml cheese, shredded (optional)
Add ingredients except cheese with the onion and squash, cover, and steam until tender. Top with cheese just before serving.

∙∙∙

Option 2: Ⓥ Ⓖⓕ

¼ cup / 60 ml fresh parsley, chopped
½ teaspoon lemon peel, grated
½ teaspoon lemon pepper (replaces ¼ teaspoon pepper, above)
Add and simmer about 2 minutes longer.

∙∙∙

Option 3: Ⓥ

Add soy sauce to taste to the sautéed squash before serving.

∙∙∙

Option 4: Ⓥ Ⓖⓕ

2 tablespoons pesto (p. 193)
Add to the sautéed squash before serving.

∙∙∙

DAWN SHOWALTER, HARRISONBURG, VIRGINIA
MARY MEYER, FRESNO, OHIO
RUTH ISAAC WIEDERKEHR, GUELPH, ONTARIO

Fresh Corn Sauté

"I always make this when sweet corn is in season after we have had lots of corn on the cob," says contributor Bev Kennel.

. . . .

3 tablespoons butter
1 cup / 250 ml green pepper, chopped
½ cup / 125 ml onion, chopped
Melt butter in frypan. Sauté green pepper and onion 2 minutes.

4 cups / 1 L corn
¼ cup / 60 ml water
1 tablespoon honey
1 teaspoon salt
pepper to taste
2 tablespoons red sweet pepper, diced (optional)
Add and stir well. Cover and cook over medium heat 10–12 minutes.

½ cup / 125 ml cheddar cheese, shredded
4 slices bacon, cooked and crumbled
Sprinkle over corn and serve.

Serves 6

. . . .

BEV KENNEL, POWHATAN, VIRGINIA

Vegetable gardeners get a double boost to their health: the fresh produce is packed with nutrients, and the labor is good exercise. But gardening can also improve mental and spiritual health. Today horticultural therapy can be found in hospitals, domestic abuse shelters, nursing homes, mental health institutions, and prisons.

"For four years I have taught gardening skills to inmates at Western Correctional Institution in Cumberland, Maryland. They find great satisfaction in being able to contribute to the beauty of this place," says Wayne A. Yoder of Ridgeley, West Virginia.

Once nothing but grass, the prison yard now boasts landscaping mostly designed, planted, and maintained by inmates.

"This may be the most important rehabilitative function of prison gardening: showing inmates that they can make a positive contribution and give back to the society they have wronged in some way," Yoder says. "They learn that whatever they sow, they also reap. That goes two ways, and is always in season."
—CHW

Green Bean Sides

. . . .

1 pound / 500 g green beans, cut in 1-inch / 2.5-cm pieces
Cook in small amount of water until crisp-tender, 5–10 minutes.
Drain (save liquid for soup) and add one of the options below.

Serves 4

. . . .

Parsley-lemon option: Ⓥ Ⓖⓕ

In 1 tablespoon butter or oil lightly sauté 2 cloves minced garlic
and 2 tablespoons finely chopped fresh parsley. Add the cooked
beans, season to taste with salt and pepper. Stir gently and heat
through. Sprinkle with the juice of 1 lemon and serve.

. . . .

Mint option: Ⓥ Ⓖⓕ

In 1 tablespoon butter or oil sauté ¼ cup / 60 ml minced onion.
Add 2 tablespoons minced fresh mint. Add cooked beans and
season to taste with salt and pepper. Serve.

. . . .

Basil-tomato option: Ⓥ Ⓖⓕ

In 1 tablespoon oil sauté ¼ cup / 60 ml minced onion and 1 clove
minced garlic. Add 2 tablespoons minced fresh basil, 1 cup /
250 ml chopped tomatoes, and cooked green beans. Cover and
cook about 5 minutes. Season to taste and serve.

. . . .

Ham or bacon option:

In 1 tablespoon butter or oil sauté ¼ cup / 60 ml minced onion and
1 clove minced garlic. Add ¼ cup / 60 ml cooked ham or bacon.
Add cooked beans and season to taste with salt and pepper. Serve.

. . . .

Almond-Parmesan option: Ⓥ Ⓖⓕ

In 2 tablespoons olive oil sauté 2 cloves minced garlic and ¼ cup /
60 ml slivered almonds. Add cooked beans and season to taste
with salt and pepper. Sprinkle with 2 tablespoons grated Parmesan
cheese and serve.

. . . .

MARY ELLEN LEHMAN, BOSWELL, PENNSYLVANIA
RON BLOUGH, LOUISVILLE, OHIO
HELEN THOMAS, CHARLESTON, WEST VIRGINIA
DAWN SHOWALTER, HARRISONBURG, VIRGINIA
STEPHANIE KNUDSEN, LANCASTER, PENNSYLVANIA

In LaGrange, Indiana, Greg and Lei Gunthorp are fourth-generation pastured pork producers, raising more than one thousand hogs—plus thousands of chickens and ducks—on about one hundred acres of land. The hogs spend most of their time foraging on fields planted with clover and corn. Few immunizations are necessary.

The Gunthorps find it much more pleasant to work with healthy, happy animals. Back when the family used a hog-finishing building, the fumes inside made it hard to breathe. The stressed animals also were much more likely to bite. It certainly wasn't a place where children could interact with the animals. In contrast, the Gunthorps' three children can safely run around in the pastures where the sows spend their days.

There's really only one drawback to raising pigs this way, Lei says: they don't grow as fast as with conventional methods. "But," she adds, "what's time to a pig?"
—CHW

Curried Beans and Potatoes

Tester says, "The more I ate the more I liked it!"

. . . .

3 tablespoons mustard oil or vegetable oil
1 teaspoon mustard seeds (black if available)
4 cloves garlic, thinly sliced
Heat oil in medium frypan over medium-high heat. When hot, add mustard seeds. As soon as mustard seeds begin to pop, add garlic. Stir for 1 minute until garlic turns golden.

½ teaspoon ground turmeric
⅛–¼ teaspoon ground red pepper
¼ teaspoon pepper
1 medium potato, quartered and thinly sliced
Add and stir 1 minute.

4 cups / 1 L green beans, whole or cut
Add and stir until mixed. Salt to taste. Add small amounts of water to keep from sticking and to allow vegetables to steam. Cook until potatoes are tender, stirring occasionally. When done, increase heat to evaporate remaining liquid.

Serves 4–6 Ⓥ ⓖⓕ
. . . .

RUTH MASSEY, COLUMBUS, OHIO

Vegetable Fritters

. . . .

⅓ **cup / 75 ml flour or whole wheat flour**
½ **teaspoon baking powder**
½ **teaspoon salt**
⅛ **teaspoon pepper**
2 eggs, beaten
Mix to form a smooth batter. Add one of the options below and mix gently. Very lightly spray a frypan with oil and heat to medium hot. Drop a large spoonful of batter onto frypan. Fry until golden, turn, and cook on other side until done.

Serves 4 Ⓥ

. . . .

Summer squash option:

3 cups / 750 ml summer squash, shredded
⅓ **cup / 75 ml onion, minced; or 2 cloves garlic, minced**
1 tablespoon fresh parsley, chopped (optional)

. . . .

Corn option:

2 cups / 500 ml corn
2 tablespoons milk

. . . .

LORRAINE PFLEDERER, GOSHEN, INDIANA
MARY KATHRYN YODER, HARRISONVILLE, MISSOURI
NAOMI FAST, HESSTON, KANSAS

If you've eaten conventionally raised eggs all your life, the first time you crack open an egg from a free-range hen you might think something is wrong with it. The yolk has a darker color, bordering on orange. That color signals extra beta-carotene and other nutrients for you.

Foraging hens eat up to 30 percent fresh clover and greens, a diet that yields powerhouse eggs. Compared to commercial eggs, pasture-raised eggs have seven times more beta-carotene, a fourth less saturated fat, a third less cholesterol, two-thirds more vitamin A, and twice the omega-3 fatty acids, one of the fats essential for good health.

Milk from a pasture-raised cow: well, it still looks white. Its butter and cream are a little more yellow than usual. But all these contain a significant nutritional boost from the cow's diet of grass.[2]
—CHW

As Gloria Luster worked in a neighborhood garden in a low-income area of Baltimore, Maryland, she was frequently visited by Mr. Robert, an alcoholic neighbor. "Miss Gloria, I want a little piece of land. I know how to grow things," he'd pester her.

Finally she gave in. That was several years ago. And Mr. Robert has become one of the neighborhood's best gardeners.

"He's taught others how to grow things," Luster says, "and he's almost stopped drinking. He takes a chair into that garden and just sits a lot of the time. This is the therapeutic portion of gardening. Gardening is a very spiritual enterprise."

Mr. Robert now gardens two plots side by side, producing much more food than he could ever eat himself. "He grew such beautiful okra, and since many of the people in that area have southern roots, he was giving it away as fast as he could cut it," Luster says. "He doesn't have any money but what he has, he's been giving. It's what I tell people: it doesn't always take money. Give of yourself, give of your time, your knowledge, and then your life becomes richer."
—CHW

Okra Curry

. . . .

½ cup / 125 ml onion, sliced
¼ teaspoon garlic, minced
¼ teaspoon ground ginger
¼ teaspoon ground turmeric
¼ teaspoon chili powder
In frypan sauté onion in 2 tablespoons oil until golden. Add ginger, garlic, and spices, and sauté for a few minutes.

1 pound / 500 g okra, cleaned and trimmed
½ teaspoon salt
Add and cook a few minutes.

1 cup / 250 ml tomatoes, sliced
Add and fry for a few minutes until liquids evaporate.

Serves 6 Ⓥ Ⓖⓕ
. . . .

RICHARD SARKAR, EPHRATA, PENNSYLVANIA

Spicy Roasted Eggplant

. . . .

½ cup / 125 ml packed fresh cilantro sprigs, chopped
¼ cup / 60 ml olive oil
2 tablespoons lemon juice
2 teaspoons ground cumin
1 teaspoon ground coriander
pinch of ground cinnamon
Stir together.

1 large eggplant, cut in ¼-inch / 5-mm slices
Brush cilantro mixture on both sides of eggplant slices and transfer
to greased baking pan. Broil eggplant 5–6 inches / 12–15 cm from
heat until golden and cooked through, about 10 minutes. Salt and
pepper to taste.

Serves 4 Ⓥ Ⓖⓕ

. . . .

CAROL BORNMAN, LOUGA, SENEGAL

Fried Okra

. . . .

½ cup / 125 ml cornmeal
1 teaspoon salt or seasoned salt
¼ cup / 60 ml Parmesan cheese, grated (optional)
¼ teaspoon chili powder (optional)
Mix together.

3 cups / 750 ml okra
⅔ cup / 150 ml milk
Dip whole or sliced okra in milk then in cornmeal mixture until coated.

Heat 2 tablespoons oil in frypan over medium heat. Add cornmeal-
coated okra and fry on all sides until golden brown.

Serves 4–6 Ⓥ Ⓖⓕ

. . . .

To oven-fry: Oil a shallow baking pan. Spread cornmeal-coated
okra evenly in pan. Bake in preheated oven at 400° F / 200° C for
30–45 minutes, stirring often.

. . . .

AL MORTENSON, LOUISVILLE, KENTUCKY
DAWN JOHNSON, FORT LAUDERDALE, FLORIDA
LARRY MILLER, MACON, MISSISSIPPI

Roasted Summer Vegetables

A versatile summer recipe that can be used as a side dish, main dish, or salad. Be sure to make enough for leftovers to put on pizza. Try a variety of vegetables: any summer squash, onions, potatoes, tomatoes, green beans, green or red peppers, mild chili peppers, carrots, eggplant, mushrooms, or fennel.

. . . .

8–10 cups / 2–2.5 L fresh vegetables
Cut into bite-sized pieces for even cooking time (i.e., thinly slice potatoes but chop summer squash in larger chunks). Toss with one of the seasoning options below. Then spread seasoned vegetables in a thin layer on a baking sheet and bake in preheated oven at 425° F / 220° C for 20 minutes. Stir occasionally.

Serves 8 (side dish), 4–6 (main dish) Ⓥ
. . . .

For a main dish: Serve over cooked penne pasta, wild rice, or couscous. Top with freshly grated Parmesan cheese.

. . . .

For a salad: Cool vegetables (or use the leftovers) and add 2 cups / 500 ml diced tomatoes, 3 ounces / 90 g feta cheese, and additional vinaigrette dressing.

. . . .

Seasoning 1:

3 tablespoons fresh basil, chopped
2 tablespoons fresh cilantro, chopped
1½ tablespoon fresh thyme, chopped
1 tablespoon olive oil
½ teaspoon salt
½ teaspoon pepper
1–4 cloves garlic, minced

. . . .

Seasoning 2:

1 tablespoon olive oil
1 teaspoon chili powder
½ teaspoon salt
¼ teaspoon dried thyme
⅛ teaspoon pepper

. . . .

. . . .

Seasoning 3:

¾ cup / 175 ml Italian dressing or vinaigrette dressing

. . . .

Seasoning 4:

4 cloves garlic, minced
⅓ cup / 75 ml olive oil
2 tablespoons each fresh thyme, oregano, basil, chopped
2 tablespoons balsamic vinegar
1 tablespoon Dijon mustard
½ teaspoon salt
¼ teaspoon pepper
Good with onion, eggplant, zucchini, green peppers, and tomatoes.

. . . .

Kabob variation: Soak wooden skewers, if using, at least 30 minutes in water to prevent scorching. Thread a variety of seasoned vegetables on each skewer, keeping mushrooms separate, as they will cook faster; carrot chunks and small whole potatoes should be boiled a few minutes in advance. Grill over medium heat until vegetables are tender.

. . . .

SUSAN LOHRENTZ, SEATTLE, WASHINGTON
ELAINE GIBBEL, LITITZ, PENNSYLVANIA
AL MORTENSON, LOUISVILLE, KENTUCKY
ESTHER KREIDER EASH, NEWTON, KANSAS
LOIS KLASSEN, VANCOUVER, BRITISH COLUMBIA

Pesto Pizza

*For a different crust, try the Focaccia (pp. 112–13) or
Zucchini Yeast Roll (p. 111) recipes.*

· ·

1 heaping tablespoon active dry yeast
1¼ cup / 300 ml warm water
Stir together in a large bowl until yeast is
dissolved.

2 cups / 500 ml flour
1 cup / 125 ml whole wheat flour
1 teaspoon salt
Add enough flour to make a soft dough. Knead 8–10 minutes
until smooth and elastic. Place in greased bowl, turn to grease
both sides, cover with a damp cloth, and let rise until doubled
in bulk, about 45–55 minutes. Generously grease pizza stone or
baking sheet with olive oil. Roll or press dough onto pan. Bake in
preheated oven at 450° F / 230° C for 5–8 minutes.

½ cup / 125 ml pesto (p. 193)
3 medium tomatoes, sliced
2 cups / 500 ml mozzarella cheese, shredded
Spread pesto on crust. Top with tomatoes and cheese. Garnish
with fresh basil leaves (optional). Bake in preheated oven at 450° F /
230° C until cheese is melted, 5–8 minutes.

Serves 3–4 Ⓥ
· ·

Vegetable Pizza: Arrange on the unbaked pizza crust 4 cups /
1 L diced fresh vegetables (choose a variety such as broccoli,
cauliflower, green pepper, mild chili peppers, mushrooms, summer
squash, onions), 1½ cup / 375 ml diced fresh tomatoes, and ¼ cup /
60 ml chopped fresh herbs (basil, parsley, oregano). Sprinkle with
1 cup / 250 ml shredded mozzarella cheese and ⅓ cup / 75 ml
grated Parmesan cheese. Bake in preheated oven at 400° F /
200° C for 10–15 minutes.

· ·

MARIA CLYMER KURTZ, STEPHENS CITY, VIRGINIA
JUDY LEATHERMAN, PHILADELPHIA, PENNSYLVANIA
HELEN BROWN, HUNTINGTON, WEST VIRGINIA

Creamy Pesto Pasta

. . . .

3 tablespoons butter
¼ cup / 60 ml flour
3 cups / 750 ml milk
Melt butter in a large saucepan. Add flour and cook 3 minutes; do not brown. Add milk and bring to a boil. Cook gently 5 minutes.

1 cup / 250 ml pesto (p. 193)
1 teaspoon salt
¼ teaspoon ground nutmeg
Stir in. Remove from heat.

1 pound / 500 g spaghetti, fettuccine, or linguine
Cook and drain. Combine with sauce. Toss well until sauce thickens. Taste and adjust seasoning if necessary.

Serves 6 Ⓥ
. . . .

GUDRUN MATHIES, EPHRATA, PENNSYLVANIA

Fresh Tomato and Basil Pasta

So simple and so delicious on a summer evening.

. . . .

4 large cloves garlic, minced
2 pounds / 1 kg tomatoes, chopped, seeded, and drained
½ cup / 125 ml fresh basil, chopped
¼ cup / 60 ml olive oil
1 teaspoon salt
Combine and let stand at room temperature 1–2 hours.

1 pound / 500 g whole wheat pasta shells or ziti
Cook according to package directions. Combine hot pasta and sauce. Garnish with freshly grated Parmesan cheese or feta cheese. Serve immediately.

Serves 6–8 Ⓥ
. . . .

Mint variation: Replace basil with ⅓ cup / 75 ml chopped fresh mint plus the juice and grated rind of 1 lemon.

. . . .

REGINA BEIDLER, RANDOLPH CENTER, VERMONT
DEANNA RISSER, GOSHEN, INDIANA
CARA ULRICH, ARCHBOLD, OHIO

Great Green Vegetable Pasta

Substitute other green vegetables to suit your tastes and what you have on hand.

. . . .

1 cup / 250 ml cottage cheese or ricotta cheese
½ cup / 125 ml milk (optional if using cottage cheese)
⅓ cup / 75 ml Parmesan cheese, freshly grated
1 clove garlic, minced
2 tablespoons fresh basil, chopped; or 2 teaspoons dried
2 tablespoons fresh parsley, chopped; or 2 teaspoons dried
½ teaspoon salt
Stir together in a bowl and set aside. Or for a smooth texture, purée in blender.

12 ounces / 350 g fusilli, linguini, or spaghetti
In large soup pot of boiling water, start cooking according to package directions.

2 cups / 500 ml broccoli florets
2 cups / 500 ml zucchini, sliced
1 cup / 250 ml green beans
1 cup / 250 ml peas
¼ cup / 60 ml green onions, chopped
Stir in broccoli 6 minutes before pasta is done; boil 3 minutes. Stir in zucchini and green beans slowly; boil 2 minutes. Stir in peas and green onions slowly; boil 1 minute. Remove from heat. Drain well and return to soup pot.

2 tablespoons butter
Toss with pasta and vegetables until melted. Add cottage cheese mixture; toss gently to coat. Serve immediately sprinkled with freshly grated Parmesan cheese and freshly ground pepper. Garnish with tomato slices.

Serves 4–6 Ⓥ

. . . .

Spring variation: Use spinach and asparagus for the vegetables.

. . . .

ROBERTA SCHWINKE, MORRISON, MISSOURI
JOCELE MEYER, FRESNO, OHIO
KATHI SUDERMAN, BEIJING, CHINA

Greek Fennel Skillet

Serve plain as a side dish or make it a meal by serving this savory sauté over pasta or Polenta (p. 394). It can also top Italian bread that has been brushed with olive oil and toasted.

. . . .

2 cloves garlic, minced
In a medium frypan sauté in 2 tablespoons olive oil for 1 minute.

2 medium fennel bulbs, thinly sliced
1 large onion, thinly sliced
Add and sauté until tender, 5–10 minutes.

1 tablespoon lemon juice
3 medium tomatoes, chopped
Add and cook over medium heat until part of liquid evaporates, 10 minutes. Salt and pepper to taste.

1½ cup / 375 ml feta cheese, crumbled, or mozzarella
**   cheese, shredded**
½ cup / 125 ml black olives (optional)
Stir in.

Serves 2–4 Ⓥ ⒼⒻ
. . . .

NICOLE CARLIN, PITTSBURGH, PENNSYLVANIA

Consumers are expressing health concerns about pesticide residues on their food, but another population is even more at risk. For farmworkers pesticides are a serious occupational hazard, causing both acute, immediate symptoms (like fatigue and skin rashes) and diseases like cancer or birth defects, stemming from long-term exposure.

Fieldworkers are not always adequately trained to work with pesticides or given protective gear. Even those who aren't doing the spraying are exposed—sometimes without their knowledge—through contact with the plants and soil. Fields and orchards may lack facilities for hand-washing. The chemicals spread through the air and are brought home on clothing and cars, contaminating living quarters, play areas, and food. Children are especially vulnerable; even those who do not spend time in the fields with their parents are at risk of dangerous levels of exposure.
—CHW

In annual conferences sponsored by Chefs Collaborative Portland and Ecotrust, local farmers and food buyers for restaurants and institutions get acquainted and learn what each other have to offer. To help the process along, "farmer-chef speed dating" was born. "It was like a middle school dance," says organizer Larry Lev. "Farmers were on one side of a big room, and chefs on the other. And when we set them loose they dashed across the room to find one another." The speed dating practice has since spread widely in farmer-chef circles.
—Celene Carillo, Corvallis, Oregon

Summer Garden Ratatouille

"Summer isn't summer without this dish," says contributor Sarah Myers. "It is my favorite way to enjoy all the goodness and bounty of a summer garden."

. . . .

2 onions, chopped
4 cloves garlic, minced
1 bay leaf
Sauté in 3 tablespoons olive oil about 5 minutes.

1 medium eggplant, chopped
1½ tablespoon fresh basil, chopped; or 2 teaspoons dried
1 tablespoon fresh rosemary, chopped; or 1 teaspoon dried
1½ teaspoon salt
1 teaspoon fresh marjoram, chopped; or ½ teaspoon dried
Add, cover, and cook over medium heat, stirring occasionally, until eggplant is soft, about 15–20 minutes.

2 summer squash, chopped
2 green, orange, or red sweet peppers, cut in strips
2 cups / 500 ml tomatoes, chopped
Add and simmer until peppers and squash are tender, about 10 minutes. Serve over pasta or polenta (p. 394) sprinkled with chopped fresh parsley, black olives, or freshly grated Parmesan cheese.

Serves 4–6 ⓥ

. . . .

SARAH MYERS, MOUNT JOY, PENNSYLVANIA
LINDA HERR, CAIRO, EGYPT
JOAN KREIDER, ST. PAUL, MINNESOTA

Kohlrabi with Peas and Potato

This is a mild yet flavorful dish, and it cooks up quickly.

. . . .

½ cup / 125 ml onion, chopped
1 clove garlic, minced
In a large soup pot, sauté in 1 tablespoon oil about 3–4 minutes.

½ teaspoon dry mustard
½ teaspoon ground cumin
¼ teaspoon ground turmeric
¼ teaspoon ground coriander
Add and stir-fry for about 30 seconds.

1 cup / 250 ml kohlrabi bulbs, peeled and chopped
1 cup / 250 ml potatoes, peeled and chopped
Add and stir briefly.

1 cup / 250 ml tomatoes, chopped
½ cup / 125 ml water
¾ teaspoon salt
½ teaspoon sugar
Add; bring to a boil then simmer until vegetables are crisp-tender, about 15 minutes.

kohlrabi leaves, finely chopped
Add and simmer 8–10 minutes.

½ cup / 125 ml peas
Stir in and cook until peas are done. Serve over rice.

Serves 4 Ⓥ Ⓖⓕ
. . . .

JESSICA SEEM, BROOKTONDALE, NEW YORK

Spicy Tomato Tempeh

Adjust the amount of crushed hot chilies to suit your family's tastes.

. . . .

2 tablespoons olive oil
2 tablespoons soy sauce
1 teaspoon sesame oil
1 teaspoon paprika
Combine in a medium bowl.

8 ounces / 250 g tempeh, cut into bite-sized cubes
Add and toss to coat. Spread on a baking sheet and roast in
preheated oven at 375° F / 190° C until tempeh is browned,
30 minutes. Stir after 15 minutes.

1 green pepper, thinly sliced
1 onion, thinly sliced
2 cloves garlic, minced
In a deep frypan, sauté in 2 tablespoons olive oil until softened,
about 10 minutes.

1½ pound / 750 g tomatoes, coarsely chopped
1 tablespoon paprika
¼ teaspoon crushed hot chilies
½ teaspoon dried thyme
1 bay leaf
Add and cook over medium-high heat until mixture is bubbling,
about 10 minutes.

1 tablespoon flour
Sprinkle in, stirring, and cook 2–3 minutes until the sauce is
thickened. Add roasted tempeh. Add 1 teaspoon sugar, dash
of balsamic vinegar, and salt to taste. Serve over brown rice or
polenta (p. 394).

Serves 4 Ⓥ
. . . .

AMY KAUFFMAN, NEW YORK CITY, NEW YORK

Seitan with Peanut Sauce

Seitan (p. 404) is an alternative protein food made from wheat gluten. This is a nice vegetable combination, but try others according to what's available.

. . . .

1 medium onion, chopped
6 cloves garlic, minced
In large frypan sauté in 1–2 tablespoons sesame oil for 5 minutes.

12 ounces / 350 g seitan, drained and cubed;
   set aside liquid
Add and sauté another 5 minutes.

1 large head of broccoli, cut into florets
2 carrots, sliced
1 green or red sweet pepper, chopped
⅓ cup / 75 ml liquid from seitan or water
2 tablespoons soy sauce
Add, cover, and steam 5–10 minutes, until vegetables are slightly softened but still a bit crunchy.

½ cup / 125 ml water
1 tablespoon soy sauce
2 teaspoons cornstarch
Mix in a small bowl. Stir well and pour into the seitan and vegetable mixture. Cook 1–2 minutes, stirring until sauce thickens.

½ cup / 125 ml chopped peanuts
½ cup / 125 ml fresh cilantro, chopped
Sprinkle on top and serve with rice noodles or brown rice.

Serves 4 Ⓥ
. . . .

AUDREY HESS, HANOVER, PENNSYLVANIA

Malnutrition and poverty are linked, whether the problem is eating too much of the wrong foods or eating too little of the right ones. Worldwide, overeating is the fastest growing form of malnourishment, notes the World Health Organization, and the problem can exist side by side with not eating enough. One study in Indonesia found that a startling one in ten households include both undernourished and overnourished family members.[3] In 2012, three times as many people died from obesity as undernourishment.[4]
—CHW

Thai Green Beans

Try this sauce with other steamed or stir-fried seasonal vegetables, such as broccoli, snow peas, or carrots.

. . . .

5 cups / 1.25 L green beans
Steam 8–10 minutes until bright green and lightly crunchy.

½ onion, chopped
2 tablespoons ginger root, peeled and minced
3 cloves garlic, minced
In frypan or wok sauté in 2 teaspoons sesame oil over medium heat until onion is tender, 5 minutes.

3 tablespoons soy sauce
2 tablespoons Thai sweet chili sauce
Add to taste.

1 cup / 250 ml extra firm tofu, crumbled (optional)
Add and cook 5 minutes. Add steamed beans and stir to coat with sauce. Simmer over medium-low heat for 5 minutes. Serve over rice. Garnish with lightly toasted cashews, sesame seeds, or slivered almonds (optional).

Serves 4 Ⓥ
. . . .

KENDRA LOEWEN, SURREY, BRITISH COLUMBIA

Hunger always has been the burden of the poor, but increasingly the highest rates of obesity are found among people with the lowest income and least education. The reasons encompass everything from genetics to personal habits to societal factors.

One such societal factor is cheap, high-calorie foods. Research suggests the more calories a food contains per ounce, the less it costs. Compare, for example, potato chips and fresh carrots. A dollar spent on chips (or white bread, instant noodles, or candy) doesn't buy much nutrition, but it does buy nearly five times as many calories. In this limited sense, "diets composed of whole grains, fish, and fresh vegetables and fruit are far more expensive than refined grains, added sugars, and added fats," says researcher Adam Drewnowski. "[People] become obese primarily because they are poor."[5]
—CHW

Mexican Stuffed Peppers

A pleasing variation on the traditional meat and rice stuffed vegetable. If you like spicy food, do not remove the jalapeño seeds. Hot sauce also can be added at the table by those who dare.

. . . .

4 green, yellow, orange, or red sweet peppers
Cut ½ inch / 1 cm off top of peppers and discard seeds. Steam whole peppers in 1 inch / 2.5 cm boiling water until tender, about 5–8 minutes. Remove peppers from water and set aside.

⅓ cup / 75 ml onion, chopped
2 cloves garlic, minced
In large frypan sauté in 1 tablespoon oil.

2 cups / 500 ml tomatoes, chopped
1 jalapeño pepper, minced after seeds removed
2 tablespoons fresh parsley, chopped
1 tablespoon fresh oregano, chopped; or 1 teaspoon dried
1 teaspoon ground cumin
½ teaspoon salt
1 bay leaf
Add and cook 5 minutes.

2 cups / 500 ml corn
1½ cup / 375 ml cooked black beans
Add and simmer 10 minutes. Remove bay leaf. Place peppers in ovenproof dish so that they stand upright, cut ends up. Stuff peppers with vegetable mixture. Any extra filling can be placed in dish next to peppers.

¼ cup / 60 ml Parmesan cheese, freshly grated
Sprinkle on top. Bake at 350° F / 180° C to heat through, 20 minutes.

Serves 4 Ⓥ Ⓖⓕ

. . . .

LISA LOEWEN EBERSOLE, CORVALLIS, OREGON

Super Stuffed Tortillas

"My family absolutely loves this dish," says contributor Nicole Carlin. "We freeze vegetables for this recipe in bags with the right amounts of corn, peppers, and zucchini to eat in the winter."

. . . .

1–2 cloves garlic, minced
1 large onion
1 green pepper
Sauté garlic in 2 teaspoons oil for 1 minute. Add onion and pepper and sauté until crisp-tender.

2 cups / 500 ml corn
1 small-medium zucchini, sliced
1½ tablespoon ground cumin
Add and continue to sauté until all vegetables are tender but not browned.

2 cups / 500 ml cooked black beans
1 cup / 250 ml chicken or vegetable broth
6 tablespoons salsa
Add and cook until there is no excess moisture. Remove from heat and add salt, pepper, sliced green onions or chives, and chopped fresh cilantro to taste.

flour or corn tortillas
**cheddar cheese, feta, or queso blanco, shredded or
     crumbled**
Preheat a frypan with a bit of oil and place a tortilla in pan. Add cheese in center of tortilla and add ¼–½ cup / 60–125 ml vegetable filling. When the tortilla is crispy, remove, and fold in half. Or place a second tortilla on top, flip, and fry until crisp.

Serves 6–8
. . . .

Variation: Add or substitute spinach, roasted poblano peppers, or other vegetables for corn and zucchini. For a heartier meal, add leftover grilled, chopped chicken.

. . . .

NICOLE CARLIN, PITTSBURGH, PENNSYLVANIA
MELANIE BAER-DRESCHER, LITITZ, PENNSYLVANIA

Students at Henry North Elementary in Lansing, Michigan, begin each school year with a chorus of munching and crunching. They arrive just in time for the North Children's Garden harvest of cantaloupes and watermelons.

Teacher Ying Zheng and her special education class started this organic garden in 1997 as a single plot in the community garden on school property. These days, it is over three thousand square feet, involves several classes, and has caught the heart of the school. Students with low-level writing skills craft descriptive sentences about the garden. An introduction to botany is brought to life while growing seedlings. Budding designers create virtual garden tours on computers. Still, eating the garden's produce is the favorite classroom activity. The most popular item? Yellow pear tomatoes.
—Sarah Anderson, Kitchener, Ontario

Stacked Vegetable Quesadillas

Good recipe for quick weekday suppers—filling, flavorful, and low-fat. Use whatever vegetables you have on hand.

. . . .

½ sweet onion, thinly sliced
In frypan sauté in 1 tablespoon oil until translucent, 1–2 minutes.

1 clove garlic, minced
4 ounces / 125 g mushrooms, thinly sliced
2 carrots, julienned
1 zucchini or other summer squash, julienned
1 green or red sweet pepper, thinly sliced
Add and cook 5 minutes more just until vegetables are tender. Salt and pepper to taste.

12 corn tortillas
1½ cup / 375 ml pepper jack cheese, shredded
Assemble 4 stacks simultaneously on a baking sheet. Start with a tortilla, top with a large spoonful of vegetables, some grated cheese, and then another tortilla. Repeat layers, ending with a third tortilla. Place tortilla stacks in preheated oven at 400° F / 200° C for 10–15 minutes, until cheese is melted and stacks are hot. Cut into quarters and serve warm with salsa, sour cream, avocado, and/or chopped fresh cilantro.

Serves 4 Ⓥ Ⓖⓕ
. . . .
KARIN SHANK, RALEIGH, NORTH CAROLINA

Plum Tomato Galette

This rustic pie is delightful potluck or picnic fare.

....

1½ cup / 375 ml flour or whole wheat pastry flour
7 tablespoons butter, chilled
Cut together until crumbly.

⅓ cup / 75 ml extra sharp cheddar cheese, shredded
3–4 tablespoons water
½ teaspoon salt
Add and mix until dough just comes together, adding more water
if necessary. Turn onto floured surface and quickly bring together
into a ball. Cover with plastic wrap and refrigerate 30 minutes. Roll
out pastry on lightly floured surface into a circle about 15 inches /
38 cm in diameter. Wrap pastry around rolling pin and carefully lift
onto a greased baking sheet.

1 egg yolk, lightly beaten
3 tablespoons dried bread crumbs
2 pounds / 1 kg fresh plum tomatoes, sliced
Brush most of the yolk lightly over pastry. Sprinkle bread crumbs
on top, then arrange tomato slices so they overlap in a circle,
leaving a wide border.

4 ounces / 125 g goat cheese or feta cheese, crumbled
Scatter over top of tomatoes. Turn edge of pastry in over tomato
filling and brush with remaining egg yolk (mix with a little milk if
there's not enough egg left). Bake in preheated oven at 350° F /
180° C until pastry is golden, 30 minutes.

2–4 tablespoons olive oil
handful of fresh basil leaves, chopped
Remove galette from oven and drizzle with olive oil. Season well
with salt and pepper. Scatter basil leaves on top and serve.

Serves 2–4 Ⓥ

....

PAUL HUNT, LANCASTER, PENNSYLVANIA

Italian Zucchini Pie

"This is one of our favorite zucchini recipes of all time," writes contributor Sheryl Shenk. "It takes some work to make, so it's a time-saver to make two at once."

. . . .

¼ cup / 60 ml warm water
1 tablespoon active dry yeast
Mix until yeast dissolves. Set aside.

¼ cup / 60 ml milk
1 tablespoon olive oil
1 egg, beaten
Combine in a mixing bowl or food processor. Add dissolved yeast and stir.

¼ cup / 60 ml whole wheat flour
¼ cup / 60 ml Parmesan cheese, freshly grated
1 teaspoon salt
1–2 teaspoons fresh basil, chopped
Blend in.

2 cups / 500 ml bread flour
Add ½ cup / 125 ml at a time to make a smooth but slightly sticky dough. Place in a greased bowl, turn to grease both sides, cover with a damp cloth, and place in a warm place while preparing the zucchini filling.

¼ cup / 60 ml butter
8 cups / 2 L zucchini, thinly sliced
1–2 cups / 250–500 ml onion, chopped
Melt butter in a large frypan over medium heat. Add zucchini and onions and sauté until soft, about 10 minutes. Remove from heat.

1 clove garlic, minced
1 tablespoon each fresh basil and oregano, chopped;
    or 1 teaspoon dried
1 teaspoon each fresh thyme, rosemary, sage, parsley,
    savory, and marjoram, chopped; or ½ teaspoon dried
1 teaspoon salt
½ teaspoon pepper
Stir in.

5 large eggs, beaten
4 cups / 1 L mozzarella cheese, shredded
Combine in a separate bowl, then stir into zucchini mixture.

Divide risen dough in half. Place each half on lightly floured surface
and roll into a circle 12 inches / 30 cm in diameter. Place each into
a lightly greased 10-inch / 25-cm pie dish.

4 teaspoons prepared mustard
¼ cup / 60 ml Parmesan cheese, grated (optional)
Spread the pie crusts with mustard. Divide the zucchini mixture
between the two crusts. Sprinkle Parmesan cheese on top, if
using. Bake in preheated oven at 375° F / 190° C until center is
set, 18–20 minutes. If crust begins to brown before center is done,
cover edges with aluminum foil. Let stand 10 minutes before
serving.

Yields 2 pies Ⓥ

SHERYL SHENK, HARRISONBURG, VIRGINIA

"When there's fresh corn, you eat fresh corn. When there's banana, you eat banana." I heard various versions of these statements when I lived in a poor rural community in Guatemala. My neighbors literally lived off their crops. If disaster struck and crops were destroyed, food was uncertain and large debts were incurred to buy staples of corn and beans. If the year was plentiful, excess could be sold and a different type of food purchased. Yet always, when it was *su tiempo* ("its time"), a crop was eaten and eaten and eaten.

Back in the United States, I strive to eat within the seasons, including many foods from our garden. That means eating what's available in its time. Sometimes that means a certain amount of repetition. As I look at my overabundant zucchini crop, I remember my former neighbors. It helps me see with gratitude the gift of food that God has given. I have learned to say with a thankful heart, "When there's zucchini, you eat zucchini."
—Jenn Esbenshade,
New Holland, Pennsylvania

Summer Squash Bake

This popular dish can be made ahead and refrigerated until you are ready to bake it; just give it another 20–30 minutes in the oven. Adding cheese or meat makes it a main dish, while without them it's a delicious side dish.

. . . .

6–7 cups / 1.5–1.75 L zucchini or yellow squash, shredded or chopped (remove spongy seedy part if using mature squash)
1 small onion, minced
Combine with enough water to cook or microwave until tender, 3–4 minutes (shredded zucchini may be used without cooking). Drain, reserving the water to make Cream Soup Substitute (see below). Set aside.

1 recipe Cream Soup Substitute (p. 387)
    or 1 can condensed cream soup
1 cup / 250 ml plain yogurt or sour cream
1 cup / 250 ml carrot, shredded
Mix together in a separate bowl.

2 tablespoons fresh oregano, chopped; or 2 teaspoons dried
1 cup / 250 ml cooked chicken, diced (optional)
1 cup / 250 ml cheese, shredded (optional)
Add and mix thoroughly. Stir into squash mixture.

¼ cup / 60 ml butter, melted
2–3 cups / 500–750 ml Herbed Croutons (p. 393)
    or herb stuffing mix
Mix together in a separate bowl. Put half into the bottom of a 9 x 13-inch / 3.5-L baking pan or a deep casserole dish. Add the squash mixture and top with the reserved croutons. Bake at 350° F / 180° C for 30 minutes.

Serves 6 (main dish), 8–10 (side dish)
. . . .

CAROLYN BEYER, LEOLA, PENNSYLVANIA
LOIS LOFLIN, HALSTEAD, KANSAS
MYRNA KAUFMAN, GOSHEN, INDIANA

Making compost isn't quite as simple as piling up waste materials and letting them decompose. An important step is to aerate the pile by turning it, allowing air to get through.

Most farms use heavy machinery powered by gas. But at the Polyface farm in Swoope, Virginia, the work is done by—pigs.

Widely known for his innovative farming methods, grower Joel Salatin created the "pigerator" system, in which he layers corn with cattle manure, wood chips, straw, and hay. Pigs will completely root through the pile to find the grain, which ferments, making it extra nutritious. The pigs, well, they're in hog heaven. It's just one example of how farmers can work with nature to create systems that are healthy in every way: for animals, people, the environment, and communities.
—CHW

Crustless Zucchini Tomato Quiche

2 cups / 500 ml zucchini, chopped
1 cup / 250 ml tomatoes, chopped
½ cup / 125 ml onion, chopped
⅓ cup / 75 ml Parmesan cheese, grated
Place in greased 10-inch / 25-cm pie pan or casserole dish.

1½ cup / 375 ml milk
¾ cup / 175 ml Baking Mix (p. 390)
½ teaspoon salt
¼ teaspoon pepper
3 eggs
Beat in blender until smooth, 15 seconds or more. Pour over vegetables. Bake in preheated oven at 400° F / 200° C until knife inserted in center comes out clean, about 30 minutes. Let stand a few minutes to cool before serving. Garnish with fresh parsley.

Serves 6 Ⓥ

Autumn variation: Substitute finely chopped broccoli, spinach, or kale for the zucchini and tomatoes.

RUTH K. HEATWOLE, HARRISONBURG, VIRGINIA
TARYN PADIAK, BAINGRIDGE, NEW YORK
NANCY MUCKLOW, KINGSTON, ONTARIO

Stuffed Zucchini

A way to use those overgrown zucchini that hide under the leaves until they are too big for most dishes.

....

1 extra-large zucchini
Split lengthwise, scoop out the seeds, and discard. Cut away (and reserve) flesh to form two shells, each ½ inch / 1 cm thick.

¾ pound / 350 g ground beef or venison
1 small onion, chopped
1 red sweet pepper, chopped
Cook in frypan until meat is browned. Drain off fat.

1 cup / 250 ml corn
1 cup / 250 ml stewed tomatoes
2–3 tablespoons mild chili peppers, seeded and chopped
1 clove garlic, minced
1 tablespoon chili powder
1½ teaspoon fresh oregano, chopped; or ½ teaspoon dried
½ teaspoon ground cumin
Add, along with chopped zucchini flesh. Turn heat to high and boil, stirring often, until liquid evaporates, about 5 minutes.

¼ cup / 60 ml bread crumbs
¼ cup / 60 ml Monterey Jack cheese, shredded
2 tablespoons fresh cilantro, chopped
Add to filling and mix well. Place the zucchini shells in a baking dish and fill with the meat mixture. Bake in preheated oven at 350° F / 180° C for 30–35 minutes.

¼ cup / 60 ml Monterey Jack cheese, shredded
Sprinkle on the filled zucchini halves. Return to the oven and bake until cheese begins to brown, 12–15 minutes. Remove from the oven and let stand 5 minutes. Garnish with 2 tablespoons chopped fresh cilantro and serve.

Serves 2–4
....

GLORIA SNIDER, RICHMOND, VIRGINIA

Eggplant Cheese Pie

This is good served with a fresh fruit salad or a salad of field greens with sliced green apples.

....

4½ cups / 1.1 L eggplant, cut into ½-inch / 1-cm cubes
1 medium onion, minced
2 cloves garlic, minced
In large frypan sauté in 1½ tablespoon oil, 2 minutes. Cover and cook until eggplant is soft, about 5 minutes, stirring as needed.

1 tablespoon fresh oregano, chopped; or 1 teaspoon dried
1 tablespoon fresh basil, chopped; or 1 teaspoon dried
Add and salt to taste.

1 small zucchini, sliced
Line bottom and sides of greased 10-inch / 25-cm pie pan with zucchini slices. Spoon eggplant mixture on top.

2 cups / 500 ml mozzarella cheese, shredded
⅔ cup / 150 ml evaporated milk
1 egg
Combine in a bowl then pour over vegetables. Bake in preheated oven at 375° F / 190° C for 30 minutes.

Serves 6 Ⓥ Ⓖⓕ
....

CLARA YODER, HARRISONBURG, VIRGINIA

Eggplant Burgers

A delicious late summer meatless grill—or make it under the broiler. You might need a knife and fork to eat these hearty sandwiches.

. . . .

2 tablespoons oil
2 teaspoons wine vinegar or balsamic vinegar
1 teaspoon Dijon mustard
¼ teaspoon salt
¼ teaspoon pepper
Whisk together in a small bowl.

1 large eggplant
Cut crosswise into ¼-inch / 5-mm thick slices to make 12–16 slices. Brush with the oil mixture. Place on grill over medium-high heat. Close lid and cook, turning and brushing occasionally with remaining oil mixture, until tender, 5–10 minutes. Remove from grill. (Eggplant slices may be cooked under the broiler or sautéed in a frypan until tender, 4–5 minutes per side.)

8 thin slices provolone, Gouda, or other cheese
2 tomatoes, thinly sliced, or 4 large pieces roasted red
    sweet peppers (p. 199)
8–16 leaves fresh basil
freshly ground pepper
Place a slice of cheese on 1 eggplant slice; top with another eggplant slice. Top with 2 tomato slices or a piece of roasted red sweet pepper, then 2–4 basil leaves. Top with third eggplant slice, then another slice of cheese. Top with fourth eggplant slice. Repeat to make 4 stacks, adding a grind of pepper at the end (optional). Place on grill; close lid and cook for about 2 minutes, turning once.

4 crusty rolls or 8 thin slices sturdy bread
Drizzle balsamic vinegar on inside of split rolls. Or brush the bread with olive oil, toast it on the grill, and lightly rub a cut clove of garlic over the toasted surface. Add vegetable stacks and serve immediately. Or allow to cool, wrap tightly, and refrigerate several hours or overnight, allowing flavors to blend.

Serves 4 ⓥ
. . . .

LORI BOHN, WINNIPEG, MANITOBA
JANET YODER, PHOENIX, ARIZONA

Marinated Tofu and Vegetables

. . . .

½ cup / 125 ml vinegar or white wine vinegar
⅓ cup / 75 ml soy sauce
6 tablespoons olive oil
2 tablespoons sesame oil
2 tablespoons ginger root, peeled and minced
1 tablespoon brown sugar
2 cloves garlic, minced
2 teaspoons Tabasco pepper sauce
Mix together. Divide into two shallow pans.

2 blocks firm tofu, drained and sliced in ¼-inch / 5-mm slices
Place slices in one pan of marinade, making sure all sides are
covered with liquid. Marinate in refrigerator 8–24 hours; the longer
the tofu is in the marinade the more flavorful it will be. Remove
from marinade and fry in frypan over medium heat until lightly
browned. (The oil in the marinade will prevent sticking without
adding more to the pan.)

7 cups / 1.75 L fresh vegetables such as summer squash,
    Asian eggplant, peppers, potatoes, or carrots, cut in
    1-inch / 2.5-cm chunks, whole mushrooms, or onion
    wedges
Potatoes and carrots should be precooked 5 minutes. Add all
vegetables to other pan of marinade and refrigerate 8–24 hours.
Drain off excess marinade.

1 cup / 250 ml cherry tomatoes
Add to vegetables. Place in nonstick grilling pan (with sides and
drain holes) and grill over medium-high heat until crisp-tender. Or
stir-fry on stovetop. Or spread on baking sheets in a single layer
and roast in preheated oven at 425° F / 220° C until tender.

Serves 4–6 Ⓥ
. . . .

For kabobs: If using wooden skewers soak at least 30 minutes in
water to prevent scorching. Thread a variety of vegetables on each
skewer, keeping mushrooms separate, as they will cook faster.
Grill over medium-high heat until vegetables are tender, turning
occasionally for even cooking.

. . . .

MARIE HARNISH, INDIANAPOLIS, INDIANA
SAMIRA MUSLEH, ABBOTSFORD, BRITISH COLUMBIA

Apricot Chicken

For an attractive presentation arrange the apricots around the outside of the plate with the rice in the middle and the chicken on top.

. . . .

2 teaspoons butter
4 ripe apricots, halved and pitted
Melt butter in a frypan. Place apricots in melted butter cut side down and cook over medium heat until light brown, about 5 minutes. Turn and cook several minutes more. Remove to plate.

4 boneless, skinless chicken breasts, whole or cut
    into strips
salt and pepper
Roll chicken in mixture of salt and pepper. Sauté in 1 tablespoon olive oil on medium-high heat for 3 minutes, then medium-low heat for 7 more minutes or until no longer pink inside. Remove chicken to plate with apricots.

1 teaspoon ginger root, peeled and minced
1 green onion or 2 tablespoons onion, chopped
Combine in frypan and sauté briefly.

½ cup / 125 ml dry white wine, apple juice, or water
2 tablespoons maple syrup or apricot preserves
½ teaspoon lime peel, grated
Add to frypan along with the apricots and chicken. Simmer 10 minutes to combine flavors. Serve alone or over brown rice or couscous. Garnish with ¼ cup / 60 ml toasted sliced almonds.

Serves 4 (Gf)
. . . .
JEAN AND GALE HESS, MOUNT JOY, PENNSYLVANIA

Chicken Cacciatore

Using a crockpot keeps you from heating up the kitchen.

. . . .

3-pound / 1½-kg whole chicken, skinned and cut into pieces
4 cups / 1 L tomatoes, chopped
1 green, yellow, orange, or red sweet pepper, cut in strips
2 onions, thinly sliced
2 cloves garlic, minced
1 bay leaf
1 teaspoon salt
1 tablespoon fresh oregano, chopped; or 1 teaspoon dried
1 tablespoon fresh basil, chopped; or ½ teaspoon dried
¼ teaspoon pepper
¼ cup / 60 ml white wine (optional)
1 cup / 250 ml mushrooms, chopped (optional)
Combine in slow cooker and cook on low for 8 hours. Serve over pasta or noodles.

Serves 6

. . . .

MARY BETH LIND, HARMAN, WEST VIRGINIA

Menno Wiebe, who lived among Canada's native people, was struck by the way they ate. People from communities steeped in the traditions of hunting and gathering now would go to the store and buy frozen and processed foods. It contributed to the deteriorating physical health of many individuals, he says, but also affected the social and spiritual health of their community.

In response Wiebe helped to start Mennonite Central Committee Canada's Native Gardening project, introducing new ways for Aboriginal communities to feed themselves. The program was formed to address increasing problems such as diabetes, and university studies confirmed that participating communities experienced better health. But it was also intended to be an antidote to an economic system that hindered self-sufficiency and to bring people together.

"Our exchange with the native communities was as much about friendship as food," says Wiebe. "I believe in a gospel that reaches right into the digestive system."
—Rich Preheim, Elkhart, Indiana

Fajitas

Two fantastic, flavorful options.

. . . .

1 pound / 500 g boneless chicken breasts or thighs, lean sirloin beef, or venison round steak

Cut meat in thin strips. Choose the paste or marinade option below and cook as directed.

4 cups / 1 L vegetables: onion, chopped; green or red sweet pepper, sliced; carrots, thinly sliced; yellow squash, sliced
ground red and black pepper

Toss vegetables with several dashes of pepper. Stir-fry over high heat in 2 teaspoons oil (none needed if using a nonstick frypan). Serve meat and vegetables in warm flour tortillas with each person adding shredded cheese or crumbled queso blanco, sliced banana peppers, diced tomatoes, salsa, and sour cream to taste.

Serves 4

. . . .

Cilantro spice paste:

1 cup / 250 ml fresh cilantro leaves, finely chopped
2 tablespoons soy sauce
1 tablespoon oil
1 tablespoon chili powder
2 teaspoons ground cumin
juice of one lime

Mix together. Coat meat well with cilantro paste; let stand at least 15 minutes. Stir-fry over high heat in 2 teaspoons oil. Remove from pan and keep warm while stir-frying vegetables.

. . . .

Barbecue marinade:

¼ cup / 60 ml olive oil
2 cloves garlic, minced
2 tablespoons each red wine vinegar and barbecue sauce
2 teaspoons dry mustard
1 teaspoon each Worcestershire sauce and salt
¼ teaspoon each pepper and Tabasco pepper sauce

Combine and add meat. Stir to coat and refrigerate at least 12 hours. Remove meat from marinade and stir-fry in 1 tablespoon oil until browned. Leave in pan while stir-frying vegetables.

. . . .

NATHAN REGIER, NEWTON, KANSAS
MARY FARRAR, MARKHAM, ONTARIO

Green Enchiladas

. . . .

3 poblano peppers
Roast and peel (p. 199). Scrape out seeds.

3–4 tomatillos
½ cup / 125 ml water
Remove and discard dry husks, cut tomatillos into quarters, and place in microwavable bowl with water. Microwave on full power until tender, 3–4 minutes. (Tomatillos also may be broiled in the oven alongside the roasting poblanos. Turn them every few minutes and remove tomatillos when soft but barely scorched. Some may cook faster than others, so check and remove them from pan as necessary.)

¼ cup / 60 ml unsalted dry roasted peanuts
½ medium onion
2 tablespoons cilantro, chopped
½ teaspoon salt, or to taste
Place with roasted peppers, cooked tomatillos, and cooking liquid in blender or food processor and process until smooth. Add additional water to desired consistency.

8 (6-inch / 15-cm) corn tortillas
2 cups / 500 ml cooked chicken or turkey, shredded
½ cup / 125 ml feta cheese or queso blanco, crumbled
Fill a shallow bowl or pie pan with boiling water. Dip each tortilla in water to soften, 10–15 seconds. Fill with ¼ cup / 60 ml chicken and 1 tablespoon cheese. Roll up and place in 9 x 9-inch / 2.5-L baking pan. Pour sauce evenly over filled enchiladas, covering all tortilla edges.

¼ cup / 60 ml feta cheese or queso blanco, crumbled
Sprinkle on top. Bake in preheated oven at 350° F / 180° C until heated through, 15 minutes (feta cheese or queso blanco will not melt).

Serves 3–4 Ⓖ
. . . .

LUCILE "PILY" HENDERSON, DAVIS, WEST VIRGINIA
BERNITA BOYTS, SHAWNEE MISSION, KANSAS

Slow Cooker Enchiladas

"I have used various combinations of beans, substituted chopped chicken for the ground meat, and used different cheeses," says contributor Jocele Meyer. "This recipe can be baked in the oven for about 30 minutes at 350° F / 180° C or heated in the microwave. With the flexibility it is a great dish for carry-in meals."

. . . .

1 pound / 500 g ground beef, turkey, or venison
1 cup / 250 ml onion, chopped
½ cup / 125 ml green pepper, chopped
Cook together in a large skillet until meat is browned and vegetables are tender. Drain off fat.

2 cups / 500 ml cooked pinto or kidney beans
2 cups / 500 ml cooked black beans
2 cups / 500 ml tomatoes, chopped
⅓ cup / 75 ml water (¼ cup / 60 ml If using summer squash)
1 teaspoon chili powder
½ teaspoon ground cumin
¼ teaspoon pepper
1 cup / 250 ml summer squash or carrots, shredded (optional)
1 cup / 250 ml corn (optional)
ground red pepper to taste (optional)
Add and brIng to a boil. Reduce heat; cover and simmer for 10 minutes.

1 cup / 250 ml sharp cheddar cheese, shredded
1 cup / 250 ml Monterey Jack cheese, shredded
Combine separately.

7 (6- to 7-inch / 15- to 18-cm) flour tortillas
In a slow cooker layer about 1 cup / 250 ml meat-bean mixture, one tortilla and ⅓ cup / 75 ml cheese. Repeat layers to use all ingredients. Cover and cook on low for 5–7 hours or until heated through.

Serves 6–8
. . . .

JOCELE MEYER, FRESNO, OHIO

A culinary proverb holds that the quality of one's ingredients largely determines the quality of the finished dish. Likewise, an animal's diet greatly affects the character of its meat, not only in terms of taste but in nutritional value.

Animals like cows (ruminants) have digestive systems best suited for eating grass. When they are fed mostly grains—as is the case in confined growing operations and feedlots—it affects the biochemistry of their bodies, including their meat. Studies have shown that in comparison to grainfed meat, the meat of pasture-raised animals has less fat and fewer calories; more healthy fats, such as omega-3 fatty acids; more conjugated linoleic acid (CLA), a potential cancer fighter; and more antioxidants and vitamins.[6] —CHW

Beef Burritos

"Lupe Sanchez of Oaxaca, Mexico, taught me this recipe," says contributor Judy Weaver. "She is a careful market shopper and incredible in-season cook."

. . . .

1½ pound / 750 g beef chuck roast
Boil until tender with some chopped onion, garlic, water, and salt or roast to medium-well done. Let cool. (May also use leftover roast beef or venison.) Pull into shreds with two forks.

2 cups / 500 ml mozzarella cheese, shredded
2–3 avocados, chopped
2–3 medium tomatoes, chopped
½ cup / 125 ml red onion, diced
handful of fresh cilantro, chopped
corn tortillas
Combine all ingredients except tortillas in a large bowl. Sprinkle with lemon juice and salt and pepper. Soften a pile of corn tortillas by heating them for 1 minute in the microwave or by heating each one briefly in a frypan. At the table, each person scoops the mixture into tortillas. Roll and eat.

Serves 4–6 (Gf)
. . . .

JUDY WEAVER, SALEM, OREGON

Summer Poached Halibut

. . . .

1–2 cloves garlic, minced
1 onion or handful of fresh chives or onion tops, chopped
3–4 tomatoes, chopped in ½-inch / 1-cm chunks
3–4 handfuls of fresh spinach or Swiss chard leaves
⅓–½ cup / 75–125 ml fresh basil leaves, coarsely chopped
In large frypan sauté garlic and onion in 1 tablespoon olive oil until soft. Add tomatoes and heat briefly. Slowly stir in spinach or Swiss chard until wilted. Add basil and cook a few more minutes.

2–3 fillets fresh halibut or trout, rinsed and patted dry
Add to sauce and simmer over medium heat for a few minutes, turning fillets while still raw enough to turn without falling apart. Continue to simmer until fillets are opaque. Salt and pepper to taste. Gently slide onto a warmed platter, keeping fillets intact. Surround with sauce. Squeeze with fresh lemon and serve with rice.

Serves 2–4 (Gf)

. . . .

BRENDA LEENDERS, TRURO, NOVA SCOTIA

Campfire Salmon

"There's nothing like catching a salmon and eating it right away!" says contributor Susan Miller Huyard.

. . . .

6 salmon fillets
Place each fillet in the middle of a separate piece of aluminum foil. Season with salt, pepper, and garlic to taste.

6 lemons, thinly sliced
1 onion, thinly sliced
1 green or red sweet pepper, thinly sliced
1 zucchini, thinly sliced
1 cup / 250 ml Italian dressing
Divide lemon slices and vegetables on top of the fish and pour on dressing. Seal the foil, leaving a little space at the top for each package to expand. Place directly in the coals of a campfire or in a preheated oven at 450° F / 230° C and bake about 15–20 minutes. The packet will puff slightly. Transfer to plates. Open carefully to avoid being burned by the steam inside.

Serves 6

. . . .

SUSAN MILLER HUYARD, ANCHORAGE, ALASKA

Healthy food and children

How do I get my child to make healthy food choices?
It's amazing how many two- to five-year-olds control the family food choices. Too often the parent allows the child to choose what and when to eat. Ellyn Satter, author of several widely read books on feeding children, says, "It is very clear that parents are responsible for what and when the child eats. The child, however, is responsible to choose how much of those foods to eat." So how do parents get children to eat healthy foods?

Make family meal times a priority. Sit down together as a family. Everything tastes better when you are happy, relaxed, and part of a group.

Have set meal and snack times. Serve nothing but water between these times. This helps the child learn to listen to his or her body, and learn the feeling of hunger and fullness.

Create "no food zones." Unfortunately food seems to be everywhere, so having a place free from food in our homes is important. For example, try having no food in the living room or no food while working on the computer.

Involve children in gardening. Start with a simple pot of fresh parsley. Let them sprinkle "their" parsley on a dish.

Set an example. Show your own enjoyment of healthy foods.

Try and try again. Remember that it may take ten to fifteen tries for a child to accept a new food.

—MBL

Tempt their taste buds

Freeze it. Make popsicles of fruit juices, fruit purées, or fruit yogurt.

Drink it. Make smoothies of blended fruits and milk or yogurt.

Top it. Sprinkle steamed vegetables with a little flavored vinegar, soy sauce, toasted nuts, or cheese.

Dip it. Serve raw or blanched vegetables with a healthy dip. To blanch vegetables immerse in boiling water for 1 minute, drain, chill immediately in ice water, and refrigerate until ready to serve. Carrots and broccoli are especially good this way. It intensifies the color and makes them crisp-tender.

Hide it. If all else fails, just hide the vegetables in a favorite food. Try adding shredded carrots or zucchini to spaghetti sauce. Put shredded cabbage or spinach in meat loaf. Purée a variety of cooked vegetables and add to pizza sauce.

—MBL

Make good food fun

Create food faces. Our kids are more likely to eat their veggies if the veggies look fun. Try making "salad faces" using whatever you have. For example, sliced beets with a slice of carrot in the middle make great eyes. To make a meal out of a face, use leftover spaghetti with cheese for hair. Be creative!

Serve food restaurant style. Go into the eating area with a tray and welcome your "guests." Help them get seated and give them drink and appetizer choices (such as carrot sticks, applesauce, or yogurt) in a mock-formal tone. ("Good afternoon, ma'am. Would you like to hear our special for today?") The beverage and "appetizers" give them something to eat while you whip up the main course.

Include kids in food preparation. You'll need to allow extra time, but kids like to help in the kitchen. They often are more open to eating something if they helped prepare it.

—Kent Dutchersmith, Goshen, Indiana

Four Fruit Crisp

Don't have four kinds of berries or fruits? Use more of the same kind. This recipe works well with fresh, frozen, or canned fruits. Adjust the amount of sugar to the sweetness of the fruit.

. . . .

**1½ cup / 375 ml each of four fruits (6 cups / 1.5 L total):
raspberries, blueberries, blackberries, marionberries,
boysenberries, huckleberries, saskatoons, mulberries,
strawberries, sour cherries, peaches, apples**

Mix together and pour into 10-inch / 25-cm deep dish pie pan. Alternatively, the fruits can be cooked with ¼ cup / 60 ml water, ¼–½ cup / 60–125 ml sugar (depending on the sweetness of the fruit), and 2 tablespoons cornstarch to thicken before baking.

**¾ cup / 175 ml flour
¾ cup / 175 ml rolled oats
3 tablespoons butter
2 tablespoons oil
¾ cup / 175 ml brown sugar
⅓ cup / 75 ml nuts, chopped (optional)**

Mix until crumbly. Sprinkle topping over fruit. Bake in preheated oven at 375° F / 190° C until fruit bubbles and top is golden brown, about 30 minutes; may take longer if using frozen fruit.

Serves 8 Ⓥ

. . . .

MARY KATHRYN STUCKY, MOUNDRIDGE, KANSAS
ARLENE GUNDY, FLANAGAN, ILLINOIS
AUDREY HARDER, SASKATOON, SASKATCHEWAN

**As I set a bowl of fresh raspberries in front of my guest, I remarked, "I feel so rich with all this wonderful fruit fresh from my garden." My guest from Colombia gently reminded me, "Anyone who has enough food is rich."
—MBL**

Blueberry Peach Delight

A marvelous fruit-on-the-bottom cobbler, best served warm as is or with milk or frozen yogurt.

· ·

¾ cup / 175 ml water or juice from fruit
⅓ cup / 75 ml brown sugar or honey
1½ tablespoon cornstarch
Mix in 2-quart / 2-L casserole.

3 cups / 750 ml peaches, sliced
1½ cup / 375 ml blueberries
1½ tablespoon lemon juice
Add peaches and blueberries and microwave until mixture thickens; stir a few times as the mixture heats. Remove and stir in lemon juice.

1 cup / 250 ml flour (part or all whole wheat)
½ cup / 125 ml sugar
1½ teaspoon baking powder
½ teaspoon salt
Sift together in a bowl.

½ cup / 125 ml milk
¼ cup / 60 ml applesauce or butter, softened
Add and stir until blended. Pour over fruit; top with 1 tablespoon sugar and ⅛ teaspoon nutmeg (optional). Bake in preheated oven at 350° F / 180° C for 30 minutes.

Serves 6 Ⓥ

· ·

Variation: Use other fruits, such as blackberries. Can also be made with frozen fruits.

· ·

CECILE EYLER, PHILIPPI, WEST VIRGINIA
JEANNIE LEHL, GRANTS PASS, OREGON

Whole Wheat Peach Kuchen

Good with fresh peaches. Also a great way to use up a quart of canned peaches that are a bit less attractive than others on the shelf.

. . . .

¾ cup / 175 ml whole wheat pastry flour
½ cup / 125 ml flour
2 tablespoons sugar
¼ teaspoon salt
¼ teaspoon baking powder
¼ cup / 60 ml walnuts, ground (optional)
Combine in a large bowl.

¼ cup / 60 ml butter
Cut in until crumbly. Pat mixture over bottom and sides of a pie pan or oven-safe frypan.

4 cups / 1 L peach halves, peeled
Arrange in pastry, cut side down.

3 tablespoons sugar
1 teaspoon ground cinnamon
Mix together and sprinkle on top. Bake in preheated oven at 400° F / 200° C for 15 minutes.

1 cup / 250 ml plain yogurt or sour cream
1 egg, beaten
2 tablespoons sugar
½ teaspoon vanilla
Combine and pour over peaches and bake 30 minutes longer or until set.

Serves 6–8 Ⓥ
. . . .

Variation: Substitute 3 cups / 750 ml blueberries for the peaches.

. . . .

VALERIE BAER, BAINBRIDGE, PENNSYLVANIA
RUTH BOWMAN, SALEM, OHIO

Plum Tart

"This was my grandmother's recipe—without any measurements, of course, as measurements were not used much in her day," says contributor Pat Meadows. "It's my very favorite dessert."

. . . .

Shortbread Tart Crust (p. 381)
1 tablespoon tapioca (optional)
Sprinkle tapioca on the unbaked crust.

small blue plums, halved and pitted
Arrange in the crust, cut side up, making slightly overlapping concentric circles starting at the outside. Fit as many plums into the pan as possible.

¾ cup / 175 ml sugar
2 teaspoons ground cinnamon
Mix and pour over the plums. Bake in preheated oven at 350° F / 180° C until plums are soft and filling is boiling, about 45 minutes. Cool on a wire rack. Serve with whipped cream.

Yields 1 tart Ⓥ
. . . .

PAT MEADOWS, WELLSBORO, PENNSYLVANIA

Berry Grunt

A fun camping dessert: just take along some biscuit mix and sweetener, pick some wild berries, and cook over your camp stove.

. . . .

3 cups / 750 ml berries
⅓ cup / 75 ml berry syrup, maple syrup, honey, or sugar
1 tablespoon each water and lemon juice
Combine in a frypan. Stir gently, cover, and bring to a simmer.

1 cup / 250 ml Baking Mix (p. 390)
½ cup / 125 ml milk
3 tablespoons sugar
Mix together and drop by spoonfuls into the simmering berries. Cover tightly and simmer 15 minutes or until dumplings are done.

Serves 4–6 Ⓥ
. . . .

PEARL HOOVER, FAIRFAX, VIRGINIA

Fruit Platz

Use any number of fruits in this traditional Russian Mennonite dessert, sometimes known as "pie-by-the-yard." "Mennonites in Ukraine, particularly in the Crimea, had plentiful summer fruit, especially plums and apricots," notes contributor Arli Klassen. "Platz was a frequent treat."

. . . .

1 cup / 250 ml flour
½ cup / 125 ml whole wheat pastry flour
1½ teaspoon baking powder
¼ teaspoon salt
Combine.

½ cup / 125 ml butter or oil
½ cup / 125 ml milk
Mix in butter or oil until crumbly. Add milk. Mix with fork until a ball of soft dough forms. Press into 9 x 13-inch / 3.5-L baking pan.

4 cups / 1 L assorted fruits, cut into large chunks:
**   peaches, plums, apricots, nectarines, sweet cherries,**
**   gooseberries, blueberries, raspberries, halved green figs**
1 cup / 250 ml sugar, more or less depending on the
**   sweetness of the fruit**
Mix and spread over dough.

¾ cup / 175 ml sugar or brown sugar
¾ cup / 175 ml flour
1 tablespoon butter
1 teaspoon ground cinnamon (optional)
½ teaspoon ground nutmeg (optional)
Mix and spread over fruit. Bake in preheated oven at 375° F / 190° C for 30–45 minutes. Best served the day made.

Serves 8–10 (V)
. . . .

Autumn or winter variation: Use apples and cranberries, with a teaspoon of grated orange rind in the crumb topping. May use frozen fruits.

. . . .

JUDY WILSON, NANAIMO, BRITISH COLUMBIA
ARLI KLASSEN, KITCHENER, ONTARIO
TINA BOHN, GOSHEN, INDIANA

Ground Cherry Squares

"A light, flavorful dessert," notes one tester. The batter puffs up around the filling while baking, resulting in bars that resemble stained glass windows. Never heard of ground cherries? They are a type of tomato similar to tomatillos (p. 36).

. . . .

3 cups / 750 ml ground cherries, outer husk removed
½ cup / 125 ml brown sugar
3 tablespoons water
Mix in a saucepan and bring to a boil. Reduce heat.

3 tablespoons cornstarch
3 tablespoons water
Mix together and add to saucepan. Heat slowly, stirring constantly, until thickened. Ground cherries should still be whole; do not overcook. Cool to lukewarm.

1 cup / 250 ml butter, softened
1¼ cup / 300 ml sugar
1 teaspoon vanilla
½ teaspoon lemon extract or lemon juice (optional)
Cream together with an electric beater until light and fluffy.

4 eggs, slightly beaten
2 cups / 500 ml flour
Add to the creamed mixture. Spread batter into greased 10 x 15-inch / 25 x 40-cm jelly roll pan. Use knife to lightly score surface of batter, making 30 squares. Place a spoonful of cooked ground cherries in center of each square. Bake in preheated oven at 350° F / 180° C for 35–40 minutes. Cool and cut into squares.

Yields 30 squares Ⓥ
. . . .

MARY ELLEN LEHMAN, BOSWELL, PENNSYLVANIA

Yogurt Fruit Pie

. . . .

1 cup / 250 ml plain yogurt or sour cream
⅔ cup / 150 ml sugar
1 egg
2 tablespoons flour
½ teaspoon vanilla
¼ teaspoon salt
Combine and mix well.

2½ cups / 625 ml peaches, chopped, or berries
9-inch / 1-L unbaked pie crust (p. 380)
Add fruit and pour in pie crust. Sprinkle with ground cinnamon.
Bake in preheated oven at 400° F / 200° C for 25 minutes.

⅓ cup / 75 ml brown sugar
⅓ cup / 75 ml flour
2 tablespoons butter
Combine. Remove pie from oven and cover evenly with topping.
Return to oven and bake at 375° F / 190° C for 25–30 minutes.

Yields 1 pie Ⓥ

. . . .

GALE AND JEAN HESS, MOUNT JOY, PENNSYLVANIA
LINDA MAST, CORVALLIS, OREGON
MARGARET WYSE, WAXHAW, NORTH CAROLINA

When I lived in Argentina, the indigenous people I worked with collected wild honey: thick, dark, delicious honey that's nothing like any I've found in U.S. stores. Many sold the honey in nearby Paraguayan border towns. Thanks to a favorable exchange rate, they got a good price that helped them buy, among other things, what I call the "white" foods: white sugar, white flour, white rice. Honey is a traditional part of their diet, but economic conditions encouraged them to sell it and buy sugar.

When the Argentine peso was devalued after an economic crash, honey prices also crashed. Several months later, people told me they could no longer afford sugar but were eating the honey they couldn't sell—and noticing that their children seemed healthier.
—Eric Kurtz, Elkhart, Indiana

Fruit Pie

. . . .

Prepare a 9-inch / 1-L pie crust (p. 380). In the bottom of the crust sprinkle a small amount of the sugar. Mix remaining sugar and thickener (flour, cornstarch, or tapioca) together then add the fruit and liquid (juice, water, yogurt); pour into the pie crust. Sprinkle with spices and butter (if any). Cover with a second crust into which vent holes have been made, or sprinkle with crumb topping. Bake in preheated oven at 425° F / 220° C for 10 minutes. Reduce heat to 350° F / 180° C and continue baking for 25–30 minutes.

Yields 1 pie Ⓥ

. . . .

Ground cherry pie:

3 cups / 750 ml ground cherries, outer husk removed
1 tablespoon lemon juice
⅓ cup / 75 ml sugar
½ cup / 125 ml brown sugar
⅓ cup / 75 ml flour
1 teaspoon ground cinnamon
1 tablespoon butter

. . . .

Elderberry pie:

2½ cups / 625 ml elderberries
3 tablespoons lemon juice
½–¾ cup / 125–175 ml sugar
2 tablespoons flour

. . . .

Apple pie:

4–5 cups / 1–1.3 L apples, sliced
2 tablespoons water
½ cup / 125 ml sugar or brown sugar
1 tablespoon flour
1 tablespoon cornstarch
1 teaspoon ground cinnamon
¼ teaspoon each ground nutmeg and ground allspice

. . . .

. . . .

Blackberry pie:

**4 cups / 1 L blackberries; or replace 1 cup / 250 ml with
sliced apples**
½ cup / 125 ml sugar
3 tablespoons quick-cooking tapioca

. . . .

Saskatoon or blueberry pie:

3 cups / 750 ml saskatoons or blueberries
½ cup / 125 ml rhubarb
⅔ cup / 150 ml sugar
¼ cup / 60 ml quick-cooking tapioca

. . . .

Currant pie:

3 cups / 750 ml currants
⅓ cup / 75 ml water
1 cup / 250 ml sugar
3 tablespoons flour

. . . .

Pear pie:

4 cups / 1 L pears, diced
1 cup / 250 ml plain yogurt or sour cream
3 tablespoons lemon juice
⅔ cup / 150 ml sugar
3 tablespoons quick-cooking tapioca

. . . .

Crumb topping: Mix together 1 cup / 250 ml flour, ½ cup /
125 ml sugar, ½ cup / 125 ml chopped nuts (optional). Cut in 3
tablespoons butter and 1 tablespoon oil to make crumbs.
For pear or apple pies try replacing nuts with 1 cup / 250 ml grated
sharp cheddar cheese for a cheese crumb topping.

. . . .

GROUND CHERRY: MERVIN AND MARILYN SWARTZENTRUBER, GOSHEN, INDIANA
ELDERBERRY: CONNIE ZEHR, AKRON, NEW YORK
APPLE: CATHERINE MUMAW, HARRISONBURG, VIRGINIA
BLACKBERRY: ALICE KEPPLEY, BOYERTOWN, PENNSYLVANIA
SASKATOON: ELSIE REMPEL, WINNIPEG, MANITOBA
CURRANT: JUDITH UNRUH, HILLSBORO, KANSAS
PEAR: LOIS MASON, UPLAND, CALIFORNIA

Fruit Custard Pie

"A favorite summer pie," says contributor Helen Thomas. "We change the fruit as the summer progresses and the fruits ripen."

. . . .

9-inch / 1-L unbaked pie crust (p. 380)
2 cups / 500 ml apricots, plums, cherries, or berries
¼ cup / 60 ml sugar (adjust to the sweetness of the fruit)
Arrange fruit in pie crust. Sprinkle with sugar.

2 eggs, beaten
1¼ cup / 310 ml milk
¼ cup / 60 ml sugar
1 teaspoon vanilla
Mix together until well combined. Pour over fruit. Bake in preheated oven at 450° F / 230° C for 15 minutes. Reduce heat to 350° F / 180° C and continue baking until custard is set, about 25 minutes.

Yields 1 pie Ⓥ

. . . .

HELEN THOMAS, CHARLESTON, WEST VIRGINIA
LAVONNE DYCK, GLENBUSH, SASKATCHEWAN

Gingered Blueberry Slush

Light and refreshing on a hot day.

. . . .

1 cup / 250 ml orange juice
¼ cup / 60 ml powdered sugar
1 tablespoon lemon juice
1 tablespoon candied ginger root, finely chopped
Combine in a medium bowl 1 hour before serving.

2 cups / 500 ml frozen blueberries
Stir in. Place in refrigerator and let rest for 1 hour; as the blueberries start to melt, the juices get slushy. Before the berries are completely thawed, serve dusted with ground nutmeg and powdered sugar. (Note: Large berries thaw more slowly than small ones.)

Serves 3–4 Ⓥ Ⓖ︎ⓕ

. . . .

CATHERINE MUMAW, HARRISONBURG, VIRGINIA

We three women—two who are trying to raise their own food and make part of their livelihood from the soil, along with a third woman who is a biologist at a national wildlife refuge—are picking blueberries. One finds a horned worm, which none of us can positively identify. Interestingly, the two gardeners are sure it is a tomato hornworm, a dreaded garden pest that should be killed immediately. On the other hand the biologist suggests that it might become a very special kind of butterfly. Although we could not concur on its potential harm, we did agree that it would metamorphose into some kind of butterfly.

I wonder, if instead of killing those we fear, we loved or at least tolerated them, what beautiful metamorphosis would happen?
—MBL

Zucchini Brownies

"This was one of almost thirty recipes I tested, with taster comments provided by friends at Pittsburgh Mennonite Church and Ten Thousand Villages," says Julie Swartzentruber. "The original recipe was a delicious, fluffy cake. After six or seven tries, I came up with an adaptation that's denser and chewier like traditional brownies."

· ·

1 cup / 250 ml flour
¾ cup / 175 ml whole wheat flour
⅓ cup / 75 ml baking cocoa
½ teaspoon baking soda
½ teaspoon salt
Combine in large bowl.

2–3 cups / 500–750 ml zucchini, shredded
Stir in.

1 egg
¾ cup / 175 ml sugar
¾ cup / 175 ml brown sugar
½ cup / 125 ml plain yogurt
½ cup / 125 ml oil
1 teaspoon vanilla
Combine in separate bowl and beat with fork. Stir into zucchini mixture. Spread evenly into greased 9 x 13-inch / 3.5-L pan.

½–1 cup / 125–250 ml semisweet or mint chocolate chips
½ cup / 125 ml nuts, chopped (optional)
Sprinkle on top of batter. Bake in preheated oven at 350° F / 180° C until toothpick inserted in center comes out clean, 35–40 minutes.

Serves 18–24 Ⓥ
· ·

JULIE SWARTZENTRUBER, PITTSBURGH, PENNSYLVANIA
MARY KEITH, SEFFNER, FLORIDA

Pesto

Pesto is a very forgiving recipe; measurements given below need not be followed exactly. Pesto is wonderful in soups and also can be used to flavor sandwiches (try mixing a spoonful with mayonnaise), deviled eggs, and salads. Or brush on meat or fish before grilling or baking.

. . . .

1 cup / 250 ml packed fresh basil leaves and tender stems (may use part fresh spinach)
1–3 cloves garlic
⅓ cup / 75 ml pine nuts, walnuts, or hazelnuts, toasted
3–6 tablespoons Parmesan cheese, grated
½ teaspoon salt, or to taste
2 sprigs flat parsley (optional)
Finely chop together in food processor.

⅓–½ cup / 75–125 ml olive oil
Add gradually while food processor runs to make a thick paste. Serve at room temperature with any kind of hot pasta. The flavor is intense; a little goes a long way. (For a lower-fat version, use broth for part of the oil.)

Yields about 1 cup / 250 ml Ⓥ Ⓖⓕ
. . . .

To freeze: Freeze in ice cube trays. When frozen, remove cubes and place in a resealable plastic bag, removing from the freezer as needed. When making pesto to freeze, omit the garlic and cheese if desired. When using the pesto, stir in freshly grated Parmesan and minced garlic.

. . . .

Cilantro variation: Grind in food processor ½ cup / 125 ml sesame seeds (optional). Add and process together 4 cups / 1 L fresh cilantro, 4 cloves garlic, 1 teaspoon ground cumin (optional), ¼ cup / 60 ml fresh lime juice or red wine vinegar, 5–6 tablespoons olive oil, and salt and pepper to taste.

. . . .

BARBARA RESSLER, APPLE CREEK, OHIO
ANITA DERSTINE, PORTLAND, OREGON
LOIS BAERG, SASKATOON, SASKATCHEWAN

Grilled Peach Salsa

Salsa (at left) can be used with pork or chicken, but it is wonderful with chips.

. . . .

5 large peaches, washed and halved, pits removed
Brush grill grate with vegetable oil and grill peaches face down for several minutes. With tongs, flip peaches until skins begin to darken. (This can also be done in a vegetable grill basket.) Remove peaches from grill when they can be pierced easily with a fork or skewer. Allow to cool. Remove skins. Chop.

5 tomatoes, chopped
1½ jalapeño peppers, minced, seeds removed
Add to peaches.

½ cup / 125 ml honey
2 tablespoons fresh cinnamon basil or cilantro, chopped
salt and pepper to taste
Stir in.

Yields 4 cups / 1 L Ⓥ Ⓖⓕ
. . . .
MARSHALL KING, GOSHEN, INDIANA

Fresh Summer Salsa

. . . .

6 medium fresh tomatoes, diced
1 medium red onion, diced
1 large green pepper, diced
2–3 hot chili peppers, diced
¼ bunch fresh cilantro, chopped
4 cloves garlic, minced
3 tablespoons fresh basil, chopped
2 tablespoons vinegar
1 tablespoon lemon juice
½ teaspoon salt, or to taste
Combine in bowl. Let stand 30 minutes and serve.

Serves 6 Ⓥ Ⓖⓕ
. . . .
MARC AND HANNAH GASCHO REMPEL, CORVALLIS, OREGON
ARDIS DILLER, BELLEVILLE, PENNSYLVANIA
JO ANN HEISER, URBANA, ILLINOIS

Roasted Eggplant Cilantro Dip

. . . .

2 medium eggplants, peeled, cut into 1-inch / 2.5-cm cubes
Soak in a bowl of cold water for 20 minutes. Drain. Place in a single layer on a baking pan.

2–3 cloves garlic, peeled
1 tablespoon olive oil
Add to baking pan. Stir to coat eggplant with oil and sprinkle with salt and pepper. Bake in preheated oven at 350° F / 180° C, stirring occasionally, until brown and soft, 20–30 minutes. Remove from oven and cool to room temperature.

2–3 tablespoons olive oil
Mix with eggplant and garlic in food processor or with a fork until smooth.

1 cup / 250 ml fresh cilantro, chopped
juice of 2 lemons
Add half the lemon juice and cilantro. Let the mixture stand about 5 minutes; taste and adjust the flavor with more lemon or cilantro if needed.

Yields 2 cups / 500 ml Ⓥ Ⓖf
. . . .

CAROLYN AND CARL ANDERSON, TUCSON, ARIZONA

Imagine modern-day dietary laws for right eating.

Food shall be washed, chopped, sautéed, stirred, and baked with a grateful attitude and with tender, loving care.

While eating you shall restrict yourself from all actions that distract you from the food, such as driving, watching TV, or working.

Whenever possible, food shall be eaten in the company of others. When that is not possible, eat in the presence of the holy. Light a candle or place yourself in harmony with God's creation by eating outside, near a window, or with a flower or plant.

Each eating experience should include a time of centering, remembering God's goodness, and offering an expression of thanks.

All negative emotions surrounding eating shall be avoided. You shall come to God's table free from guilt and shame and leave from God's table filled with the grace and love God is offering to us in this food.

By grace we are given the chance to live each new day in right relationship with God, our neighbors, and our food.
—Ingrid Friesen Moser, Goshen, Indiana

Layered Greek Dip

. . . .

1½ cup / 375 ml yogurt cheese (p. 387)
2 tablespoons chives, minced
Mix together. Spread in glass 10-inch / 25-cm pie pan.

1 cup / 250 ml Hummus (p. 396)
Drop by small spoonfuls over yogurt cheese; spread evenly.

1 cucumber, peeled, seeded, and chopped
3 plum tomatoes, seeded and chopped
¼ cup / 60 ml olives, sliced
4 ounces / 125 g feta cheese, crumbled
¼ cup / 60 ml green onions, chopped
Layer on top in order given. Sprinkle lightly with chopped fresh
oregano or dried oregano. Serve with pita wedges. (May brush
pita lightly with olive oil, sprinkle with garlic powder, and bake in a
preheated oven at 350° F / 180° C until crisp, about 8–10 minutes.)

Serves 4–6 Ⓥ
. . . .

AUDREY METZ, WASHINGTON, DISTRICT OF COLUMBIA

Herb Veggie Dip

*"This recipe is quick to make and is a great substitute for the onion soup mix
and sour cream standby," says contributor Marie Moyer.*

. . . .

½ cup / 125 ml mayonnaise
½ cup / 125 ml plain yogurt or yogurt cheese (p. 387)
½ teaspoon salt
Mix together in a small bowl.

1 tablespoon each fresh dill, parsley, chives, chopped
1 teaspoon lemon juice
1 teaspoon celery seed
½ teaspoon garlic powder
½ teaspoon paprika
Add a combination or all of the above. Chill for 1 hour and serve
with fresh vegetables. In winter use dried herbs (1 teaspoon each)
in place of fresh ones.

Yields 1 cup / 250 ml Ⓥ
. . . .

MARIE MOYER, LETHBRIDGE, ALBERTA

Vegetable Pizza Bites

. . . .

2 cups / 500 ml Baking Mix (p. 390)
½ cup / 125 ml cold water
Mix and spread on a greased 12-inch / 30-cm pizza pan.
Bake in preheated oven at 375° F / 190° C until brown, about
10–12 minutes.

4 ounces / 125 g cream cheese
¼ cup / 60 ml mayonnaise
2 teaspoons fresh dill, chopped; or ½ teaspoon dried
⅛ teaspoon each onion powder and garlic powder
Mix together.

¾ cup / 175 ml fresh spinach or parsley, chopped
⅓ cup / 75 ml red sweet pepper, diced
Mix in. Spread on cooled crust.

2 cups / 500 ml fresh vegetables: broccoli, carrots,
green onions, tomatoes, green pepper, summer squash,
cucumber, cauliflower, finely chopped
Arrange on top of cream cheese mixture. Cut and serve or chill up
to 24 hours.

Yields 12 slices Ⓥ
. . . .

SHERYL JANTZI, OLATHE, KANSAS
MARY ELLEN LEHMAN, BOSWELL, PENNSYLVANIA

For us as CSA farmers, having direct contact with our customers is incredibly meaningful and rewarding. It's been a pleasant surprise to find that many people, especially those with young children, will spend hours at the farm when they come to pick up their produce. They'll sit in the shade and talk while munching on carrots and pick basil until their fingers are pungent. From year to year we get to see the children of our returning customers grow up, and we have a sense of privilege in knowing that our vegetables are helping their bodies grow strong and healthy. This feeling is especially keen as we watch expectant mothers select their vegetables and know that we are contributing to the health of their growing babies.
—Jon and Beth Weaver-Kreider, Goldfinch Farm, York, Pennsylvania

Bruschetta with Grilled Bread

· ·

1 loaf French bread, sliced
Grill slices lightly on both sides (or broil in oven on a baking sheet).

2 large yellow tomatoes, diced
2 large red tomatoes, diced
½ cup / 125 ml mozzarella cheese, diced
½ cup / 125 ml green olives, chopped
½ cup / 125 ml olive oil
½ cup / 125 ml fresh basil, chopped
2 tablespoons lemon peel, grated
1 tablespoon capers or dill pickles, chopped
6 cloves garlic (minced)
salt and pepper to taste
Combine and spoon over grilled bread.

Serves 8–12 (appetizer)
· ·

LINDA LONGACRE, TELFORD, PENNSYLVANIA

Roasted Peppers

Roasted peppers can be expensive to buy but are very easy to make. When peppers are in abundance, roast some and freeze for later use. One way to do this is in freezer boxes, separating the layers with waxed paper.

· ·

peppers (sweet or hot, any color)
Roast whole peppers under broiler or over a gas flame. Turn frequently, until the skin blackens. Remove from heat and put in a bag or covered pot to allow the pepper to steam and cool. Then rub or wash off the blackened skin. Remove the stem and seeds. Use in any recipe calling for roasted peppers.

· ·

MARY BETH LIND, HARMAN, WEST VIRGINIA

Tomato Sauce

"I use this for spaghetti sauce, pizza sauce, or any time I need a marinara-type sauce," says contributor Mary Beth Lind. *"I really like the added nutrition of the carrot."*

. . . .

1 onion, chopped
2 cloves garlic, minced
Sauté until soft in 2 tablespoons olive oil.

2 carrots, shredded
½ green pepper, chopped
2 bay leaves
¼ cup / 60 ml fresh parsley, chopped
2 tablespoons fresh basil, chopped; or 2 teaspoons dried
1 tablespoon fresh oregano, chopped; or 1 teaspoon dried
1 tablespoon fresh thyme, chopped; or 1 teaspoon dried
Add. Stir well.

6 cups / 1.5 L plum tomatoes, peeled and chopped
6 ounces / 175 g tomato paste
1 tablespoon honey (optional)
salt and pepper to taste
Add and season to taste. Simmer 15 minutes. Remove bay leaf and serve or freeze. To can, ladle into hot, sterilized pint jars to within ½ inch / 1 cm of top, add 1 tablespoon lemon juice or vinegar per pint jar to assure acidity, seal with sterilized lids, and process full jars in boiling water bath for 35 minutes.

Yields 3 pints / 1.5 L Ⓥ Ⓖⁱ
. . . .

Squash variation: Add 1 cup / 250 ml cooked, puréed winter squash. Do not can this variety.

. . . .

MARY BETH LIND, HARMAN, WEST VIRGINIA
ELLEN MILLER, WATERLOO, IOWA

Pictured (from top)>>>
Tomato Sauce (recipe above)
Zucchini Relish (recipe on p. 202)
Favorite Canned Salsa
(recipe on p. 203)

Zucchini Relish

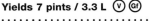

1 large red sweet pepper, chopped
1 large green pepper, chopped
10–12 cups / 2.5–3 L zucchini, chopped
2–4 cups / 500 ml–1 L onion, chopped
5 tablespoons salt
Combine and let stand overnight. Drain. Rinse twice.

2¼ cups / 560 ml vinegar
4 cups / 1 L sugar
2 tablespoons cornstarch
1 tablespoon ground nutmeg
1 tablespoon dry mustard
1 tablespoon ground turmeric
1 teaspoon celery salt; or 2 tablespoons celery seed
  (optional)
½ teaspoon pepper (optional)
Combine in a soup pot. Add drained vegetables and bring to a
boil. Lower heat and simmer 10–15 minutes, stirring frequently.
Ladle into hot, sterilized pint jars to within ½ inch / 1 cm of top,
seal with sterilized lids, and process full jars in boiling water bath
for 10 minutes.

Yields 7 pints / 3.3 L Ⓥ Ⓖⓕ

SARAH MYERS, MOUNT JOY, PENNSYLVANIA
NANCY K. GAVIN, HUDSON, WISCONSIN
NANCY FRIESEN, ALBANY, OREGON

**Finally there is enough not only
to feed us now, but also later.
Spring starts out as a season of
net loss, like winter, when we are
using more from our root cellar,
canned goods, and freezer than
we are producing. Then spring
moves to that marvelous break-
even point when there is enough!**

**Summer and fall are the blessed
times of being able to store food.
There is enough for both now
and later. In the midst of the
accompanying busyness, may we
be most grateful.
—MBL**

Favorite Canned Salsa

"Making salsa was becoming an annual summer family event until my bout with cancer changed that. We all anticipate salsa-making returning as a family event," writes contributor Sarah Myers. "One year we made 104 pints in one day. Those pints are long gone but the memory of that fun day and the taste of the salsa is still fresh!"

. . . .

14 cups / 3.5 L tomatoes, peeled, chopped, and drained
3 cups / 750 ml onion, chopped
½ cup / 125 ml chili peppers, chopped; more for increased heat
1–3 cups / 250–750 ml green, yellow, and red sweet peppers, chopped
8–10 cloves garlic, minced
Combine and set aside.

1 cup / 250 ml tomato sauce
1 cup / 250 ml ketchup
¾ cup / 175 ml vinegar
10 tablespoons cornstarch or Thermflo
2½ tablespoons salt
1 tablespoon chili powder
1½ teaspoon ground cumin
Combine. Cook until thick and a clear dark color.

2–3 cups / 500–750 ml corn (optional)
2–3 cups / 500–750 ml cooked black beans (optional)
Add sauce to drained vegetables and optional ingredients if using. Ladle into hot, sterilized pint jars to within ½ inch / 1 cm of top, seal with sterilized lids, and process full jars in boiling water bath for 35 minutes. If you use the optional corn and/or black beans, due to the lower acidity of this variation, do not can in a boiling water bath; only pressure canning is recommended.

Yields 9–11 pints / 4–5 L (v) (GF)
. . . .

SARAH MYERS, MOUNT JOY, PENNSYLVANIA

Hundreds of jars crowd the shelves of Grandma's cellar. Once these jars, filled with summer's treasures, were the family's savings account: sustenance for the lean months of winter. Today I do not need to preserve garden bounty. But as I tend plants, harvest their fruit, and seal it in the same jars that my grandmother and mother filled before me, I sense that I am part of something larger than myself. Preserving food also preserves connections: with my foremothers and with the Creator and Sustainer of life.
—Karla Stoltzfus, Iowa City, Iowa

Bruschetta Preserve

Enjoy a taste of the summer year-round. Bruschetta makes a great appetizer, snack, or light lunch.

. . . .

5–7 cloves garlic, minced
1 cup / 250 ml white wine vinegar
1 cup / 250 ml dry white wine or white grape juice
½ cup / 125 ml water
2 tablespoons balsamic vinegar
2 tablespoons sugar
2 tablespoons dried basil
2 tablespoons dried oregano
Combine in a large saucepan. Bring to a full boil, then reduce heat and boil gently, uncovered, for 5 minutes. Remove from heat.

9 cups / 2.3 L tomatoes, peeled, chopped, and drained
Pack into hot, sterilized half-pint jars to within ¾ inch / 1.5 cm of top. Add hot liquid to cover tomatoes. Seal with sterilized lids and process full jars in boiling water bath for 20 minutes. To serve, spoon over thick slices of crusty bread that have been toasted and lightly brushed with olive oil (not a gluten-free option). Sprinkle with garlic salt and grated Parmesan or mozzarella cheese, then broil until cheese melts.

Yields 9 half-pints / 2.25 L (V) (Gf)
. . . .

NANCY MUCKLOW, KINGSTON, ONTARIO

Pickled Green Beans

A family favorite.

. . . .

5–6 pounds / 2.5–3 kg straight green beans
ground red pepper
10–12 cloves garlic
10–12 heads dill

Put 1 large garlic clove, ¼ teaspoon ground red pepper, and 1 head dill in each pint jar. Fill with straight green beans, packing them in as tight as possible. Make sure the length of the beans is about ½ inch / 1 cm from top of jar.

8 cups / 2 L water
5 cups / 1.3 L apple cider vinegar
½ cup / 125 ml pickling salt

Bring to a boil. Fill jars with brine to ½ inch / 1 cm of top. Seal with sterilized lids and process in boiling water bath for 10 minutes. Let stand 2–4 weeks before eating.

Yields 10–12 pints / about 5 L Ⓥ Ⓖⓕ

. . . .

JEANNE HEYERLY, CHENOA, ILLINOIS

Pizza Sauce

Very good on spaghetti, too.

∙∙∙

12 pounds / 6 kg tomatoes, peeled and chopped
2 medium onions, halved
2–4 chili peppers
¼ cup / 60 ml fresh basil
2 tablespoons fresh oregano
1 tablespoon fresh marjoram
2 teaspoons fresh thyme
2 teaspoons fennel seeds
6 cloves garlic; or 2 teaspoons garlic powder
Purée in blender or food processor. (If fresh herbs aren't available, use half or less of dried.) Put purée in large stainless steel soup pot.

⅓ cup / 75 ml sugar
3 tablespoons salt
30 ounces / 900 g tomato paste
⅓ cup / 75 ml olive oil
Add to purée. Cook for 1½–2 hours until very thick, stirring occasionally to keep from sticking. Ladle into hot, sterilized pint jars to within ½ inch / 1 cm of top, add 1 tablespoon lemon juice or vinegar per pint jar to assure acidity, seal with sterilized lids, and process full jars in boiling water bath for 35 minutes.

Yields 12–14 pints / about 6 L Ⓥ ⒼⒻ

∙∙∙

JEANNE HEYERLY, CHENOA, ILLINOIS

"For I do not do the good I want, but the evil I do not want is what I do." (Romans 7:19)

Sometimes as I try to live justly, I feel like the author of the above quote. Making tomato sauce is one example. Instead of using lots of fuel to cook down the tomato sauce to thicken it, I often use a can of tomato paste from the grocery store. Alas, tomato paste, unless organic, concentrates the pesticides as well as the tomatoes. So do I use extra fuel or increase my exposure to pesticides?
—MBL

Hot Pepper Marmalade

A food processor is helpful for chopping the peppers, but if you chop them by hand, use gloves to protect your skin. This preserve is a lovely appetizer served with cream cheese or Brie on crackers.

. . . .

3–5 chili peppers, minced
2 medium green peppers, minced
1 medium red sweet pepper, minced
1 medium yellow sweet pepper, minced
1 cup / 250 ml white vinegar
2 cups / 500 ml sugar, or more to taste
Combine in a large saucepan.

1 package no-sugar-needed pectin
Gradually add, stirring until dissolved. Boil 1 minute. Skim off foam. Ladle into hot, sterile half-pint jars to within ½ inch / 1 cm of top, seal with sterilized lids, and process full jars in boiling water bath for 10 minutes.

Yields 6 half-pints / 1.5 L (V) (Gf)

. . . .

BARBARA MCMILLAN, HERMINIE, PENNSYLVANIA

Blueberry Raspberry Jam

. . . .

4 cups / 1 L fresh blueberries
4 cups / 1 L fresh raspberries
Pick over to remove stems and soft berries. Wash berries.

2 tablespoons lemon juice
2 tablespoons water
1 (1.75-ounce / 50-g) package pectin
Combine with berries in a soup pot. Place over high heat and bring
to a hard boil (continues boiling when stirred), stirring often.

5½ cups / 1.3 L sugar
Add and stir constantly until mixture returns to a boil. Boil for
exactly 1 minute. Ladle the hot jam into hot, sterile jars to within
¼ inch / 5 mm of top. Seal with sterilized lids and process in a
boiling water bath for 10 minutes.

Yields 4 half-pints / 1 L

. . . .

BONITA SUTER, RED WING, MINNESOTA

Generous God,

Source of all we enjoy around this table,
Thank you for the rich flavors, crisp colors,
and simple foods
that fill us and please us.

We remember those who have labored long
on our behalf.
For farmers near and far,
for their households,
their land and their communities,
we ask your sustaining grace.
Give hope, health, and fruitfulness
to your people who farm.

Fill us with the Spirit's generosity and joy
so that we may fittingly eat at the table
you have set
and serve the world you have made.
Amen.

—JENNIFER DAVIS SENSENIG, HARRISONBURG, VIRGINIA

For everything there is a season . . .
a time to plant, and a time to pluck up what is planted.
(Ecclesiastes 3:1a, 2b)

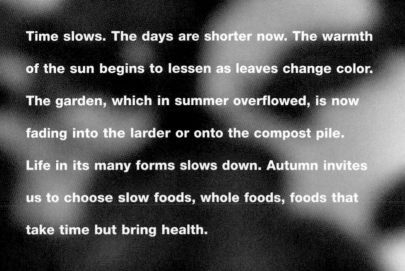

Time slows. The days are shorter now. The warmth
of the sun begins to lessen as leaves change color.
The garden, which in summer overflowed, is now
fading into the larder or onto the compost pile.
Life in its many forms slows down. Autumn invites
us to choose slow foods, whole foods, foods that
take time but bring health.

a u t u m n

Main Dishes

Desserts

Extras

broccoli

brussels sprouts

cauliflower

celery

collards

cranberries

grapes

kale

pears

persimmons

pumpkin

swiss chard

winter squash

Invitations to Action

Eat mindfully. Savor your food.

Eat meals together as a family. Start with a goal of three or four family dinners a week.

Practice rituals of thankfulness, like saying grace at each meal.

Try eating slow foods such as whole grains or dry beans three times a week.

Become a fan of less-than-perfect fruits and vegetables. Foods don't have to be flawless or of a certain shape or size to be delicious and nutritious.

Increase the amount of fresh, locally produced food that you preserve: Freeze green peppers for chili, can a batch of salsa, dry some rosemary, use windfall apples to make applesauce. If this is your first time, invite someone with experience to help.

Vegetarian Menu

Weeknight Menu

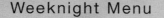

Weekend Menu

Make double recipes of soups, stews, breads. Freeze half for a quick meal on another day.

Instead of "buying time" with processed foods, try "spending time" working with others to prepare and preserve food.

Share meals with others: Cook together with friends, then eat together. Or start a supper club.

slow life down

Nutty Pumpkin Bread

"I developed this recipe for a nutrition class while studying at Messiah College in Grantham, Pennsylvania," says contributor Lisa Mast. "We were to make a 'traditional' favorite recipe lower in fat and sugar—and I boosted fiber content as well."

. . . .

1½ cup / 375 ml flour
1½ cup / 375 ml whole wheat flour
1 cup / 250 ml wheat germ
1 cup / 250 ml sugar
1 cup / 250 ml brown sugar
2 teaspoons baking soda
1½ teaspoon salt
2 teaspoons ground cinnamon (optional)
½ teaspoon each ground ginger, nutmeg, cloves (optional)
Mix together in a large bowl and make a well.

2½ cups / 625 ml pumpkin or winter squash, cooked and puréed; may substitute part applesauce
4 eggs, lightly beaten
½ cup / 125 ml oil
½ cup / 125 ml pecans or other nuts, chopped
1 cup / 250 ml raisins or dates, chopped (optional)
Add into the well and mix just until all the dry ingredients are moistened. Pour batter into two greased 9 x 5-inch / 2-L loaf pans. Bake in preheated oven at 350° F / 180° C until toothpick inserted in center of loaves comes out clean, 50 minutes. Cool in the pan on a wire rack for 10 minutes. Loosen edges and turn the loaves out onto the rack to cool completely before slicing.

Yields 2 loaves or 48 mini muffins Ⓥ
. . . .

Muffin variation: Pour batter in greased mini muffin tins; bake about 10 minutes.

. . . .

LISA MAST, BALTIMORE, MARYLAND
KENDRA LOEWEN, SURREY, BRITISH COLUMBIA
BETTY CLIFTON, MIDDLETOWN, VIRGINIA

Fall—time is of the essence.
Both the squirrel and I are
scurrying around gathering up
our winter store.
—MBL

Cranberry Nut Loaf

A delightful holiday gift.

· ·

1 cup / 250 ml whole wheat flour
1 cup / 250 ml flour
⅓ cup / 75 ml flaxseed meal
1½ teaspoon baking powder
½ teaspoon baking soda
¼ teaspoon salt
Mix in a large bowl.

1 egg
¾ cup / 175 ml sugar
¾ cup / 175 ml orange juice
¼ cup / 60 ml oil
2 tablespoons orange peel, grated
1 teaspoon vanilla
Whisk together in a separate bowl. Add to dry ingredients and mix just until everything is moistened.

1½ cup / 375 ml cranberries, coarsely chopped
½ cup / 125 ml walnuts or pecans, chopped
Fold in cranberries and half the nuts. Spread evenly into a greased 9 x 5-inch / 2-L loaf pan. Sprinkle with the remaining nuts. Bake in preheated oven at 350° F / 180° C until the top is golden and toothpick inserted in the center comes out clean, 55–60 minutes. Cool in the pan on a wire rack for 10 minutes. Loosen edges and turn the loaf out onto the rack to cool completely before slicing.

Yields 1 loaf Ⓥ

· ·

MEGAN GOOSSEN, DINUBA, CALIFORNIA
JILL HEATWOLE, PITTSVILLE, MARYLAND

Oat Bran Cranberry Pancakes

. . . .

¾ cup / 175 ml oat bran
½ cup / 125 ml whole wheat flour
1 tablespoon baking powder
1 teaspoon salt
¼ teaspoon ground cinnamon
¼ teaspoon ground ginger
Stir together in a large bowl.

1 cup / 250 ml milk
1 egg
1 tablespoon oil
2 teaspoons honey, slightly warmed
Combine separately. Mix into dry ingredients.

½ cup / 125 ml cranberries, chopped
½ cup / 125 ml apple, chopped
Fold in. Fry in a medium-hot, greased frypan. Serve with cranberry syrup (optional).

Serves 3–4 Ⓥ
. . . .

Cranberry syrup: Boil together 1 cup / 250 ml cranberry juice, 2 tablespoons honey, 1 tablespoon cornstarch, and a pinch of ground ginger.

. . . .

DIANE JONSON, CARSTAIRS, ALBERTA

Time is health. Unfortunately, I've been brainwashed into thinking that time is money. I'm trying to reprogram myself to think of time as health. I know that slow foods such as whole grains, dried beans, and vegetables are better for me than fast foods. Wellness programs suggest thirty minutes of exercise daily. My spiritual director recommends thirty minutes of meditation and prayer daily. I guess, for my health, I'll keep spending time in my garden; it provides for both.
—MBL

Cranberry Coffee Cake

Especially pretty when baked in a glass dish.

. . . .

3 cups / 750 ml cranberries
⅔ cup / 150 ml sugar
Combine and spread over bottom of a greased 9 x 13-inch / 3.5-L baking pan.

1 cup / 250 ml walnuts, chopped
Sprinkle over cranberries.

¾ cup / 175 ml butter, softened
⅔ cup / 150 ml sugar
3 eggs, lightly beaten
1 teaspoon vanilla
Cream together butter and sugar with an electric mixer. Add eggs and vanilla and mix well.

1⅓ cup / 325 ml flour
1 teaspoon baking powder
½ teaspoon salt
Combine in a separate bowl then add to creamed mixture, mixing well. Drop batter by large spoonfuls over cranberry mixture. Bake in preheated oven at 350° F / 180° C until toothpick inserted near center comes out clean, 40 minutes.

Serves 12–15 (v)
. . . .

CAROL WOFER, LEBANON, OREGON

All the things we use, all the things we make, everything we manipulate, everything we accumulate, derives from the creation itself. If we learn to seek godly contentment as our great gain, we will take and shape less of God's earth. We will demand less from the land. We will leave room for other creatures. We will responsibly exercise dominion over the earth and will preserve it. We will thus allow creation to heal itself and to perpetuate its fruitfulness, to the praise of its Creator.
—Calvin B. DeWitt, president of Au Sable Institute of Environmental Studies[1]

Eating in season has become part of my spiritual journey and an easy tie-in with the church calendar. My family has come to expect and look forward to certain foods at certain times of the year—and only those times.

In the spring, we eat bowls and bowls of fresh spinach salad and lettuce salads with special dressings. In July, when the onions peak in production here, I make big batches of French onion soup that my children beg for. In fall I make recipes with Napa cabbage that I can't grow well in the spring or summer. Fall and winter is also time for making carrot chowder to load up on vitamins A and C for when cold and flu season hits.

Starting with Advent, soon after a hard freeze, I begin to make kale potato soup once a week. This is warm, comfort food. It is green and fun to serve with a swirl of something red, like spaghetti sauce.
—Marie Harnish, Indianapolis, Indiana

Kale Potato Soup

. . . .

1 large bunch kale, chopped
Steam and set aside. (Don't try to cook it with the potatoes; the flavor will be too strong.)

1 tablespoon butter
1 large onion, chopped
1 clove garlic, minced
Melt butter in soup pot. Add onion and sauté until golden. Add garlic and sauté another minute.

2 large potatoes, diced
2 cups / 500 ml hot water or vegetable broth
Add, bring to boil, reduce heat, and simmer until potatoes are soft. Remove half of the cooked potatoes; purée the rest with the cooking liquid and return to the soup pot. Return reserved potatoes and steamed kale to soup pot. (Purée everything if a smooth texture is desired.)

3 cups / 750 ml water or vegetable broth
½ teaspoon salt, or to taste
pepper to taste
Add along with additional hot water or milk to preferred consistency. Heat gently until hot and serve.

Yields 6 cups / 1.5 L Ⓥ
. . . .

MARIE HARNISH, INDIANAPOLIS, INDIANA

Hearty Broccoli Soup

As with any soup, you can use more or less vegetables or even different ones.
This soup can be served chunky or puréed.

. . . .

2 cups / 500 ml potatoes, diced
1 cup / 250 ml onion, chopped
1 cup / 250 ml carrots, thinly sliced
½ cup / 125 ml celery, minced
1 cup / 250 ml water
Cook together for 5 minutes.

2 cups / 500 ml broccoli, chopped
Add and continue to cook an additional 5–10 minutes.

3 cups / 750 ml milk
2 chicken or vegetable bouillon cubes
1 teaspoon Worcestershire sauce
salt and pepper to taste
Add and heat to boiling.

1 cup / 250 ml milk
⅓ cup / 75 ml flour
Blend until smooth in a small bowl. Stir into the soup and cook just
until thickened. Turn off heat.

1 cup / 250 ml Swiss or sharp cheddar cheese, shredded
Add and stir until melted.

Yields 8 cups / 2 L
. . . .

Broccoli-cauliflower variation: Replace the carrots and celery
with chopped cauliflower.

. . . .

ESTHER SHANK, HARRISONBURG, VIRGINIA
BECKY GEPFORD, AURORA, OREGON
TAMARA BRUBAKER, MOUNT JOY, PENNSYLVANIA

Butternut Bisque

Toast the cleaned, dried squash seeds with a little oil and salt, and then put them on the table to sprinkle over soup.

. . . .

2 tablespoons butter
1 medium onion, chopped
1 cup / 250 ml carrots, diced
Melt butter in a large saucepan. Add onion and carrots and sauté over medium-low heat for 5 minutes.

3 cups / 750 ml chicken or vegetable broth
Add, cover, and simmer for 10 minutes.

2 cups / 500 ml winter squash, cooked
½ cup / 125 ml plain yogurt
1 cup / 250 ml evaporated milk or additional plain yogurt
2 tablespoons maple syrup
Add and transfer mixture to a blender or food processor in small batches; purée until smooth. (Skip this step if a chunky soup is preferred.) Return to saucepan and cook over medium heat until hot. Season to taste with salt, pepper, garlic, and onion powder. Garnish with sour cream or plain yogurt.

Serves 4–6
. . . .

TERRI CARUFEL-WERT, MADISON, WISCONSIN

"The heavens are telling the glory of God. . . . There is no speech . . . yet their voice goes out through all the earth." (Psalm 19:1)

Looking down, I know what's above. Backpacking through the forest in the fall has always been a treasured spiritual experience. Constantly alert to the uneven ground, I turn my gaze downward instead of up. However, if I am observant, looking down I know what's above. Black cherry seeds on the ground tell me there are cherry trees above. Acorns tell me there are oak trees above. So, too, looking at the earth tells me, without speech, the glory of God. —MBL

Food is a gift from God. And as such, especially when so many people are hungry, it's just not right for good food to go to waste. This is the belief at the heart of the Fraser Valley Gleaners in Abbotsford, British Columbia. Through the program and a sister organization, hundreds of volunteers collect and process donated vegetables that may not be marketable: perhaps they're blemished, too small, or a bit wilted. Trimmed and dried, the vegetables make a nutritious soup mix for pennies per cup. Millions of servings are distributed each year through various international relief organizations, bringing waste and need together to lessen both.

"We often feel so helpless, listening to the news. We think, 'I'm just one person; how can I do anything to help?'" says manager Carl Goosen. "Well, every hour a volunteer works here yields the equivalent of 120 servings of soup."
—CHW

Gingery Butternut Squash Soup

Fresh ginger provides a bright flavor to this comforting soup.

. . . .

2 onions, chopped
2 tablespoons fresh ginger, peeled and minced
In a large soup pot sauté in 1 tablespoon oil until onion is translucent.

2 apples, peeled, seeded, and chopped
1 butternut squash, peeled, seeded, and cut into cubes;
**   may use 2 cups / 500 ml cooked winter squash**
4 cups / 1 L chicken or vegetable broth
Add to pot and bring to a boil. Reduce heat and simmer until squash and apples are tender. Purée in blender until smooth. Salt and pepper to taste. Garnish with chopped fresh parsley (optional) and serve.

Serves 4
. . . .

RAMONA HARTZLER, NORTH LAWRENCE, OHIO

Celery Cream Soup

Nothing remotely like the gloppy stuff out of a can. Much of the flavor depends on a good stock.

. . . .

2 cups / 500 ml onion, chopped
2 cloves garlic, crushed
In soup pot sauté in 1 tablespoon oil until soft, 4–5 minutes.

3 cups / 750 ml celery, finely chopped
Add, cover, and cook over medium heat 10 minutes, stirring occasionally.

2 cups / 500 ml vegetable broth
1 cup / 250 ml dry white wine or additional broth
Add and bring to a low boil. Cook uncovered until vegetables are soft and liquid is reduced in half, about 15 minutes. Remove from heat, cool slightly, and purée until smooth (this may require two batches). Return to soup pot.

1 cup / 250 ml evaporated milk
Stir in. Reheat over medium heat until hot but do not boil. To serve, pour into bowls and sprinkle with a pinch of crushed celery seeds, freshly ground pepper, and Herbed Croutons (p. 393; optional).

Serves 3–4 ⓥ
. . . .

STEVEN LONT, CORVALLIS, OREGON

Early one morning during Peace Corps training in Yemen, we found our cook bent over the kitchen trash can. He was muttering to himself as he fished out a crust of old bread. Usually jovial, he shook the piece of dry bread at us and launched into a rapid lecture in Arabic. Our clueless look softened his angry eyes to those of a patient father. "*Haram*—it's a sin," he said, slowly gesturing toward the garbage can where we had tossed the bread the night before.

In simple, slow Arabic and sign language, he told us that no bread, no matter how small or dry or old, is ever thrown away here. He placed the crust on the windowsill to dry out completely. Later it could be given to the hungry or softened in soup. It was now destined to be useful.
—Lyn Kawai, Shedd, Oregon

225

Autumn Vegetable Soup

This is a very adaptable soup that welcomes whatever vegetables are on hand. Try different grains or pastas; vary the herbs; use just a few vegetables or small amounts of many kinds. Vary the quantity of vegetables and grains to make a thicker or thinner soup.

. . . .

½ cup / 125 ml onion, chopped
2 cloves garlic, minced
In soup pot, sauté onion in 1 tablespoon olive oil over medium heat until soft. Add garlic and sauté 1 minute.

½ cup / 125 ml each kale, cabbage, carrots, red or green
    sweet pepper, chopped
½ teaspoon each salt, dried basil, dried oregano
⅛ teaspoon pepper
Add and sauté briefly, then turn heat down to low, cover, and let cook about 5 minutes, stirring occasionally.

2 cups / 500 ml bean cooking liquid or vegetable broth
1 cup / 250 ml tomato juice
¾ cup / 175 ml cooked beans
½ cup / 125 ml corn
2 teaspoons dried instant barley
2 teaspoons alphabet or orzo pasta
1½ tablespoon red cooking wine (optional)
Add and bring to a gentle boil and simmer about 15 minutes.

½ cup / 125 ml tomatoes, chopped
1 tablespoon fresh parsley, chopped
Add tomatoes and parsley, simmer another few minutes.

Serves 4 Ⓥ
. . . .

NANCY BRUBAKER, LANCASTER, PENNSYLVANIA

On sunny fall days I purposely park my car facing the sun. I spread a layer of fresh herbs on a baking sheet and place it in the car. Several hours later I have dried herbs and a wonderful-smelling car.
—MBL

Chicken and Chickpea Soup

Serve with rice (pilaf or steamed) or couscous. These flavors are a common combination in North Africa and parts of the Middle East.

. . . .

3-pound / 1½-kg whole chicken, cut up; or equivalent pieces
8 cups / 2 L water
1 onion, cut in wedges
2 whole cloves garlic, peeled
1 stick cinnamon; or 1 teaspoon ground
1 teaspoon whole cardamom pods; or ½ teaspoon ground
¼ teaspoon ground nutmeg
salt and pepper to taste
Simmer together until tender, about 1 hour. Remove chicken. Strain broth to remove spices (using whole spices makes a clearer broth, but ground spices are fine). Push cooked garlic and onion through sieve into the broth. Chill broth and skim off fat.

2 cups / 500 ml cooked chickpeas
2 cups / 500 ml pumpkin, peeled and chopped
1 large potato, chopped
3 cups / 750 ml tomatoes, peeled and quartered
1 tablespoon ground turmeric
Add to broth and reheat. Simmer until vegetables are tender, about 20 minutes. Remove chicken from bones, cut into small pieces, and stir into soup. Or brown chicken pieces under broiler as vegetables are cooking and serve separately.

Serves 6–8 (Gf)
. . . .

LINDA HERR, CAIRO, EGYPT

My chickens, which range through the orchard eating grass and bugs, have many parts. They have legs, thighs, necks, backs, giblets, wings, bones, and skin, as well as breasts. I welcome recipes that use more than just boneless, skinless chicken breasts—recipes that use the whole chicken.
—MBL

Butternut Harvest Stew

A marvelous combination of flavors, perfect served with homemade biscuits and honey.

. . . .

2 tablespoons butter
1½ pound / 750 g boneless pork, cut in ¾-inch / 2-cm cubes
1 medium onion, chopped
2 cloves garlic, minced
Melt butter in a large saucepan. Add pork, onion, and garlic and sauté until meat is no longer pink; drain off fat.

3 cups / 750 ml chicken broth
¾ teaspoon salt
¼ teaspoon dried rosemary, crushed
¼ teaspoon rubbed or ground sage
1 bay leaf
Add, cover, and simmer 20 minutes.

1 medium butternut squash, peeled and chopped
2 medium apples, peeled (if desired) and chopped
Add and simmer uncovered until squash and apples are tender, 20 minutes. Discard bay leaf.

Serves 4–6
. . . .

RUTHIE VOTH, CLAYHOLE, KENTUCKY

If a pie represented all the food grown, how much would you guess goes to waste? Unfortunately, it's much more than a sliver. A study by anthropologist Timothy W. Jones indicates that 40–50 percent of all food ready for harvest never gets eaten. The average U.S. household wastes 14 percent of its food purchases.

Cutting food waste would save tens of billions of dollars each year and result in a healthier environment. Less waste means reduced landfill use, soil depletion, and applications of fertilizers, pesticides, and herbicides.

Jones lists three simple ways to reduce your own food waste. First, carefully plan your purchases: devise menus and make up grocery lists accordingly. Second, keep track of what lurks in the refrigerator and pantry that needs to be used while it is still good. Third, remember to refrigerate or freeze foods that can be eaten later.
—CHW

Green Salad with Autumn Fruit

. . . .

1–2 pears or tart apples, thinly sliced
2 tablespoons lemon juice
Toss together in a medium bowl.

6–8 cups / 1.5–2 L lettuce or mixed greens, torn
Add to fruit along with any of the following:
¼–½ cup / 60–125 ml cheese such as blue, Gorgonzola,
    feta, Parmesan, Asiago, or Gouda, crumbled or shredded
½ cup / 125 ml dried cranberries
½ cup / 125 ml walnuts, hazelnuts, or almonds, coarsely
    chopped and toasted (or caramelized: see below)

⅓ cup / 75 ml oil
1 tablespoon Dijon mustard
1 tablespoon sugar
1 tablespoon lemon juice
½ teaspoon salt
¼ teaspoon pepper
Shake together in jar with a tight lid (or use another favorite poppy
seed dressing or vinaigrette). Add dressing to salad and toss gently
or arrange on individual serving plates.

Serves 5–8 Ⓥ

. . . .

Caramelized nuts:

½ cup / 125 ml walnuts, hazelnuts, or almonds
1–2 tablespoons corn syrup
1–2 tablespoons sugar
Mix together and toast in oven at 350° F / 180° C until sugar
begins to melt and nuts are toasted and coated. Watch carefully to
avoid burning.

. . . .

GWEN PEACHEY, CORVALLIS, OREGON
KERRY STUTZMAN, GREENWOOD VILLAGE, COLORADO
MIRIAM HUEBERT-STAUFFER, CANTON, KANSAS

Sweet Potato Salad

. . . .

3 cups / 750 ml sweet potatoes, cooked, peeled, and diced
1 cup / 250 ml celery, diced
¾ cup / 175 ml green or red sweet pepper, chopped
½ cup / 125 ml onion, chopped
2 tablespoons fresh parsley or cilantro, chopped
3 green onions, thinly sliced (optional)
Combine in a large bowl. Top with dressing of choice below.

Serves 4–6
. . . .

Honey-mustard dressing: Ⓥ ⒼⒻ

½ cup / 125 ml cider vinegar
2 tablespoons oil
1½ tablespoon prepared mustard
1 tablespoon honey
Combine and pour over vegetables. Toss until well coated. Serve
on lettuce (optional) and sprinkle with shredded cheese.

. . . .

Spicy chipotle dressing: Ⓥ

¼ cup / 60 ml fresh lime juice
¼ cup / 60 ml canned chipotle chilies, seeds removed
1 tablespoon ketchup
1½ teaspoon Dijon mustard
1 clove garlic, minced
⅓ cup / 75 ml olive oil
Combine and purée dressing ingredients except oil using an
immersion blender or food processor. Add oil and process until
thick. Pour half of the dressing over the potato mixture and toss to
combine. Add salt and pepper to taste. The salad should be moist
but not runny. Add more dressing as needed. Cover and chill at
least 2 hours or overnight. Serve cold.

. . . .

MARGARET WYSE, WAXHAW, NORTH CAROLINA
KURT KUIPERS, MONROE, WISCONSIN

May you have turkey in season
Cranberries for squeezin'
Gravy (within reason)
And leftovers worth freezin'! Amen.
—Merrill Miller, Scottdale,
Pennsylvania

Broccoli Salad

This recipe is known to turn broccoli-haters into broccoli-lovers.

. . . .

3 cups / 750 ml broccoli florets
1 cup / 250 ml raisins
10 slices bacon, fried and crumbled;
  or ½ cup / 125 ml bacon bits
½ cup / 125 ml red onion, diced
½ cup / 125 ml raw sunflower seeds
½ cup / 125 ml cheese, shredded (optional)
Mix together in a large bowl. Set aside.

2 tablespoons sugar
1 tablespoon apple cider vinegar
¾ cup / 175 ml plain yogurt or mayonnaise
Combine sugar and vinegar and stir to dissolve. Stir in yogurt until
well blended. Pour over the broccoli mixture and stir together.

Serves 6
. . . .

ALLAN REMPEL, RICHMOND, BRITISH COLUMBIA
MARCEIL YODER, GRANGER, INDIANA
SHARON GARBER, MAHWAH, NEW JERSEY

Cranberry Salad

"On Canadian Thanksgiving Day in early October we go up to the mountain
bogs and pick wild cranberries," says contributor Mary Beth Lind. "We freeze
them until November when we make this salad for our traditional U.S.
Thanksgiving dinner."

. . . .

1 pound / 500 g cranberries
4 red apples, unpeeled, seeded
1 orange, unpeeled
Grind together with a food grinder or food processor.

1–2 cups / 250–500 ml sugar, to taste
Mix in, to taste. Chill and serve as salad or relish with roast poultry.

Serves 8–10 Ⓥ Ⓖⓕ
. . . .

MARY BETH LIND, HARMAN, WEST VIRGINIA

Place an order in a fast food franchise and you can count on at least two things. The food will be ready quickly. And no matter where you are, all over the world, the taste will be pretty much the same. Fast food is often eaten on the run, often alone.

Slow Food is about the opposite, on all counts. Founded in Italy in 1989, the Slow Food movement has grown to at least 100,000 members in more than 150 countries. Participants emphasize taking the time to savor food in a community of eaters. But Slow Food is about much more than a good meal. As founder Carlo Petrini puts it, "The pleasures of the table are the gateway to recovering a gentle and harmonious rhythm of life."
—CHW

Venison Broccoli Pasta Salad

. . . .

¼ cup / 60 ml water
¼ cup / 60 ml soy sauce
1 clove garlic, minced
1½ teaspoon sugar
½ teaspoon ginger root, peeled and minced
¼ teaspoon ground red pepper
Combine in a small saucepan and cook until about half the liquid evaporates.

1½ teaspoon sesame oil
Add to sauce and stir. Set aside.

8 ounces / 250 g venison or beef tenderloin, cut ¾ inch / 2 cm thick
Sprinkle with coarsely ground pepper. Grill on both sides until medium done. Slice thinly and add meat to sauce. Refrigerate 1 hour or more.

4 ounces / 125 g linguine, cooked and cooled
2 cups / 500 ml broccoli florets, blanched and cooled
When ready to serve, mix together with the meat and sauce. Garnish with 1 tablespoon chopped onion and 1 tablespoon toasted sesame seeds.

Serves 2–3
. . . .

MARY BETH LIND, HARMAN, WEST VIRGINIA

Greens in Peanut Sauce

"This works well as a side dish with almost anything, but I often serve it with curry meals or over polenta," says contributor Maynard Kurtz. "Sometimes I use curry powder instead of the various spices. Italian spices (oregano, thyme, basil) also work well."

. . . .

1 medium onion, chopped
2–3 cloves garlic, minced
In a large soup pot sauté in 1 tablespoon oil.

1 medium tomato, diced (optional)
Add and simmer 2–4 minutes.

½ teaspoon ground coriander
½ teaspoon ground cumin
¼ teaspoon salt, or to taste
⅛ teaspoon ground cloves
Add, cook, and stir 2 minutes.

1 pound / 500 g kale or collards (8 cups / 2 L chopped)
½ cup / 125 ml water
Add and steam until greens are soft but not mushy. Avoid overcooking. Stir occasionally to coat greens with the spices.

2–3 tablespoons chunky peanut butter
1–2 teaspoons hot water
Combine and add to greens at end of cooking time.

Serves 4–6 Ⓥ ⓖⓕ

. . . .

MAYNARD KURTZ, ELKHART, INDIANA

David Bontreger doesn't just believe he needs Sabbath rest. He believes his land needs it, too. Through reading and experience, this Amish vegetable grower near Shipshewana, Indiana, has learned that soil needs to rebuild itself. He allows fields or portions of them to not produce a crop. For example, he sowed clover in a field, plowed it under after it grew, and replanted it in sweet corn the following year. "The corn is the darkest green I have seen on this farm for many a year," he said.
—Marshall V. King, Elkhart, Indiana

Confetti Kale

A gorgeous dish full of color and nutrients.

· ·

6 cups / 1.5 L kale, chopped
1 clove garlic, minced (optional)
In large frypan sauté in 2 tablespoons olive oil over medium heat, stirring constantly, for 10 minutes.

¾ cup / 175 ml corn
½ cup / 125 ml red sweet pepper, chopped
¼ cup / 60 ml water
½ teaspoon salt
¼ teaspoon pepper
Mix in and cook for 10 minutes. Serve immediately.

Serves 4 Ⓥ Ⓖⓕ

· ·

KANDACE HELMUTH, AKRON, PENNSYLVANIA

Kale Chips

You can bake these crispy chips at different oven temperatures, but a lower temperature helps to avoid burning.

· ·

1 pound / 500 g kale, curly recommended
2 tablespoons olive oil
1 teaspoon salt, or to taste
Wash kale and dry thoroughly. Remove hardy stems by stripping off leaves starting at the base of the stem. Place kale leaves in bowl, drizzle with olive oil, and sprinkle with salt. Gently massage oil and salt into the kale leaves until evenly distributed. Place in one even layer on a baking sheet, being careful not to overlap leaves. Bake in preheated oven at 300° F / 150° C for 10–12 minutes. Rotate pan and bake for another 10–15 minutes until leaves are just turning light brown. Watch to avoid scorching. Let kale chips cool on pan for a few minutes before eating.

Serves 4 Ⓥ Ⓖⓕ

· ·

AVERY PETERS, WOLFVILLE, NOVIA SCOTIA

Savory Kale

A tasty side dish that can be tucked into wrap-type sandwiches. "Refried beans, shredded cheese, and kale in a whole wheat, homemade chapati is a favorite combination at our house," notes contributor Nancy Brubaker.

. . . .

1 onion, thinly sliced
In a large frypan sauté in 1–2 tablespoons olive oil over medium heat until brown and crisp, not just soft. Remove to a serving dish.

1 large bunch fresh kale, collards, or Swiss chard
Stack leaves, roll together, and slice about ¼ inch / 5 mm thick. Sauté in the frypan for 1 minute.

several tablespoons water
¼ teaspoon salt, or to taste
Add, cover, reduce heat, and steam until tender. Add water as needed. Kale and collards cook in 10–15 minutes; Swiss chard cooks a bit faster. When the greens are tender, drain in a colander. Return onions to pan and heat to sizzling.

1 tablespoon tomato paste
Add and stir. When this mixture is hot, return the greens to the pan. Mix, heat through, and serve.

Serves 4–6 Ⓥ ⒼⒻ
. . . .

NANCY BRUBAKER, LANCASTER, PENNSYLVANIA

In stories of earlier times, we read of rare delights: the first greens after a long winter. The miracle of an orange. We can almost taste the pleasure of such moments—the exquisite experience of luxury. Yet those pleasures are no longer ours. Oranges are nice but hardly an occasion to feel blessed. The idea of a winter without lettuce is unthinkable, and we'd probably turn up our noses at those dandelion leaves—or whatever—that our forebears were so thrilled to eat.

Are we better off? In some ways I'm sure we are. Yet when abundance breeds an inability to appreciate, we are the losers.

Our family joined a CSA, buying a share of the produce of a nearby farm. In July I was surprised when we stopped getting lettuce. They said it was too hot. I noticed my feeling of entitlement and how put off I felt by their inability to come up with it. What, exactly, makes me entitled to lettuce?
—Pamela Haines, Philadelphia, Pennsylvania

When I moved into a cabin on a friend's property, we began to share evening meals and took turns cooking. After I got married, the daily meals with these friends shifted into weekly potlucks. Some of the crazier themes were around a color (only eating red food, for example, and dressing in red) or around a culture. Indian food with music and a Bollywood movie was fun. Another time we had Spanish tapas with flamenco music played by musician friends around a fire. Fun, celebratory events like these allow us to build community, share our values and lives, and have memorable experiences together.
—Elsie Wiebe Klinger, Abbotsford, British Columbia

Sweet and Sour Swiss Chard

"The first year we bought a share of an organic co-op garden we were astounded by the quality and sheer quantity of greens we received," says contributor Alison Froese-Stoddard. "We had to find ways to eat several pounds of lettuce, kale, and Swiss chard every week! This recipe became a quick favorite."

. . . .

1 pound / 500 g Swiss chard (multiple colors preferred)
Rinse, pat dry, and remove stems. Chop stems diagonally into small pieces. Stack leaves, roll up, and slice in 1-inch / 2.5-cm strips; keep separate from stems. Set aside.

1 medium onion, diced
In deep frypan sauté in 2 teaspoons olive oil over medium heat until softened, 5 minutes.

¼ cup / 60 ml dried cranberries or raisins
2 cloves garlic, minced
3 tablespoons white or cider vinegar
1½ teaspoon sugar
salt and pepper to taste
Add along with chard stems, cover, and cook for 8 minutes. Place chopped leaves on top of the mixture (do not stir in), cover, and cook another 2 minutes. Remove from heat, stir, and serve.

Serves 4 Ⓥ Ⓖ
. . . .
ALISON FROESE-STODDARD, WINNIPEG, MANITOBA

Broccoli Gratin

. . . .

5–6 cups / 1.25–1.5 L broccoli (or cauliflower), cut in chunks
Steam broccoli just until crisp-tender, 6–8 minutes. Drain well and set aside.

1 onion, thinly sliced
1 clove garlic, minced
In small saucepan sauté in 2 tablespoons oil until fragrant and tender, about 5 minutes.

¼ cup / 60 ml flour
Sprinkle on onions and garlic. Cook, stirring constantly, 3 minutes without browning.

2 cups / 500 ml milk
Whisk in and bring to a boil.

1 teaspoon salt, or more to taste
¼ teaspoon pepper
pinch each ground nutmeg and ground red pepper
Add and cook 5 minutes.

1 cup / 250 ml cheddar cheese, shredded
Stir in and remove from heat. Combine with broccoli. Transfer to a 2-quart / 2-L casserole dish or glass baking pan.

1 cup / 250 ml bread crumbs
1 tablespoon butter, melted
¼ cup / 60 ml Parmesan cheese, grated
1 tablespoon dried parsley; or 2 tablespoons fresh, chopped
Combine and sprinkle on top of broccoli mixture. Bake in preheated oven at 350° F / 180° C until thoroughly heated, 20 minutes.

Serves 4–6 Ⓥ
. . . .

GUDRUN MATHIES, EPHRATA, PENNSYLVANIA

Brussels Sprouts with Leeks

1 pound / 500 g brussels sprouts, sliced in thirds
2 leeks, thinly sliced
In large frypan sauté in 1 tablespoon olive oil and 1 tablespoon butter.

¼ cup / 60 ml water
2 tablespoons mixed fresh herbs such as oregano, thyme, rosemary, basil, chopped; or 2 teaspoons dried
Add and cook until sprouts are tender, about 10 minutes. Salt and pepper to taste. Serve plain or on top of rice.

Serves 6–8 Ⓥ Ⓖf

JESSICA SEEM, BROOKTONDALE, NEW YORK

Roasted Cauliflower and Sprouts

When stirring an oven dish, quickly remove the dish from the oven, close the oven door, then stir. Do not stir with the oven door open, as you lose heat each second the oven door is open.

1 medium cauliflower, cut into 1-inch / 2.5-cm florets
2 cups / 500 ml brussels sprouts, halved lengthwise
2 tablespoons olive oil
Combine in a large bowl, drizzling the oil on top.

3 large cloves garlic, sliced as thin as possible
1½ teaspoon fresh rosemary, chopped; or ½ teaspoon dried
½ teaspoon pepper
Add and mix well; refrigerate overnight. The next day spread vegetables in single layer on greased jellyroll pans. Sprinkle with ¾ teaspoon coarse salt. Roast in preheated oven at 450° F / 230° C until vegetables are crisp-tender and beginning to brown at edges, 15–20 minutes. Stir occasionally. Serve hot or at room temperature.

Serves 4–6 Ⓥ Ⓖf

JOANNA BOWMAN, BROOKLINE, MASSACHUSETTS

Butternut Sage Orzo

Use orzo (tiny rice-shaped pasta) to achieve a taste similar to risotto without the constant stirring. If using dried sage, add it to the simmering butternut.

. . . .

1 cup / 250 ml onion, chopped
In large frypan sauté over medium heat in 1 tablespoon oil until tender, about 6 minutes.

1 clove garlic, minced
Add and sauté until fragrant, about 1 minute.

4 cups / 1 L butternut squash, peeled, seeded, and cut into
    ½-inch / 1-cm pieces
Add and stir to coat.

½ cup / 125 ml vegetable broth
½ cup / 125 ml white wine or additional broth
Add and simmer until squash is almost tender and liquid is absorbed, about 10 minutes.

4 cups / 1 L water or vegetable broth
1 cup / 250 ml orzo
While squash cooks bring liquid to a boil in a large saucepan and add orzo. Boil until tender but still firm to bite, about 8 minutes. Drain. Transfer to a large bowl. Stir in squash mixture.

½ cup / 125 ml Parmesan cheese, freshly grated
2 tablespoons fresh sage, chopped; or 1½ teaspoon dried
Stir in. Salt and pepper to taste.

Serves 4 Ⓥ
. . . .

ALISON FROESE-STODDARD, WINNIPEG, MANITOBA

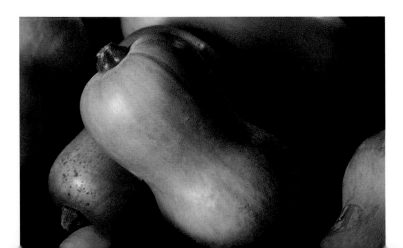

Baked Squash and Apples

Use red-skinned apples, peels on, for an attractive, colorful dish. To make it easier to slice the squash, pierce with a sharp knife a few times and microwave whole on high for 1 minute.

. . . .

2 pounds / 1 kg butternut or buttercup squash, peeled, seeds and fibers removed, cut into ½-inch / 1-cm slices
Arrange in an ungreased rectangular baking dish.

2–3 baking apples, cored and cut into ½-inch / 1-cm slices
Arrange on top of squash.

⅓ cup / 75 ml brown sugar
3 tablespoons butter, melted
1 tablespoon flour
1 teaspoon salt
¼ teaspoon ground mace (optional)
Combine in a small bowl then sprinkle on top of apples and squash. Cover and bake at 350° F / 180° C until squash is tender, 40–50 minutes.

Serves 6 Ⓥ
. . . .

DORIS SHOEMAKER, DAKOTA, ILLINOIS
RUTH STAUFFER, NICHOLVILLE, NEW YORK
CONNIE ZEHR, AKRON, NEW YORK

I spent several August weekends at the top of a ladder, threading my arms through leafy branches to pluck crisp, sweet apples from a stranger's tree. The tree owners had allowed volunteers for Seattle's Community Fruit Tree Harvest to gather their unwanted apples to give to food banks and shelters.

Gleaning groups are springing up all along the West Coast, where our fruit trees, once celebrated for their bounty, have become a nuisance for many. Some trees are the remnants of orchards that have been developed into subdivisions; others are backyard trees planted by a generation that thought nothing of canning one hundred pounds of plums every fall. Over a nine-year period, Seattle volunteers harvested 62,000 pounds of apples, plums, and pears.

To me, gleaning is one small way to respond to the news I read of overstressed, underfunded food banks and the lack of access to nutritious food that shadows poverty. Spending a few enjoyable hours a week amid the leaves reminds me how much the earth already provides, if only we can take her up on the offer.
—Jonathan Kauffman, Seattle, Washington

Chard or Kale Enchiladas

. . . .

1 pound / 500 g Swiss chard or kale
Rinse and remove stems. Finely chop leaves and set aside.
Finely chop stems.

2 onions, diced
2 cloves garlic, minced
In deep frypan sauté in 2 teaspoons oil with chopped stems until
softened, 10 minutes.

1 teaspoon ground cumin
¼ teaspoon pepper
Add with chopped greens. Cook until greens are wilted, 5 minutes.
Add water if necessary. Remove from heat.

1½ cup / 350 ml ricotta cheese or cottage cheese
Mix in. Set aside.

3 cups / 750 ml tomato sauce
2 tablespoons taco seasoning
Combine and pour 1 cup / 250 ml sauce in bottom of a
9 x 13-inch / 3.5-L baking pan.

8 corn or flour tortillas
If using corn tortillas, fill a shallow bowl or pie pan with boiling
water; dip each tortilla in water to soften, 10–15 seconds. Spoon
greens/cheese mixture into tortillas, roll up, and place seam side
down in baking pan. Pour remaining sauce evenly on top, covering
all tortilla edges. Cover and bake in preheated oven at 350° F /
180° C for 40 minutes.

1 cup / 250 ml cheese, shredded
Sprinkle on top. Bake uncovered another 10 minutes.

. . . .

Taco seasoning: Combine ¼ cup / 60 ml chili powder,
3 tablespoons ground cumin, 2 tablespoons dried oregano,
2 tablespoons ground coriander, 1 tablespoon garlic powder,
and ½ teaspoon ground red pepper. To make taco filling, add
2–3 tablespoons seasoning plus ½ cup / 125 ml water with salt to
taste for each 1 pound / 500 g ground beef and/or cooked beans.

Serves 4 Ⓥ
. . . .

JULIE HURST, EAST WATERFORD, PENNSYLVANIA

Chard Cheese Bake

. . . .

1 pound / 500 g Swiss chard or spinach, chopped
Steam and thoroughly drain.

4 eggs, beaten
1 cup / 250 ml milk
1 cup / 250 ml Swiss cheese or another cheese, shredded
1 cup / 250 ml bread, cubed
½ cup / 125 ml green onions, sliced
¼ cup / 60 ml Parmesan cheese, grated
Combine with cooked greens. Pour into a greased 2-quart / 2-L
baking dish. Cover and bake in preheated oven at 375° F / 190° C
until set, 25–30 minutes.

Serves 4 Ⓥ

. . . .

MARIANNE K. MILLER, LITTLE RIVER, KANSAS

"I am only beginning to understand thankfulness and appreciation for the food that is so necessary for life," says Ruth Leonard, an English teacher in China. "Simple foods. Basic foods. Such hard struggles to coax them from the ground."

She recalls a student whose father had died; his mother couldn't harvest the rice alone. When the rest of the class heard, they all traveled to their classmate's home on a Friday night. "For the next two days, they stooped in the fields cutting rice, their toes oozing into the chilly mud," Leonard says. "On Monday I saw them all in class. They were quiet, a bit bent, but smiling. I felt truly humbled when I heard their story—a story of love and care for one another."

But how easy it is to forget, she continues. A month later Leonard taught a lesson about weddings in the West, complete with a mock wedding. At the end, she writes, "I did the unthinkable. The wedding over, the bouquet tossed, we tossed small handfuls of rice onto the smiling 'couple.' The young men were gracious— but the touch of irony in their smiles did not elude me. Rice. Grace. Forgiveness. I felt them all in six ironic smiles."
—adapted from *A Common Place* magazine[2]

Gingered Kale and Tofu

"This is my new favorite way to cook tofu," one tester reported. "It can be made from beginning to end in the forty minutes it takes to cook brown rice."

. . . .

½ cup / 125 ml soy sauce
½ cup / 125 ml dry sherry or vegetable broth
¼ cup / 60 ml rice vinegar or white vinegar
3 tablespoons brown sugar
Bring to a boil in a medium saucepan. Simmer 1 minute and remove from heat.

2 cakes firm tofu, cut in 1-inch / 2.5-cm squares
Place in a single layer in an ovenproof pan. Pour marinade over the tofu and set aside for 10 minutes (or more). Occasionally turn tofu squares over. Drain, reserving remaining marinade.

2 tablespoons peanut oil
Sprinkle over tofu. Broil for 4 minutes then turn squares over. Continue broiling until tofu is golden brown, another 3–4 minutes.

6–12 cups / 1.5–3 L kale, coarsely chopped
3 tablespoons ginger root, peeled and minced
While tofu broils, in a large frypan sauté in 2 tablespoons peanut oil over high heat until kale wilts, stirring constantly.

¼ cup / 60 ml fresh lime juice
¼ cup / 60 ml fresh cilantro, chopped
pinch of ground red pepper (optional)
Add and remove from heat. When tofu is browned, gently toss with cooked kale and as much reserved marinade as desired. Serve on hot rice topped with toasted cashews or peanuts.

Serves 4 Ⓥ

. . . .

LISA LOEWEN EBERSOLE, CORVALLIS, OREGON

Our culture encourages us to be dissatisfied with what we have instead of nurturing contentment and gratitude for what we do have. Imagine an ad that says, "Cooking rice in twenty minutes is perfect." Instead we've got the rice-cooking down to two minutes of impatiently staring at the microwave.
—Brenda Tiessen-Wiens, Calgary, Alberta[3]

Food magazines boast of meals that can be cooked in thirty minutes, fifteen minutes, or, better yet, just five minutes. Occasionally, I want to fix a meal quickly, but usually I like slow food. Slow food is like brown rice that takes about an hour to cook. Or dried beans that soak overnight and cook for several hours. Slow food is like sprouts that take several days to mature. Sourdoughs, cheeses, and wines all get better with age.
—MBL

Chard Utopia

A tasty spin on spanakopita using Swiss chard, more abundant and seasonably available than spinach.

. . . .

2 cups / 500 ml onion, minced
1 teaspoon dried basil
1 teaspoon dried oregano
¼ teaspoon salt
In large frypan sauté in 1 tablespoon olive oil for 5 minutes.

2½ pounds / 1.2 kg Swiss chard, stemmed, finely chopped
Add and cook until wilted, 5–8 minutes.

4–6 cloves garlic, minced
1 tablespoon flour
Sprinkle in, stir, and cook over medium heat, 2–3 minutes. Remove from heat.

2 cups / 500 ml feta cheese, crumbled
1 cup / 250 ml cottage cheese
pepper to taste
Mix in.

1 pound / 500 g frozen phyllo pastry sheets, thawed
Place a sheet of phyllo in an oiled 9 x 13-inch / 3.5-L pan. Brush or lightly spray sheet with olive oil. Repeat 7 times. Spread half the filling evenly on top. Add 8 more sheets of oiled phyllo. Cover with the rest of the filling and follow with remaining sheets of phyllo, oiling each, including the top sheet. Tuck in the edges and bake uncovered in preheated oven at 375° F / 190° C until golden and crispy, 45 minutes.

Serves 8–10 Ⓥ
. . . .

AMARYAH DEGROOT, WATERLOO, ONTARIO

Nutty Cauliflower Skillet

· ·

1 tablespoon ginger root, peeled and minced
2 cloves garlic, minced
In large soup pot sauté in 2–3 tablespoons olive oil over medium-high heat for 30 seconds.

1 head cauliflower, cut into ¾-inch / 2.75-cm florets
1 teaspoon each ground coriander and ground cumin
½ teaspoon each ground turmeric, paprika, and salt
¼ teaspoon pepper
Add and mix to coat.

½ cup / 125 ml tomatoes, chopped, or ⅓ cup / 75 ml
    tomato juice
1 cup / 250 ml peas or green soybeans (edamame)
Add tomatoes, reduce heat to medium, and simmer until cauliflower is crisp-tender, 8–10 minutes. If using green soybeans, add with tomatoes; peas will take just 1–2 minutes to cook.

2 tablespoons peanut butter
Stir in. Serve over brown rice topped with peanuts and chopped fresh cilantro (optional).

Serves 4–5 Ⓥ Ⓖⓕ

· ·

BRENDA LEENDERS, TRURO, NOVA SCOTIA

How often would you eat French fries if you had to peel, wash, cut, and fry them yourself—and then clean up the mess? Or ever eat Twinkies if you had to bake the little cakes and then squirt the filling into them and clean up?

Recently a group of Harvard economists seeking to advance an economic theory for the obesity epidemic correlated the rise in the average weight of Americans with a decline in the "time cost" of eating—cooking, cleaning up, and so on. They concluded that the widespread availability of cheap convenience foods could explain most of the twelve-pound increase in the weight of the average American since the early 1960s. [The twelve-pound increase has now expanded to twenty-four pounds.] —Michael Pollan, *In Defense of Food*[4]

Red Lentil Coconut Curry

"This recipe was inspired by cooking with Gary's Malaysian brother-in-law, Ken, whose joyous abandon in the kitchen raises food preparation to both art and spiritual highs," says contributor Linda Nafziger-Meiser.

. . . .

Place can of coconut milk in freezer 20 minutes before starting to cook. Open can and remove solidified coconut butter from the top to use in sautéing.

1 large onion, minced
In large soup pot sauté in coconut butter or 1 tablespoon oil over medium-high heat until transparent but not browned.

1 tablespoon garlic, minced
1 tablespoon ginger root, peeled and minced
2 teaspoons curry powder
½ teaspoon each ground turmeric, ground cumin, pepper
¼ teaspoon ground red pepper
¼ teaspoon ground cinnamon
2–3 bay leaves
Add and reduce heat to medium-low. Cook and stir constantly for 3 minutes; do not let spices and onion brown.

1 (13.5-ounce / 400-ml) can coconut milk
¼ cup / 60 ml tamari or soy sauce
1 cup / 250 ml tomato sauce
Add and simmer on low heat for 20 minutes, stirring often.

2 cups / 500 ml dried red lentils, rinsed
5 cups / 1.3 L water
In saucepan cook for 15 minutes. Add, with liquid, to soup pot.

1 medium head cauliflower, cut into 1½-inch / 4-cm florets
1 large sweet potato, peeled and cut into 1-inch / 2.5-cm cubes
¼ head cabbage, cut in 1½-inch / 4-cm chunks
1–2 cups / 250–500 ml peas (optional)
Add to soup pot and cook over medium heat just until tender. If using peas, add at the end of the cooking time. Serve over brown rice with toppings (optional): Indian chutneys and pickles, fresh diced pears, roasted sunflower seeds, plain yogurt.

Serves 8–10 Ⓥ
. . . .
LINDA NAFZIGER-MEISER, BOISE, IDAHO

Autumn Tagine

Tagine (tah-ZHEEN) is a Moroccan stew named after the traditional heavy clay pot in which it is cooked. This colorful vegetarian version made one tester's eleven-year-old exclaim, "We should have this every night!" Adjust the amount of crushed hot chilies to suit your family's tastes.

. . . .

2 cups / 500 ml onion, diced
In large soup pot sauté in 1–2 tablespoons oil until soft, 4–5 minutes.

6 cloves garlic, minced
1 teaspoon ginger root, peeled and minced
2 teaspoons ground cumin
1 teaspoon paprika
½ teaspoon salt
½–1 teaspoon pepper
¼–1 teaspoon crushed hot chilies (optional)
Add and stir for 1 minute.

3 cups / 750 ml sweet potatoes, peeled and cut into 1-inch /
**   2.5-cm cubes**
2 cups / 500 ml cooked chickpeas
1½ cup / 350 ml vegetable broth
Add and bring to a boil. Cover; reduce heat. Simmer 5 minutes.

½ medium head cauliflower, cut into 1-inch / 2.5-cm florets
2 cups / 500 ml peas
Stir in cauliflower, cover, and simmer until vegetables are nearly tender, about 12 minutes. Add peas, cover, and simmer until hot, 2 minutes. Serve over steamed couscous or rice, garnished with chopped fresh cilantro (optional).

Serves 6–8 ⓥ
. . . .

BETHANY J. OSBORNE, TORONTO, ONTARIO

Vegetarian Groundnut Stew

This dish was inspired by peanut stews served in West Africa. The contributor adapted a recipe and prepared it for her December wedding feast using ingredients she had helped to grow during the previous summer.

. . . .

2 cups / 500 ml onion, chopped
2–3 cloves garlic, minced
In large frypan sauté in 1 tablespoon oil until translucent.

3 cups / 750 ml winter squash such as butternut, peeled and chopped
2 cups / 500 ml cabbage, chopped
1 dried chili pepper, or ground red pepper to taste
Add and sauté for a few minutes.

3 cups / 750 ml tomato juice or puréed canned tomatoes
1 cup / 250 ml apple juice
1–2 teaspoons ginger root, peeled and minced
Add, cover, and simmer until squash is tender, about 20 minutes.

1–2 cups / 250–500 ml green beans
Add and simmer 5 minutes more.

½ cup / 125 ml peanut butter
Stir in and simmer at very low heat until ready to serve. Serve on top of brown rice or millet with toppings (optional): chopped green onions, parsley, cilantro, peaches or other fruit, crushed peanuts, flaked coconut.

Serves 6 Ⓥ Ⓖf

. . . .

JENNIFER DEGROOT, WINNIPEG, MANITOBA

"You give them their food in due season." (Psalm 145:15)

It's funny—in the spring I can hardly wait for fresh lettuce and tomato salads, but now after several months of eating fresh tomatoes at least once a day, if not three times a day, I'm secretly hoping for a frost. I'm ready; it's "due season," for soups and stews.
—MBL

Savory Squash Bread Pudding

Sautéed kale or mustard greens offer a nice counterpoint to the sweet butternut squash.

· ·

**3 cups / 750 ml butternut squash, peeled and cut in
½-inch / 1-cm pieces**

Arrange squash in a single layer on jelly roll pan coated with cooking spray. Sprinkle with salt. Bake in preheated oven at 400° F / 200° C until tender, 12 minutes. Remove from oven; reduce temperature to 350° F / 180° C.

**1 cup / 250 ml onion, chopped
1 clove garlic, minced**

In a frypan sauté onion in 1 teaspoon olive oil over medium-high heat until tender, 5 minutes. Add garlic and sauté 1 minute. Remove from heat; cool slightly.

**3 large eggs
2 large egg whites
2 cups / 500 ml milk
½ cup / 125 ml Parmesan cheese, freshly grated
¼ teaspoon salt
¼ teaspoon pepper
⅛ teaspoon ground nutmeg**

Whisk together in a large bowl. Stir in squash, onion, and garlic.

**9 cups / 2.3 L day-old French bread, cut in 1-inch / 2.5-cm
cubes**

Add and stir gently to combine. Let stand 10 minutes. Spoon into a greased 2-quart / 2-L baking dish.

½ cup / 125 ml Parmesan cheese, freshly grated

Sprinkle on top. Bake in preheated oven at 350° F / 180° C until custard is set and top is lightly browned, 45 minutes.

Serves 4–6 Ⓥ

· ·

MEGAN GOOSSEN, DINUBA, CALIFORNIA

Stuffed Acorn Squash

. . . .

2–3 large acorn squash or other winter squash
Cut squash in half and remove seeds and strings. (To make this easier, pierce squash with a knife and microwave a minute or two.) Place cut side down on lightly greased baking sheet with sides. Bake at 350° F / 180° C until almost soft but not mushy, 40–50 minutes. (Or cook in the microwave for about 10 minutes, covered.) May do this step in advance. Remove from oven, fill with one of the following stuffing options, and finish baking as directed.

Serves 4–6
. . . .

Sausage stuffing:

1 pound / 500 g bulk sausage or turkey sausage
4 celery stalks, finely diced
1 medium onion, finely diced
2 carrots, shredded
¼ cup / 60 ml water
2 cups / 500 ml bread crumbs
Sauté sausage just until cooked through. Add celery, onion, carrots, and water. Cover and simmer 15 minutes. Mix in bread crumbs. Stuff into cooked squash and bake at 375° F / 190° C for 10 minutes.

. . . .

Apple-sausage stuffing:

1 pound / 500 g bulk sausage
1 onion, diced
1 apple, diced
2 cups / 500 ml toasted bread cubes
¾ cup / 175 ml nuts, chopped
¾ cup / 175 ml golden raisins
1 tablespoon sour cream or plain yogurt
¼ teaspoon each dried thyme, basil, and oregano
Brown sausage in large skillet. Add onion and apple and sauté just until tender. Remove from heat. Add remaining ingredients and stuff into cooked squash, cover, and bake at 375° F / 190° C for 20 minutes.

. . . .

More stuffing options >

....

Apple stuffing: Ⓥ Ⓖf

2–3 tart apples, diced
¼ cup / 60 ml maple syrup
¼ cup / 60 ml butter, melted
Combine. Stuff into cooked squash, cover, and bake at 375° F / 190° C for 30 minutes.

....

Mushroom stuffing: Ⓥ

1 onion, chopped
½ cup / 125 ml mushrooms, chopped
2 cloves garlic, minced
2 cups / 500 ml bread crumbs
½ teaspoon each sage and salt
dash pepper
In large frypan sauté onion, mushrooms, and garlic until soft. Add remaining ingredients and stuff into cooked squash. Bake at 375° F / 190° C for 20 minutes.

....

Fruit and nut stuffing: Ⓥ

1½ cup / 375 ml onion, chopped
1 stalk celery, diced
2 cloves garlic, minced
2 tart apples, chopped
1½ cup / 375 ml bread crumbs or cooked brown rice
½ cup / 125 ml sunflower seeds
6–8 dried apricots, chopped
¼ cup / 60 ml nuts, chopped
¼ cup / 60 ml raisins, dried cranberries, or currants
½ teaspoon salt
¼ teaspoon each dried thyme, sage, oregano
dash pepper
In large frypan sauté onion, celery, and garlic in 1 tablespoon oil until onion is translucent. Add remaining ingredients and mix well. Stuff into cooked squash, cover, and bake at 375° F / 190° C for 20–30 minutes.

....

SAUSAGE: NANCY HALDER, PARNELL, IOWA
APPLE-SAUSAGE: JUDITH MISHLER, SHIPSHEWANA, INDIANA
APPLE: CHRISTINE FIELD, READING, PENNSYLVANIA
MUSHROOM: SUSAN CARLYLE, BARNARDSVILLE, NORTH CAROLINA
FRUIT AND NUT: JENNIFER DEGROOT, WINNIPEG, MANITOBA

Poultry Pasta Primavera

Like creamy Alfredo-type sauces but without all the fat.

. . . .

8 ounces / 250 g angel hair pasta, cooked
2 cups / 500 ml broccoli florets
1 cup / 250 ml carrots, julienned
½ cup / 125 ml red sweet pepper, sliced
1 sweet onion, sliced

Five minutes before pasta is done add the vegetables to the cooking water. Continue cooking until pasta is done and vegetables are crisp-tender. Drain and set aside.

1 clove garlic, minced
1 teaspoon dried parsley; or 1 tablespoon fresh, chopped
½ teaspoon dried basil; or 1½ teaspoon fresh, chopped
½ teaspoon dried oregano; or 1½ teaspoon fresh, chopped

In large frypan sauté in ½ tablespoon oil.

2 tablespoons flour
1 cup / 250 ml milk

Add flour and stir briefly. Add milk, stirring constantly until thickened.

1 cup / 250 ml cooked chicken, turkey, or rabbit, chopped

Add and heat through.

½ cup / 125 ml yogurt cheese (p. 387)
¼ cup / 60 ml Parmesan cheese, freshly grated

Add and heat, but do not boil. Serve the white sauce over the pasta and vegetables. Garnish with additional freshly grated Parmesan cheese.

Serves 4

. . . .

MARY BETH LIND, HARMAN, WEST VIRGINIA

Although a beautiful time of year, fall always makes me a little melancholy. I think it is because time is moving from great abundance to perhaps scarcity. And I have an underlying fear— will there be enough? So I fill a few extra canning jars, stuff a few more things in the freezer, dry another bunch of herbs, and add some apples to the bins in the root cellar. What is enough? —MBL

Pumpkin Sausage Pasta

Especially wonderful when made with homemade sausage. Green Salad with Autumn Fruit (p. 229) is the perfect accompaniment.

. . . .

1 pound / 500 g penne pasta or other chunky pasta
Cook, drain, and set aside.

1 pound / 500 g bulk sweet Italian sausage
In large, deep frypan coated with cooking spray, brown sausage over medium-high heat. When cooked, remove meat and set aside. Drain fat from frypan and return pan to stove.

1 medium onion, finely chopped
4 cloves garlic, minced
Add to frypan and sauté until soft, 3–5 minutes.

1 bay leaf
2 tablespoons fresh sage, cut into very thin strips
1 cup / 250 ml dry white wine or chicken broth
Add and cook until half of liquid evaporates, about 2 minutes.

1 cup / 250 ml chicken or vegetable broth
1 cup / 250 ml pumpkin or winter squash, cooked, puréed
Mix in. Continue stirring until sauce starts to bubble. Add sausage and reduce heat.

½ cup / 125 ml evaporated milk
½ teaspoon ground nutmeg
⅛ teaspoon ground cinnamon
coarse salt and pepper to taste
Stir in milk. Add seasonings and simmer 5–10 minutes to thicken. Remove bay leaf. Pour sauce over cooked pasta. Combine sauce and pasta and toss over low heat for 1 minute. Garnish with freshly grated Romano or Parmesan cheese and fresh sage leaves (optional).

Serves 6
. . . .

MEGAN GOOSSEN, DINUBA, CALIFORNIA

Butternut Skillet

A cinch to throw together and absolutely delectable. Vary the amounts of squash and sausage to suit your family's tastes.

. . . .

2–3 cups / 500–750 ml butternut squash or pumpkin, peeled and chopped in 1-inch / 2.5-cm pieces
1 onion, chopped
hot chili peppers, chopped; or hot pepper sauce to taste
In large saucepan sauté in 2 tablespoons oil until onion is translucent. Cover and cook until pumpkin is cooked, 10 minutes.

1 cup / 250 ml chicken, beef, or vegetable broth
Add and cook for 10 minutes.

1 cup / 250 ml browned sausage
salt and pepper to taste
Add and cook uncovered until liquid is absorbed. Serve with rice or noodles.

Serves 4
. . . .

KAREN METZLER, CHILLICOTHE, OHIO
HAZEL HEISEY, BRIDGEWATER, VIRGINIA

Our family spent six years working with Mennonite Central Committee in Lesotho, southern Africa. About half of that time we lived in a mountain village with no electricity or running water. As we carried water up from the spring and laundry down to the river; as we hiked to school or to visit friends; as we relaxed in the evenings with a candle and a book or a pen, we often compared a life based primarily on sustainable energy sources (human, sun, wind) to a life based primarily on extracted energy (fossil fuels).

Back in the United States, we started experimenting with generating our electricity with solar and wind. Our homestead still runs with no grid electricity. This large choice dictates smaller choices, like no microwave or dishwasher. Those choices sometimes slow us down and feel like a burden; they sometimes stretch our pocketbooks. But always they give us satisfaction that we are taking small steps to share the earth with our global neighbors and pass its life on to our grandchildren.
—Brenda Hostetler-Meyer, Millersburg, Indiana

Herbed Broccoli Sandwich

"This quickly became a lunchtime favorite," one tester said; "Simple, easy, and delicious."

. . . .

2 cups / 500 ml broccoli, finely chopped
½ cup / 125 ml onion, finely chopped
In large frypan sauté in 2 tablespoons oil until broccoli is bright green.

a few dashes each of dried basil, thyme, pepper
½ teaspoon salt
Mix in.

4–6 slices French bread
Top with vegetable mixture.

¾ cup / 175 ml cheese, shredded
Sprinkle on top and broil until melted. Serve immediately.

Yields 4–6 Ⓥ

. . . .

Rainbow sandwich variation: Try adding a handful of shredded carrots, purple cabbage, or minced banana peppers while cooking the broccoli. Or top bread with a layer of thinly sliced tomatoes, add vegetable mixture, and serve without broiling.

. . . .

GLADYS LONGACRE, SUSQUEHANNA, PENNSYLVANIA

Dinner Co-ops

Recipe for success, part 1

Day after day, dinnertime arrives with the regularity of a metronome. You are left with the problem of planning, shopping, preparing, and serving food, whether you live alone or in a large household.

One day while a neighbor and I were mulling this over, we decided to do something about it. I made dinner for her family one night, she made dinner for my family another. We added a third family, and our neighborhood dinner co-op was born. That was six years ago, and all three families still swear by the system.

One evening a week a family brings dinner to each of the other two families. We don't bring appetizers or desserts, but we provide a complete dinner with some kind of protein, a starch, and a vegetable. We don't consult about menus or finances. We each pay for what we serve.

When we began I think we were all a bit nervous about whether the others would like the food we prepared. But we have all learned about cooking large quantities. It now takes little more work than preparing a meal for one family.

The easiest meals are those that do not require cooking right before delivering. Casseroles, stews, beans and rice, lasagna, soups, and pasta salads can all be made as much as three or four days ahead, which makes this system workable even for those with long workdays. If you can cook one evening a week or on one weekend day, you can make one big dinner, pack it up in casserole dishes, and you've taken care of dinner for three nights. Often you have four nights' worth because you usually get one night's worth of leftovers in the deal.

Recipe for success, part 2

When Kristi Bahrenburg of Hyattsville, Maryland, started a weekly playgroup among her friends with small children, she didn't realize how difficult arranging meeting times would be. Finally the group decided that dinnertime might work—and a dinner co-op was born.

The four women and five children gather for weekly shared dinners cooked by that week's hostess. "It's a wonderful break to be served high-quality, homemade food in a casual atmosphere where our kids can run around together before and after the meal," Bahrenburg says.

Here are some suggestions for creating your own cuisine that builds community:

Find partners. You can ask friends, coworkers, or neighbors to participate, or invite members through a community organization or place of worship.

Agree on a structure. If you have only a few participants, you can hold your shared dinners in a member's home. Or have the cooks du jour deliver meals directly to participants. Decide how often you want to have co-op dinners: daily, once a week, monthly, or whatever suits members' needs.

Make your shared food sustainable. Consider committing as a group to preparing meals with locally produced foods. Emphasize vegetables and whole grains. Buy items in bulk to minimize waste.

Bahrenburg says the co-op has helped her see a whole new side of her friends: "One mother is from Shanghai, so we get really amazing, authentic Chinese foods. Another is from Croatia, so her cooking style also has a unique, regional flair. It's rewarding because we really have enjoyed getting to know each other better."

—Karin Chenoweth at www.coopamerica.org and from *Co-op America Quarterly*[5]

Cranberry Apple Crisp

A lovely and delicious variation to traditional apple crisp.

. . . .

4 cups / 1 L cooking apples, peeled and sliced
2 cups / 500 ml cranberries
¼ cup / 60 ml brown sugar
1 teaspoon orange peel, grated (optional)
Combine in a large bowl and toss gently until fruit is coated.
Place in greased 8 x 8-inch / 2-L baking dish.

¾ cup / 175 ml brown sugar
¾ cup / 175 ml flour
¾ cup / 175 ml rolled oats
½ cup / 125 ml oat bran
1 teaspoon ground cinnamon
Combine in a medium bowl.

¼ cup / 60 ml butter
1 tablespoon oil
⅓ cup / 75 ml nuts, chopped (optional)
Cut into flour mixture until crumbly. Sprinkle evenly over apple
mixture. Bake at 350° F / 180° C until fruit is soft and topping is
crisp, 45–50 minutes. Serve warm with milk or frozen yogurt.

Serves 6–8 Ⓥ
. . . .

RUTH BOWMAN, SALEM, OHIO
JILL HEATWOLE, PITTSVILLE, MARYLAND

I stumbled across a heavy, ancient cider press at an estate sale. The price, seventy-five dollars, accurately reflected its weathered condition. But my dad helped me make the necessary repairs, and soon I was in business. I cultivated the friendship of a local orchard owner who lets me gather apples dropped from his trees. Each year I invite a group of new Goshen College students to my home. Amid the beautiful maple leaves and the gathering dusk of a crisp fall evening, we wash, shred, and press five or six bushels of apples. Making cider with my students—most of whom have never seen a cider press—is always a highlight of the season.
—John D. Roth, Goshen, Indiana

Upside-Down Pear Gingerbread

"When someone gave me a bucket of pears from her tree I looked for pear recipes. There aren't many," notes contributor Bernita Boyts. "I finally put two together: a recipe for gingerbread and the topping from a pineapple upside-down cake. A little grated fresh ginger root is a good addition with the spices."

. . . .

¼ cup / 60 ml brown sugar
2 tablespoons sugar
1 tablespoon butter
1 tablespoon water
Combine in an ovenproof, microwavable casserole dish. Microwave on low until butter melts. Stir.

2 ripe pears, peeled, cored, and sliced
Arrange on top of syrup.

1 cup / 250 ml flour
½ cup / 125 ml whole wheat flour
1 teaspoon baking soda
1 teaspoon ground ginger
½ teaspoon ground cinnamon
¼ teaspoon each ground nutmeg, ground allspice, salt
Stir together and set aside.

⅓ cup / 75 ml butter, softened
½ cup / 125 ml brown sugar
1 egg
In a mixing bowl beat together butter and brown sugar with an electric mixer until light and fluffy. Add egg and beat another minute.

½ cup / 125 ml molasses or honey
½ cup / 125 ml buttermilk
Alternately add molasses and buttermilk with dry ingredients to creamed mixture. Spoon over pears in baking dish. Bake in preheated oven at 350° F / 180° C until toothpick inserted in cake comes out clean, 30–35 minutes. Remove from oven and cool about 3 minutes. Turn onto a platter. Serve warm or cold with whipped cream.

Serves 8 Ⓥ
. . . .

BERNITA BOYTS, SHAWNEE MISSION, KANSAS

Pear Custard Bars

A pleasing way to use pears in season.

. . . .

⅓ cup / 75 ml butter, softened
⅓ cup / 75 ml sugar
Cream together with an electric mixer.

¾ cup / 175 ml whole wheat flour
¼ teaspoon vanilla
Add and beat until combined.

⅔ cup / 150 ml nuts, chopped
Stir in and press into an 8 x 8-inch / 2-L baking pan. Bake
in preheated oven at 350° F / 180° C until lightly browned,
20 minutes. Cool in pan on a wire rack.

8 ounces / 250 g cream cheese, softened,
**   or 1 cup / 250 ml plain yogurt**
½ cup / 125 ml sugar
1 egg
½ teaspoon vanilla
In a mixing bowl beat cream cheese until smooth (no need to beat
the yogurt). Mix in sugar, egg, and vanilla. Pour over crust.

3 cups / 750 ml fresh pears, peeled and sliced
Arrange over filling.

½ teaspoon sugar
½ teaspoon ground cinnamon
Combine and sprinkle over pears. Bake in preheated oven at
350° F / 180° C for 25–30 minutes. (Center will be soft and will
become firmer upon cooling.) Cool for 45 minutes, then cover and
refrigerate at least 45 minutes before cutting. Store in refrigerator.

Yields 16 bars Ⓥ
. . . .

JOCELE MEYER, FRESNO, OHIO

Pear Custard Pie

. . . .

9-inch / 1-L unbaked pie crust (p. 380)
4–5 cups / 1–1.3 L pears, peeled and sliced
Place fruit in pie crust.

2 eggs
1 cup / 250 ml sugar
¼ cup / 60 ml flour
¼ cup / 60 ml butter, softened
1 teaspoon vanilla
In small bowl beat together with an electric mixer until light and
fluffy. Pour mixture over fruit. Bake in preheated oven at 450° F /
230° C for 10 minutes. Reduce heat to 350° F / 180° C and
continue baking until set, 30 minutes.

Yields 1 pie (V)
. . . .

GWEN PEACHEY, CORVALLIS, OREGON

Pumpkin Pecan Pie

. . . .

1 cup / 250 ml pumpkin or sweet potato, cooked, puréed
¾ cup / 175 ml light corn syrup
3 eggs, beaten
⅓ cup / 75 ml brown sugar
¼ cup / 60 ml butter, softened
1 teaspoon vanilla
½ teaspoon salt
1 cup / 250 ml pecans, chopped
Beat together all ingredients but pecans with an electric mixer.
Stir in pecans.

9-inch / 1-L unbaked pie crust (p. 380)
Pour into pie crust. Bake in preheated oven at 350° F / 180° C until
set, 45–55 minutes.

Yields 1 pie (V)
. . . .

FLORENCE ZEHR, MANSON, IOWA
LOIS MASON, UPLAND, CALIFORNIA
DONALD FREDERICK, EAST PEORIA, ILLINOIS

Pumpkin Chocolate Cheesecake

Cookbook author Cathleen Hockman-Wert and designer Julie Kauffman were once part of a supper club. The most memorable dish of that experience, Cathleen says, was Julie's marbled cheesecake. This is a lower-fat version.

. . . .

1 cup / 250 ml chocolate wafer or graham cracker crumbs
1 tablespoon brown sugar
1 tablespoon oil
Combine with a little water and press into the bottom of a 9-inch / 1-L springform pan coated with cooking spray. Set aside.

3 cups / 750 ml low-fat cottage cheese (don't use nonfat)
12 ounces / 350 g cream cheese, softened
1¼ cup / 300 ml sugar
¼ cup / 60 ml cornstarch or arrowroot powder
Purée cottage cheese in blender or food processor. Add remaining ingredients and beat until smooth. Pour into a bowl.

2 eggs, beaten
2 teaspoons vanilla
¼ teaspoon salt
Mix in. Remove 2 cups / 500 ml batter and set aside.

1½ cup / 375 ml pumpkin, cooked and puréed
¼ cup / 60 ml brown sugar
¾ teaspoon ground cinnamon
⅛ teaspoon ground nutmeg
Add to remaining batter.

⅓ cup / 75 ml baking cocoa
1 cup / 250 ml chocolate chips, melted
Add to the reserved batter. Stir until thoroughly blended. Pour pumpkin mixture into crust-lined pan then spoon chocolate mixture on top in small rounds; swirl together with a knife. Bake in preheated oven at 325° F / 160° C until edge of filling is set, 60–65 minutes. Let cheesecake stand in oven with door closed for 30 minutes. Remove and cool on rack to room temperature, about 3 hours. Cover and refrigerate for several hours before serving. To bake in a 9 x 13 inch / 3.5-L baking pan, decrease baking time to 45 minutes.

Serves 12–16

. . . .

CATHLEEN HOCKMAN-WERT, CORVALLIS, OREGON
JULIE KAUFFMAN, LANCASTER, PENNSYLVANIA

Winter Squash Bars

Moist and not too sweet. These bars freeze well.

. . . .

2 cups / 500 ml winter squash or pumpkin, cooked, puréed
1½ cup / 375 ml sugar
¾ cup / 175 ml oil
4 eggs
1 teaspoon vanilla
½ teaspoon salt
Beat together in a mixing bowl.

1 cup / 250 ml flour
1 cup / 250 ml whole wheat flour
2 teaspoons baking powder
1 teaspoon baking soda
1 teaspoon ground cinnamon
Mix in. Pour into lightly greased 11 x 17-inch / 28 x 43-cm jelly roll
pan. Bake in preheated oven at 350° F / 180° C for 25–30 minutes.

Yields 24 bars Ⓥ
. . . .

ELLEN DAVIS-ZEHR AND DENNIS ZEHR, TISKILWA, ILLINOIS

Frosted Persimmon Cookies

"Every autumn, for many years, one of my clients would gather persimmons from her tree, make persimmon pulp, and then bring these frosted cookies as a gift to the office where I worked. We always anticipated the day these cookies would arrive," says contributor Evelyn Shellenberger.

. . . .

2 cups / 500 ml sugar
1 cup / 250 ml butter, softened
Cream together with an electric mixer in a large bowl.

2 cups / 500 ml persimmon pulp (p. 30)
2 eggs, slightly beaten
Blend in.

4 cups / 1 L flour
2 teaspoons baking soda
2 teaspoons ground cinnamon
1 teaspoon ground nutmeg
1 teaspoon ground cloves
Sift together then add gradually to persimmon mixture, blending well after each addition.

1 cup / 250 ml pecans or other nuts, chopped
½ cup / 125 ml raisins
Stir in. Drop by tablespoon onto ungreased baking sheets and bake in preheated oven at 375° F / 190° C for 8–10 minutes.

3 cups / 750 ml powdered sugar
3 tablespoons butter, melted
5–6 tablespoons milk
Blend together, adding enough milk to make a spreading consistency. Frost cookies while warm.

Yields 6–8 dozen Ⓥ

. . . .

EVELYN SHELLENBERGER, PAOLI, INDIANA

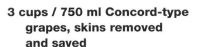

Grape Pie

*A pie with excellent flavor, packed with
all the tang of the small black grapes that
manage to survive the prairie's harsh winters.*

. . . .

**3 cups / 750 ml Concord-type
    grapes, skins removed
    and saved**

In saucepan simmer pulp for 5 minutes. Press through a sieve to
remove the seeds. Combine the pulp and the reserved skins.

1 cup / 250 ml sugar
3 tablespoons flour
1 tablespoon lemon juice
9-inch / 1-L unbaked pie crust (p. 380)

Add sugar, flour, and lemon juice to grapes. Pour into pie crust.

1 cup / 250 ml flour
½ cup / 125 ml sugar
2 tablespoons butter, softened
2 tablespoons oil

Combine and sprinkle over the grape mixture. Bake in preheated
oven at 425° F / 220° C for 10 minutes. Reduce heat to 350° F /
180° C and bake for 30 minutes.

Yields 1 pie Ⓥ

. . . .

ELEANORE AND JOHN REMPEL-WOOLLARD, EDMONTON, ALBERTA
KRISTIN SHANK ZEHR, HARRISONBURG, VIRGINIA
MARY BETH LIND, HARMAN, WEST VIRGINIA

The miraculous is not
extraordinary but the common
mode of existence. It is our
daily bread. Whoever really
has considered the lilies of the
field or the birds of the air and
pondered the improbability of
their existence in this warm
world within the cold and empty
stellar distances will hardly
balk at the turning of water into
wine—which was, after all, a
very small miracle. We forget
the greater and still continuing
miracle by which water (with
soil and sunlight) is turned into
grapes.
—Wendell Berry, author[6]

Pumpkin Dip

A dip for fruits or cookies such as gingersnaps or vanilla wafers.

. . . .

**12 ounces / 350 g cream cheese, softened;
   or 1½ cup / 375 ml yogurt cheese (p. 387)
1 cup / 250 ml brown sugar**
Beat together until well blended.

**1 cup / 250 ml pumpkin, cooked and puréed
4 teaspoons maple syrup
1 teaspoon ground cinnamon**
Add and beat until smooth.

Yields 2 cups / 500 ml Ⓥ Ⓖⓕ
. . . .

DEBRA LAYMAN, HARRISONBURG, VIRGINIA

Green Surprise Dip

A yummy addition to vegetable sticks, crackers, or tortilla chips. Kids like it, too!

. . . .

**1 cup / 250 ml steamed kale, Swiss chard, or spinach
1 cup / 250 ml plain yogurt
1 cup / 250 ml cooked chickpeas
¼ cup / 60 ml mayonnaise
2 cloves garlic
½ onion, chopped
1 tablespoon lemon juice, or to taste
½ teaspoon salt, or to taste**
Purée in blender or food processor.

Yields about 2½ cups / 625 ml Ⓥ
. . . .

TERESA DUTCHERSMITH, GOSHEN, INDIANA

Pear or Apple Chutney

Serve with curry dishes, on turkey sandwiches, or with cream cheese on a bagel.

. . . .

12 cups / 3 L pears and/or apples, peeled, cored, chopped
2 cups / 500 ml cider vinegar
1½ cup / 375 ml onion, chopped
1 jalapeño pepper, minced, seeds removed
4 cloves garlic, minced
1 cup / 250 ml currants
½ cup / 125 ml dried cranberries, cherries, golden raisins,
 apricots, or peaches, chopped
2 inches / 5 cm ginger root, peeled and minced
4 cups / 1 L brown sugar (use less if fruit is sweet)
2 teaspoons ground coriander
1 teaspoon each ground cloves, yellow mustard seed, salt
1½ teaspoon chili powder
1½ teaspoon each ground cumin and cumin seed
½ teaspoon ground cinnamon
⅛ teaspoon ground cardamom
Combine in large saucepan. Bring to a boil, lower heat to medium, and cook until mixture thickens and mounds slightly on a spoon, 50–60 minutes. Stir occasionally to prevent sticking. Ladle into hot, sterilized half-pint jars to within ½ inch / 1 cm of top. Seal with sterilized lids and process in boiling water bath for 15 minutes.

Yields 12 half-pints / 1.5 L Ⓥ Ⓖⓕ

. . . .

LISA LOEWEN EBERSOLE, CORVALLIS, OREGON

Delicious Creator God,

I taste your glory in the tangy crunch
    of a crisp apple.
I taste your glory in salty tears of emotion.
I taste your glory in cool, clear, life-giving water.
I taste your glory in the heavy sweetness
    of dark chocolate.
Your glory flavors the early peas
      and new lettuce of spring,
    the raspberries and sour cherries
      of my backyard,
    the mealy goodness of new potatoes
      and butternut squash.
It steeps in my tea
    and bakes in my peach cobbler.
For the nibbles and feasts of your glory
    and for my taste buds,
I give you thanks.

—DONNA MAST, SCOTTDALE, PENNSYLVANIA

The field of the poor may yield much food,
but it is swept away through injustice.
(Proverbs 13:23)

Nights are long. Snow blankets the landscape. The sun can only warm us around the edges. The naked trees groan as they bend in the frozen wind. Woodchucks, who in summer devastated the garden, now burrow in for a long winter nap. Winter invites us to reflect upon the food we purchase and eat in light of the dreams and values we pursue throughout the year.

winter

Breads and Breakfast

Soups

Salads

Sides

Main Dishes

Desserts

Extras

Invitations to Action

"Vote" with your dollars by spending your food budget on foods that reflect your values.

Support locally-owned grocery stores, restaurants, and cooperatives.

If you buy coffee, chocolate, or tea, buy fairly traded products. Ask your local supermarket and coffeehouse to carry fairly traded foods.

Celebrate the earth's bounty by sharing with others. Invite a newcomer to lunch. Share vegetables from your CSA box or garden with a neighbor. Offer to carpool to a farmers' market.

Advocate for government policies—both domestic and international—that permit countries to make local food production for local consumption a priority.

Start or participate in a community kitchen program in which groups cook meals together, saving money and time.

Teach a child, or share with a friend, why you choose the foods you do.

Vegetarian Menu

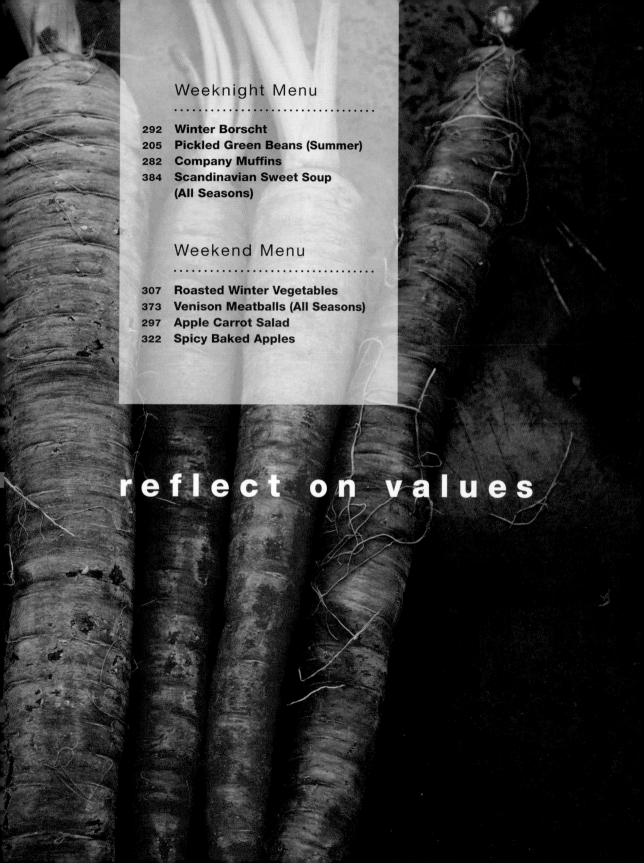

Weeknight Menu

Weekend Menu

reflect on values

Sweet Potato Crescent Rolls

Beautiful rolls for a holiday dinner. "My children loved these rolls," one tester reports. "I decided to frost them like cinnamon rolls, and then my family couldn't get enough of them."

. . . .

1½ cup / 375 ml whole wheat bread flour
¼ cup / 60 ml sugar
1 tablespoon active dry yeast
1 teaspoon salt
1 teaspoon ground cinnamon
½ teaspoon ground nutmeg
¼ teaspoon ground ginger
¼ teaspoon ground allspice
Combine in a large bowl.

1 cup / 250 ml sweet potatoes, cooked and mashed
1 cup / 250 ml milk
¼ cup / 60 ml butter
Combine in large saucepan and cook over medium heat, stirring until butter is melted and mixture is warm. Add to flour mixture. Beat with mixer set on low speed, scraping bowl often, until mixture is all moistened, 1–2 minutes.

1 large egg, beaten
Add and beat at medium speed for 3 minutes.

2–2½ cups / 500–625 ml bread flour
Stir in enough flour by hand to make dough easy to handle. Turn onto floured surface and knead until smooth and elastic, about 7–9 minutes. Place in greased bowl, turn to grease both sides, cover with a damp cloth, and let rise until doubled in bulk. Punch down dough and divide it in half. Roll each half of dough on lightly floured surface into a 12-inch / 30-cm circle.

2 tablespoons butter, melted
Brush each circle with 1 tablespoon butter. Cut into 12 wedges and tightly roll up each wedge from wide end to point. Place crescent rolls, point side down, on greased baking sheet. Cover and let rise until doubled. Bake in preheated oven at 375° F / 190° C until golden brown, 10–12 minutes.

Yields 2 dozen Ⓥ
. . . .

SHERYL SHENK, HARRISONBURG, VIRGINIA

Although no longer producing, the garden holds a cache of root vegetables. The carrots, beets, parsnips, turnips, and rutabagas are hidden beneath a layer of straw. My winter spiritual ritual involves taking the spading fork, scraping away the snow, gently removing the straw, and digging deep into the soft earth for the hidden treasures. I can never do this without reflecting on what seems cold and frozen in my soul but which hides a wealth of buried treasures that can nourish me for a "dark night."
—MBL

Company Muffins

A breakfast treat that's also a good snack when baked in a mini muffin tin.

½ cup / 125 ml flour
½ cup / 125 ml whole wheat flour
1 cup / 250 ml oat bran or rolled oats
¾ cup / 175 ml brown sugar
1 tablespoon ground cinnamon
2 teaspoons baking soda
1 teaspoon baking powder
½ teaspoon salt
In large bowl combine and stir well.

2 large tart apples, peeled, cored, and shredded
1½ cup / 375 ml carrots, finely shredded
1 cup / 250 ml walnuts, chopped, or flaxseed meal
½ cup / 125 ml raisins
Add and stir to coat. Make well in center.

2 eggs, slightly beaten
½ cup / 125 ml milk
¼ cup / 60 ml oil
In a separate bowl mix together. Pour into flour mixture. Stir just until moistened. Fill greased muffin tins about three-quarters full. Bake in preheated oven at 375° F / 190° C for 18–20 minutes.

Yields 18 muffins

ANITA HOSLER, CANBY, OREGON
KAREN REMPEL ARTHUR, WAINFLEET, ONTARIO
CHRISTY HEATWOLE, LANCASTER, PENNSYLVANIA

Nutty Sweet Potato Waffles

Appropriate for luncheon or a light supper meal as well as breakfast.

. . . .

½ cup / 125 ml butter
Melt. Set aside and allow to cool.

2 cups / 500 ml sweet potatoes, cooked and mashed
6 eggs, beaten
2 cups / 500 ml milk
Stir into cooled butter.

1 cup / 250 ml whole wheat flour
1 cup / 250 ml rolled oats, finely ground in blender
1 cup / 250 ml walnuts, pecans, or hazelnuts, finely ground
2 tablespoons baking powder
2 teaspoons salt
Sift together into the sweet potato mixture. Mix until combined.
Bake in a hot waffle iron.

Yields 8 large waffles
. . . .

ALICE KEPPLEY, BOYERTOWN, PENNSYLVANIA

We no longer have a cow and our neighbor no longer sells milk, so I go to the store to buy milk. Until recently, I would diligently check the sale papers from the major supermarkets to see where it was the cheapest. Since I live in a rural area, those stores are at least twenty-five miles away. Of course, I never made a special trip just to get milk. I would just stock up when I went through those towns for work.

One mile from home, however, a small grocery store sells milk. Unfortunately, it is usually more expensive than at the major supermarkets. So I would drive past this store and buy my milk at a major chain grocery store. I would patronize the local store in "emergencies," but not regularly. But then I realized that if everyone in my community did that, we would soon lose our local store, and then I would have to go twenty-five miles for any grocery anytime, emergency or not. Now in one small way I try to seek the good of where I find myself. I buy my milk from the small, local grocery store.
—MBL

Apple Spice Waffles

While the batter is quite thin, the flavor is full. Resist the temptation to add more flour.

. . . .

2¼ cups / 560 ml whole wheat flour
¾ cup / 175 ml rolled oats
¼ cup / 60 ml oat bran
4 teaspoons baking powder
1 teaspoon ground cinnamon
½ teaspoon salt
½ teaspoon ground ginger
¼ teaspoon ground nutmeg
Combine in a large bowl.

1 cup / 250 ml apple, diced or shredded
½ cup / 125 ml nuts, chopped (optional)
Add and toss to coat.

3 cups / 750 ml milk
2 eggs
½ cup / 125 ml butter, melted
1 tablespoon honey
Combine separately and beat well. Add all at once to dry ingredients, stirring until well combined. Bake in hot waffle iron. Serve with syrup, yogurt, apple butter, or applesauce.

Serves 4–6 Ⓥ

. . . .

DIANE JONSON, CARSTAIRS, ALBERTA

Stroll through a supermarket produce department and you'll see labels from around the world. It's easy to assume that buying these imported foods benefits the farmers of those countries.

The sad reality is that when the best agricultural land is used to grow crops for export, local people may end up going hungry.

Because of fluctuations in global markets and rules set in international trade agreements, export crops sell at widely varying prices and only a fraction of the profits trickles down from the corporations to the actual growers. Impoverished farmers end up selling their land and working for agribusinesses on huge single-crop farms. Workers who once raised crops to feed their families may not be paid enough to buy the foods they need. As a result we see countries like India, where an abundance of food is produced but millions of people are hungry because they are too poor to buy it.
—CHW

Potato Soup

. . . .

2 tablespoons butter
½ cup / 125 ml onion, chopped
Melt butter in large saucepan. Add onion. Sauté until translucent.

3 cups / 750 ml potatoes, diced
2 cups / 500 ml water or vegetable broth
½ teaspoon salt
¼ teaspoon pepper
¼ cup / 60 ml celery with leaves, chopped (optional)
½ cup / 125 ml carrots, diced or shredded (optional)
⅛–¼ teaspoon ground nutmeg, dried marjoram, celery salt,
   dried dill weed, or paprika
Add, cover, and cook until vegetables are tender, about
15 minutes. For a creamier soup, remove some of the cooked
potatoes, purée them, and return to the saucepan.

2 cups / 500 ml milk
3 tablespoons flour
Mix together until smooth. Add to soup and cook until thickened,
stirring constantly. Garnish with fresh chopped parsley.

Serves 3–4 Ⓥ
. . . .

Ham or cheese variation: Add 1 cup / 250 ml cubed cooked
ham or 1 cup / 250 ml shredded sharp cheddar cheese.

. . . .

Cheeseburger variation: Add 8 ounces / 250 g browned ground
meat and 1 cup / 250 ml shredded cheese. Right before serving,
stir in ¼ cup / 60 ml plain yogurt. In summer, garnish with finely
shredded lettuce and diced tomatoes.

. . . .

Dumpling variation: Combine 1 large beaten egg, ½ cup /
125 ml flour, and 2 tablespoons milk. Drop dough by teaspoons
into simmering soup. Simmer 5 more minutes.

. . . .

Corn variation: Use 1 cup / 250 ml potatoes and add 2 cups /
500 ml corn.

. . . .

JIM AND KAREN SKIDMORE, PHILIPPI, WEST VIRGINIA
CAROL KLINGENBERG, PEABODY, KANSAS
ANITA DERSTINE, PORTLAND, OREGON

Dilly Bean Potato Soup

This recipe serves a crowd—or makes delicious leftovers.

. . . .

1½ cup / 375 ml celery, chopped
6 carrots, shredded
3 cloves garlic, minced
In large soup pot sauté in 2 tablespoons oil.

12 cups / 3 L chicken or vegetable broth
9 large potatoes, diced
salt to taste
Add and simmer until potatoes are tender, 20–25 minutes. Mash some of the potatoes in the broth mixture for creamier texture.

8–9 cups / 2–2.3 L cooked Great Northern beans
2 tablespoons dried dill weed
Add to soup.

1½ cup / 375 ml plain yogurt or sour cream
3 tablespoons flour
¾ teaspoon pepper
Combine and stir into soup. Cook and stir until thickened.

Serves 12 or more
. . . .

MELISSA ATCHISON, MANHATTAN, KANSAS

Small local farmers may be unable to compete with imported goods. Perhaps commercial growers in Guatemala can grow green beans more cheaply than small farmers in neighboring El Salvador, for instance. Or cabbages shipped in refrigerated containers from China are more attractive than those trucked into a Filipino city by a local farmer. Imported kidney beans may be deemed tastier than a local variety. All of these examples leave local farmers without local markets for their produce.

The apparent solution is for farmers to plant specialty crops for export. Yet small farmers often don't have the means of competing in the global market. They need to work through intermediaries who process, store, move, and market their produce—for a price.

As more food moves over greater distances, the profits of those doing the moving (the food corporations) increase, but rarely do those of the farmers.
—CHW

If I had to put what I believe about food and the environment into two words of advice, I would say this: Celebrate hope. If you can find a farm, a market, a store where you can see that love for the earth and for future generations is a priority, sell all that you have and buy their food. If you can smell the Spirit of God on their sweet potatoes, buy twenty pounds!

You are not consistent in all areas of your life? Act on the one little thing you know. You can only afford one holy sweet potato and the rest is boxed macaroni and cheese? Act on what you can afford. You will love that sweet potato and the earth that grew it even more.
—Jennifer Schrock, Goshen, Indiana

Sweet Potato Soup

. . . .

1 medium onion, chopped
Sauté in 1 teaspoon oil in a soup pot until translucent.

2 large sweet potatoes, peeled and chopped
5 cups / 1.3 L beef or vegetable broth
Add and bring to a boil. Reduce heat and simmer, partially covered, until sweet potatoes are tender, 20–25 minutes. Remove from heat.

2 cups / 500 ml canned tomatoes with juice
¼ teaspoon ground white pepper
Stir in. Purée in blender or food processor until smooth (this may require two batches). Return to soup pot.

¾ cup / 175 ml orange juice
additional water to desired consistency
Add, heat gently until hot, and serve.

Serves 4–6
. . . .

Squash variation: Substitute peeled, chopped winter squash (such as butternut) for the sweet potatoes. This version freezes well.

. . . .

CATHLEEN HOCKMAN-WERT, CORVALLIS, OREGON

Maple Parsnip Soup

"I had never tasted parsnips before I received a few pounds of them in my co-op farm share. I made this soup, and I think I will forever be in love with the parsnip!" says contributor Alison Froese-Stoddard. A tester adds, "This was a unique and excellent soup. The mustard-maple syrup combination adds the perfect sweet and spicy flavors."

. . . .

3 tablespoons butter (can use part olive oil)
Melt in a heavy-bottomed soup pot until beginning to brown.

1 pound / 500 g parsnips, chopped
2 medium onions, chopped
2 cloves garlic, minced
Add and sauté until onions are translucent but not brown.

6 cups / 1.5 L chicken or vegetable broth
¼ teaspoon ground nutmeg
Add and bring to a simmer. Cook until parsnips are soft, 40 minutes.

½ cup / 125 ml evaporated milk
Add and remove from heat. Pour into blender and purée until velvety smooth.

⅓ cup / 75 ml maple syrup
2 tablespoons Dijon mustard (or more for a spicier taste)
salt to taste
Stir in. Serve garnished with ¾ cup / 175 ml toasted pine nuts or other nuts.

Serves 8
. . . .

ALISON FROESE-STODDARD, WINNIPEG, MANITOBA

**For some reason (I assume a combination of soil and weather along with care) my onions did poorly this year. While onions are cheap and readily available in the supermarkets, I find myself connecting in a small way with the feelings of those around the world to whom such a crop failure may mean the difference between life and death.
—MBL**

Curried Vegetable Bisque

This recipe works with many variations, says contributor Gwen Peachey.
"The red color and apple sweetness are key, but otherwise, any combination of
vegetables (except green ones) will work. It is great for groups and freezes well."

. . . .

5 cups / 1.3 L tart apple, peeled and chopped
2 cups / 500 ml onion, chopped
2 cups / 500 ml red sweet pepper, chopped
1½ cup / 375 ml carrots, chopped
¾ cup / 175 ml celery, diced
In large soup pot sauté in 2 teaspoons oil until vegetables are soft,
7–10 minutes.

3½ cups / 875 ml chicken or vegetable broth
3 cups / 750 ml potatoes, chopped
½ cup / 125 ml raisins
3 tablespoons curry powder
¾ teaspoon ground cardamom
½ teaspoon ground allspice
½ teaspoon dried thyme
Stir in and bring to boil. Reduce heat, cover, and simmer, stirring as
needed, until potatoes are soft, 12–15 minutes. Purée in batches in
blender or food processor. Add some broth if mixture is too thick.
For a chunkier soup do not purée about 2 cups / 500 ml soup.
Return everything to soup pot.

3½ cups / 875 ml beef or vegetable broth
3 cups / 750 ml milk
1¼ cup / 300 ml dry milk powder
⅓ cup / 75 ml tomato sauce
Add. (The soup can be made ahead up to this point and
refrigerated up to 24 hours.) Reheat soup over medium heat until
hot but do not boil, about 10 minutes.

2 cups / 500 ml cooked shrimp or chicken, chopped
    (optional)
salt to taste
Stir in. Just before serving, add 3–4 tablespoons chopped fresh
cilantro or sprinkle cilantro into the individual bowls as a garnish
(optional). Or serve with chutney.

Yields 20 cups / 5 L
. . . .

GWEN PEACHEY, CORVALLIS, OREGON

Curried Carrot Soup

A soup rich in vitamin A. Try it with
carrots, sweet potatoes, or winter squash.

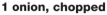

. . . .

1 onion, chopped
1 clove garlic, minced
2 stalks celery, chopped (optional)
In large soup pot sauté in 2 tablespoons olive oil until soft.

2 pounds / 1 kg carrots or sweet potatoes, chopped
6 cups / 1.5 L vegetable broth
2 teaspoons curry powder
Add and bring to a boil. Simmer until carrots are tender, about
20 minutes. Remove from heat, cool slightly, and purée.

1 teaspoon lemon juice; or 1 cup / 250 ml apple cider
salt and pepper to taste
Add and stir well. Serve with a dollop of yogurt or a sprinkle of
cilantro leaves.

Serves 4–6 Ⓥ
. . . .

PAMELA MACISAAC, TORONTO, ONTARIO
DORIS NORTH, HARRISONBURG, VIRGINIA

Members of a Goshen, Indiana, church figure if they're to follow Jesus' command of feeding the hungry, it may as well be with fresh fruits and vegetables purchased from local farmers.

The local market offered a CSA program in which $350 bought twenty-five quarter-bushel baskets of food selected by the customer from a number of market stalls over the growing season. The church decided to purchase a number of these shares as a group; any member could fill a basket and take the food home. A few brought low-income neighbors to also fill a basket. As a result, "People ate more fruits and vegetables and asked questions such as, 'What do you do with fresh spinach?'" says pastor Gwen Gustafson-Zook.

Helping to provide food for another helps to build community. "You care for each other. When someone's in need, you respond to the need," Gustafson-Zook says. "This is a way of feeding the hungry." It also builds vitality in local farming.
—Marshall V. King, Elkhart, Indiana

Winter Borscht

. . . .

¾–1 pound / 350–500 g stewing beef or chicken, chopped
1 cup / 250 ml onion, chopped
Brown in oil in a large soup pot over medium heat, 10 minutes.

8 cups / 2 L water
2 cups / 500 ml potatoes, chopped
½ head cabbage, shredded
1 cup / 250 ml beets, beet stems, or beet greens, chopped
½ cup / 125 ml carrots, diced
½ cup / 125 ml pearl barley
2 bay leaves
¼ cup / 60 ml fresh dill, chopped; or 2 tablespoons dried
1 teaspoon salt, or to taste
¼ teaspoon pepper
½ cup / 125 ml fresh chives, chopped (optional)
Add and bring to boil, cover, and simmer for 30 minutes. If using
beet greens and fresh dill, do not add until the next step.

½ cup / 125 ml fresh parsley, chopped
Add and simmer until barley is cooked and meat is tender,
another 10 minutes.

Serves 6–8
. . . .

CARL EPP, WINNIPEG, MANITOBA
DELORES PLENERT, DAWSON CREEK, BRITISH COLUMBIA

Imported bread: five cents per loaf!

What sounds like the bargain of the century sticks in the throat when you consider the impact of such a price on local wheat farmers. Imagine the farmers of an entire nation—who represent the most common occupation in developing countries—all unable to compete with foreign producers.

This is the reality caused by one of the most destructive practices of global trade: export dumping, in which products are sold abroad for less than their cost of production. The United States is one of the worst offenders. In a study of foods grown in the United States and sold abroad, wheat, for example, was sold for 40 percent less than it cost to produce.[1]

"By rigging the global trade game against farmers in developing nations, Europe, the United States, and Japan are essentially kicking aside the development ladder for some of the world's most desperate people," a July 2003 *New York Times* editorial states.
—CHW

In 1998 Kevin and Melanie Boldt founded their all-natural poultry farm, Pine View Farms, on good economic practices, environmental health, and strong relationships. Their approach has earned them a loyal customer base in nearby Saskatoon, not to mention honors like a Saskatchewan Outstanding Young Farmer Award.

The couple nurtures relationships with their customers by hosting a weekly market at their farm. The interdependency of farmer and consumer is easy to forget in the midst of big-box supermarkets. "When people choose to buy the cheapest food they can find . . . that choice has an impact right back to the farmer," says Melanie. "People say they don't want genetically modified food or pesticides, but the farmer has to use those tools when forced to survive on razor-thin margins." Melanie believes there is room for many more farms like Pine View. "The land will be farmed," she says. "It's just a question of how and by whom."
—Sarah Anderson, Kitchener, Ontario

Turkey Barley Soup

A comforting, flavorful winter soup. Chopped cooked chicken or turkey may be used in place of the ground turkey.

. . . .

4 cups / 1 L water
4 cups / 1 L chicken or turkey broth
1½ cup / 375 ml carrots, diced
1 cup / 250 ml celery, diced
½ cup / 125 ml barley
½ cup / 125 ml onion, chopped
1 teaspoon salt
½ teaspoon each poultry seasoning, pepper, ground sage
Combine in large soup pot. Cover and simmer 1 hour.

1 pound / 500 g ground turkey
2 tablespoons ketchup
1 tablespoon soy sauce
⅛ teaspoon each ground nutmeg, dried sage, dried thyme
Brown together in a frypan. Add to soup and serve.

Serves 6
. . . .

Slow cooker instructions: Brown meat with seasonings as instructed. Place in slow cooker with other ingredients (use boiling water) and cook on low for 6–7 hours.

. . . .

CHARLOTTE LONG, GOSHEN, INDIANA

Coleslaw with Fennel

Lightly dressed, fresh, and delicious.

. . . .

¼ **large head cabbage, shredded**
1 **bulb fennel, cut in quarters, cored, and thinly sliced**
2 **carrots, shredded**
¼ **onion, thinly sliced**
Toss together in a large bowl.

¼ **cup / 60 ml mayonnaise**
1½ **tablespoon apple cider vinegar**
1½ **tablespoon honey**
1 **tablespoon fresh parsley, chopped**
½ **tablespoon Dijon mustard**
½ **teaspoon fennel seeds**
Whisk together in a small bowl. Pour dressing over vegetables.
Toss until well coated. Refrigerate until ready to serve.

Serves 4–6 Ⓥ

. . . .

PAT KIGHT, ALBANY, OREGON

A few years ago I began purchasing organic grains for our breads. I was certain that I couldn't begin buying everything in organic form all at once, but I did want to start somewhere. I felt gratified knowing that something as ordinary as feeding my family healthy food could benefit the earth and profit the farmers who cared for the earth in this way. Since then I have gradually added other foodstuffs to our organic list, including local items as well.

This is my political action, our investment portfolio, the family health insurance plan, a global awareness program. I use my buying power to invest in small, local farmers instead of the huge conglomerates who control so much of the earth's precious resources.

We haven't got it all together yet, but I plan to continue the slow work of change in our household and in the world. I do this because I believe deeply that God made a wonderful and marvelous universe and asks us to care for the world, our home. Thanks be to God.
—Kristin Shank Zehr, Harrisonburg, Virginia

Shredded Beet Salad

. . . .

2 cups / 500 ml red beets, cooked, peeled, and shredded
½ cup / 125 ml fresh parsley, chopped
3 tablespoons olive oil
2 tablespoons lemon juice
2 tablespoons onion, chopped
1 tablespoon sugar
½ teaspoon salt
pepper to taste
Mix together and chill. To serve, place the red beet mixture in the middle of a dish.

1 cup / 250 ml carrots, shredded
2 hard-cooked eggs, sliced
½ cup / 125 ml fresh parsley, chopped (optional)
green olives (optional)
Arrange around the beets. Olives also may be sliced on top of the red beets as a garnish; the olive flavor really adds to this salad.

Serves 4 Ⓥ Ⓖf

. . . .

Simplest shredded beet-carrot salad: Combine equal portions of shredded carrots and shredded beets with a handful of chopped fresh parsley. Dress with oil and vinegar.

. . . .

Shredded beet-cabbage salad: Steam separately (or in sections of a steamer) until barely tender, about 5 minutes, 1 medium shredded beet, 2 shredded carrots, and 1 cup / 250 ml shredded cabbage. Let cool to room temperature. Arrange in small piles on salad plates. Dress with favorite dressing or tahini dressing below. Sprinkle with sesame seeds (optional).

. . . .

Tahini dressing: Shake together in a jar with a tight lid ½ cup / 125 ml tahini, ½ cup / 125 ml oil (combination of canola, sesame, olive), ¼ cup / 60 ml lemon juice, ¼ cup / 60 ml soy sauce or tamari, and water to desired consistency.

. . . .

SUSAN SNIDER, WEAVERVILLE, NORTH CAROLINA
JENNIFER DAVIS SENSENIG, PASADENA, CALIFORNIA
FRED YOCUM, AKRON, PENNSYLVANIA

Apple Carrot Salad

A seasonal salad with a refreshing taste.

. . . .

¼ cup / 60 ml fresh lemon or lime juice
2 tablespoons orange juice
1 tablespoon honey
Mix together in a large bowl until honey is dissolved.

2 cups / 500 ml apple, peeled (if desired)
Grate directly into juice mixture to prevent apples from browning.

2 cups / 500 ml carrots, shredded
1 tablespoon fresh mint, chopped
⅛ teaspoon salt, or to taste
¼ cup / 60 ml raisins (optional)
Toss with apples and serve immediately.

Serves 4–6 Ⓥ ⑪

. . . .

KRISTIN SHANK ZEHR, HARRISONBURG, VIRGINIA

This spring my father, who has been a farmer for more than fifty years, was in the hospital, so I asked him, "What do you think Darren [my brother] should seed this year, Dad?"

"Money," he replied.

When my uncle heard this, he requested that an acre of money be planted as well. Dad responded that Darren better plant American money. The conversation went on to crops like lentils and wheat and today's market.

Finally I said, "If you were seeding this spring, what would you plant, Dad?"

He responded, "Hope."
—Karen Martens Zimmerly, Regina, Saskatchewan[2]

Apple Lentil Salad

"Excellent flavor and texture combination," says one tester. "I was a little wary, but the tart apples and vinegar made a very nice sweet/sour combination. An excellent potluck dish!"

. . . .

1 cup / 250 ml lentils
Soak 15 minutes in hot water.

2 tablespoons curry powder
1 teaspoon salt
In large saucepan heat ¼ cup / 60 ml olive oil. Add salt and curry powder and heat until bubbly. Drain lentils, add to saucepan, and fry briefly.

2 cups / 500 ml water
Add and cook until absorbed (adding more water if needed to cook lentils until tender), about 20 minutes. Drain any excess water. Cool.

2 tart apples, cored and diced
¼ cup / 60 ml lemon juice or cider vinegar
Combine to prevent browning. Mix with cooled lentils.

2 potatoes, cooked, cooled, peeled, and chopped
½–1 small onion, thinly sliced
handful of fresh or frozen parsley, chopped
Mix in with salt to taste. Serve warm or at room temperature.

Serves 6–8 Ⓥ Ⓖⓕ

. . . .

LINDA HERR, CAIRO, EGYPT

In a recent conversation with my spiritual director about lettuce (yes, lettuce is spiritual), he complained about the high price of lettuce due to freezes in the southern states. I just said I don't eat lettuce in the winter. No salads all winter? Does salad mean lettuce? In the winter, to be present to the season, to my locality, and to the hibernating earth, salads take on a new look. There are pickled beets canned in the fall; salads made with cabbage, carrots, or apples, all of which have been preserved in the root cellar. There are sprouts of all kinds—radish, alfalfa, and bean—but no lettuce.
—MBL

Peanut Apple Salad

. . . .

8 apples, chopped
½ cup / 125 ml celery, diced
½ cup / 125 ml raisins
½ cup / 125 ml peanuts, pecans, or walnuts
¼ cup / 60 ml shredded coconut
Combine in a large bowl. Set aside.

½ cup / 125 ml peanut butter
½ cup / 125 ml mayonnaise
¼ cup / 60 ml milk
¼ cup / 60 ml sugar
Combine then pour over salad.

Serves 8 Ⓥ

. . . .

Cream dressing variation: Mix together in saucepan 1 egg, ¼ cup / 60 ml sugar, 3 tablespoons vinegar, ¼ teaspoon dry mustard, and ⅛ teaspoon celery seed. Cook until thickened. Cool. Gently fold in ¼ cup / 60 ml whipping cream (whipped) and add to salad. Toss gently.

. . . .

ANN HERSHBERGER, LINVILLE, VIRGINIA
LAVONNE DYCK, GLENBUSH, SASKATCHEWAN
MARGARET WYSE, WAXHAW, NORTH CAROLINA

When the hog market bottomed out in 1999, many Iowa farms took a devastating hit, losing hundreds of thousands of dollars in net worth. As a congregation with about twenty farming families, West Union Mennonite Church in Parnell felt the impact itself, as well as among its neighbors.

In response the church gradually developed a rural ministry aimed at supporting hurting farm families as well as at strengthening connections between area residents. In 2000 West Union hosted its first annual community hog roast, and it's been growing every year since.

"We want to celebrate rural life, which is a rich life, and do what we can to create community. People have seemed to genuinely appreciate that," says pastor David Boshart. "We are not all farmers here, but we are all impacted by the farming economy and farming practices."

As an example, he cites instances in which farmers want to build large finishing buildings close to existing nonfarming residences; such a situation can develop into real animosity, Boshart says. At events like the community hog roast, the various groups "can build relationships of trust and respect so that when those decisions are being made we have some relational capital to build on rather than seeing each other as potential adversaries."
—CHW

I live in the city with six other Mennonite Central Committee volunteers, all more or less committed to eating wisely. But it's tricky.

Should we drive half an hour to a co-op? What about fossil fuels? Should we bike a mile to Whole Foods, the 61,000-square-foot organic grocery? Supermarkets like this drive up rent prices for blocks around, forcing low-income residents to relocate. Or should we walk to Super Save, our tiny neighborhood store with bars on the windows, dusty cans, prices comparable to Safeway's, and homemade tamales?

Our solution? We drive a vanload of friends when we go to the co-op, we visit Whole Foods for special occasions, but we buy our daily bread at Super Save—because of Sonia, the cashier. Sonia knows us all by name, she scolds us for eating too much cheese, she remembers that yesterday the *other* housemate bought butter, and one day she examined my credit card receipt. "Hmm . . ." she said, "you put an extra loop in your signature."

As city trade-offs go, we figure we're getting a bargain.
—Bethany Spicher, Washington, District of Columbia

Golden Carrot Bake

"This is wonderful on a chilly day," says contributor Diane Jonson. "It is also a favorite of hungry harvest work crews."

. . . .

3 cups / 750 ml carrots, shredded
1½ cup / 375 ml water
⅔ cup / 150 ml uncooked brown rice
½ teaspoon salt
¼ teaspoon pepper
Combine in a saucepan and bring to a boil. Reduce heat, cover, and simmer for 25 minutes. Do not drain.

1½ cup / 375 ml Monterey Jack cheese, shredded
1 cup / 250 ml milk
2 eggs, beaten
¼ cup / 60 ml onion, chopped
pinch of ground nutmeg
Stir in and transfer into a 1½-quart / 1.5-L casserole dish. Bake uncovered at 350° F / 180° C for 1 hour.

½ cup / 125 ml Monterey Jack cheese, shredded
Sprinkle on top. Return to oven long enough to melt cheese, about 2 minutes.

Serves 6 Ⓥ Ⓖⓕ
. . . .

DIANE JONSON, CARSTAIRS, ALBERTA

Au Gratin Cabbage

. . . .

2 cups / 500 ml cabbage, shredded
½ cup / 125 ml carrots, shredded
⅓ cup / 75 ml green onions, chopped
Sauté until crisp-tender in frypan coated with cooking spray.
Transfer to greased 1-quart / 1-L baking dish.

½ cup / 125 ml milk
1 egg
3 tablespoons cheese, shredded
Combine in a small bowl. Pour over vegetables. Sprinkle with
1 tablespoon chopped fresh parsley and 1 tablespoon grated
Parmesan cheese. Bake at 350° F / 180° C for 30–35 minutes.

Serves 4 Ⓥ ⒼⒻ

. . . .

JUNE MARIE WEAVER, HARRISONBURG, VIRGINIA

Maple-Glazed Parsnips

*The natural sweetness of parsnips is enhanced by roasting and coating with
a maple glaze.*

. . . .

2 cups / 500 ml parsnips, peeled, cut in ½-inch /
1-cm rounds
Spray a baking pan with oil. Place the parsnip rounds in a single
layer on pan and spray lightly with oil. Sprinkle with salt. Bake in
preheated oven at 400° F / 200° C until soft, 30 minutes, stirring
occasionally; watch to avoid burning.

1 tablespoon maple syrup
½ teaspoon butter, melted
2 tablespoons walnuts, chopped and toasted (optional)
Combine maple syrup and butter and pour over the cooked
parsnips. Top with walnuts and serve.

Serves 2–4 Ⓥ ⒼⒻ

. . . .

MARY BETH LIND, HARMAN, WEST VIRGINIA

Dilly Mashed Potatoes

The ultimate in creamy winter comfort food with a sunny color.

. . . .

5 large potatoes, chopped
4 large carrots, thinly sliced
Boil together until soft. Drain, mash, and set aside.

2 tablespoons butter
¼ cup / 60 ml green onions, thinly sliced
1½ tablespoon fresh dill, chopped; or 1 teaspoon dried
Melt butter in frypan and lightly sauté onions and dill. Add to potatoes.

½ cup / 125 ml plain yogurt or sour cream
½ teaspoon salt
¼ teaspoon pepper
Stir into potatoes. Mix well and transfer to a greased 2½-quart / 2.5-L casserole dish.

½ cup / 125 ml cheddar cheese, shredded (optional)
Sprinkle on top. Bake uncovered at 350° F / 180° C for 30 minutes. May be frozen before baking. If baking from frozen, bake 1 hour covered, then 20 minutes uncovered.

Serves 6 Ⓥ Ⓖf

. . . .

CATHERINE KLASSEN, LANDMARK, MANITOBA

One out of every seven people in the world doesn't have enough food to eat, and the situation is getting worse. There's enough food available; it's just that one in seven doesn't have the means to get it: the money to buy it, the land to grow it, or the community to help provide it. Relying on goodwill clearly isn't filling the gap.

That is where the Human Right to Food comes in. It states that national governments have an obligation to respect, protect, and fulfill the right to food of their citizens to the extent of their resources. Practically speaking, in developing countries, where hunger is a major problem, governments must start by not passing laws or allowing others to take away people's ability to feed themselves. Expropriating farmland or letting others force small farmers off their land for producing biofuels or exporting food to other countries can't be done without making sure that the people affected have other ways to make a living and feed themselves.
—Stu Clark, special advisor, Canadian Foodgrains Bank, Winnipeg, Manitoba

Red Taters and Green Grannies

Delicious with a cheese omelet, a simple green salad, or pork.

. . . .

10–12 small red potatoes, unpeeled, julienned
Season with salt and pepper. Sauté in large frypan in
1–2 tablespoons olive oil.

**2–3 Granny Smith apples, unpeeled, cored, and
thinly sliced**
**½ cup / 125 ml green onions, sliced, include some
green stem**
¼ cup / 60 ml celery, diagonally sliced (optional)
Add and stir to coat with oil. Cover and cook over low heat, stirring
occasionally, until tender, 20 minutes.

½–1 cup / 125–250 ml cheddar cheese, shredded
Sprinkle on top, cover, and cook another minute to melt. Serve
immediately.

Serves 4–6 (side dish), 2–3 (main dish) Ⓥ Ⓖⓕ

. . . .

AUDREY METZ, WASHINGTON, DISTRICT OF COLUMBIA

Easy Potato Bake

. . . .

4 large potatoes, unpeeled, thinly sliced
Place in a greased 2-quart / 2-L baking dish.

¼ cup / 60 ml onion, chopped
2 tablespoons butter or oil
1 teaspoon salt
½ teaspoon dried thyme
⅛ teaspoon pepper
In saucepan heat together until butter is melted. Drizzle over
potatoes. Cover and bake at 425° F / 220° C until tender,
45 minutes.

1 cup / 250 ml cheddar cheese, shredded
Sprinkle on top and bake uncovered 15 minutes longer.

Serves 6–8 Ⓥ Ⓖⓕ

. . . .

KAREN BYLER, MONTROSE, COLORADO

Whole Beet Skillet

. . . .

4–6 medium beets with fresh greens
Cut greens off beets, leaving about 1 inch / 2.5 cm of greens on beets. Place beets in large saucepan, cover with water, and bring to a boil. Reduce heat and simmer until beets are tender when pricked with fork, 15–30 minutes, depending on size. While beets are cooking, remove stem from beet greens. Chop stems in 1-inch / 2.5-cm pieces. Chop greens separately. Drain the cooked beets and rinse with cold water. When beets have cooled enough to handle, slip peels off with fingers. Cut beets in slices. In saucepan sauté stems in 1–2 tablespoons butter until tender. Add greens and sauté until bright green and just tender. Add sliced beets and heat through.

1–2 tablespoons lemon juice
1–2 teaspoons ginger root, peeled and minced
1–2 teaspoons honey (optional)
Stir in and serve immediately.

Serves 2–4 Ⓥ Ⓖ̇ꜰ

. . . .

KRISTIN SHANK ZEHR, HARRISONBURG, VIRGINIA

Roasted Winter Vegetables

"We have some version of this at least once a week," says contributor Linda Bulson. "You can vary the vegetables, but I've found that it's best to include at least one sweet vegetable (carrot, sweet potato, parsnip) and one with a stronger flavor (turnip or rutabaga). The natural sweetness of the veggies and the garlic develops with the slow roasting."

. . . .

6–8 cups / 1.5–2 L winter vegetables: potatoes, sweet potatoes, carrots, celeriac, turnips, parsnips, rutabagas, beets, winter squash, onions, peeled and cut in 1-inch / 2.5-cm pieces, or sticks ½ inch / 1 cm thick
2 tablespoons oil
1 tablespoon dried herbs such as rosemary, thyme, parsley, oregano; or 3 tablespoons fresh

Toss ingredients together (keep onions separate, as they will roast faster; add them to the pan 10 minutes into the baking time). Spread in a single layer on greased baking pans. Roast in a preheated oven at 425° F / 220° C until tender, 30–45 minutes, stirring occasionally. Season with salt and pepper. Serve with roasted garlic sauce (optional; below).

Serves 8 (side dish), 3–6 (main dish) Ⓥ Ⓖⓕ
. . . .

Roasted garlic: Remove loose papery layers from outside of a whole garlic bulb but do not peel. Slice off top of the bulb, exposing the tip of each clove. Place on a square of aluminum foil and drizzle with 1 tablespoon olive oil or just season with salt and pepper. Wrap tightly and bake alongside the vegetables until tender.

. . . .

Roasted garlic sauce: Bake one head of garlic as directed. Squeeze soft roasted cloves into a small bowl, mash with fork, and stir in ¾ cup / 175 ml plain yogurt. (Try this sauce as a raw vegetable dip.)

. . . .

LINDA BULSON, CROPSEYVILLE, NEW YORK
JUDY HILDEBRAND, CRYSTAL CITY, MANITOBA
WILLARD ROTH, ELKHART, INDIANA

Oven Fries

"These fries remind me of boardwalk fries that we buy at the beach, which we eat sprinkled with vinegar and salt," says contributor Margaret High.

. . . .

4 medium baking potatoes or sweet potatoes
2 tablespoons oil
Scrub and dry potatoes (peeling is optional). Cut into thin sticks or wedges and place in large container with a tight lid. Pour oil on potatoes, cover, and shake to thoroughly coat fries with oil.

½ teaspoon salt
Sprinkle on fries and mix, along with a seasoning option below if desired. Spread fries in a single layer on baking sheets. Bake in preheated oven at 425° F / 220° C until golden brown and fork tender, 30–45 minutes, stirring and flipping fries every 5–10 minutes. Serve immediately.

Serves 4 Ⓥ Ⓖⓕ
. . . .

Greek-style fries:

2 tablespoons lemon juice
1 teaspoon dried oregano
¼ teaspoon pepper
2 cloves garlic, minced

. . . .

Super spicy fries:

⅓ cup / 75 ml Parmesan cheese, grated
1 tablespoon garlic, minced
1 teaspoon paprika
1 teaspoon garlic powder
½ tablespoon ground red pepper (optional)
¾ teaspoon habañero pepper flakes (optional)

. . . .

Rosemary garlic fries:

3 cloves garlic, minced
1 teaspoon dried rosemary, crushed
Especially good with sweet potatoes. Just before serving garnish with 2 tablespoons chopped parsley (optional).

. . . .

BRENDA MACDONALD, SASKATOON, SASKATCHEWAN
STEPHEN GOERTZ, ST. CATHARINES, ONTARIO
MARGARET HIGH, LANCASTER, PENNSYLVANIA
JOANNE BOWMAN, BROOKLINE, MASSACHUSETTS

You can picture our agricultural economy as an hourglass. At the top are farmers and at the bottom are consumers; food flows from one to the other through a few corporations in the middle. Those businesses—such as Archer Daniels Midland, Cargill, ConAgra, General Mills, and Philip Morris—hold enormous power. The farmers have limited options in terms of selling their products, so the corporations set the prices the farmers receive. The corporations also set the prices paid by consumers, and research indicates that market concentration results in higher prices.[3]

Here's a simple side step around this conundrum. Buy food—whole, unprocessed food—directly from farmers.
—CHW

Vegetable Vindaloo

A tangy accompaniment for any curry.

. . . .

6 medium potatoes, diced
3 medium carrots, diced
¼ cup / 60 ml vinegar
Combine, cover, and marinate at room temperature for 2 hours.

1 cup / 250 ml onion, sliced
Sauté in frypan in 2 tablespoons oil until brown.

2 teaspoons salt
1 teaspoon chili powder
1 teaspoon ground turmeric
1 teaspoon ground cumin
2 whole cardamom pods
1 cinnamon stick (1 inch / 2.5 cm long)
½ teaspoon pepper
Combine in a small bowl. Add to onion and sauté for a few minutes. Add a little water to prevent spices from burning. Drain potatoes and carrots (discard vinegar), add to frypan, and cook for 20–25 minutes.

1½ cup / 375 ml peas
Add and cook 5 minutes on low heat. Remove cinnamon stick. Serve hot with rice.

Serves 6–8 Ⓥ Ⓖⓕ
. . . .

RICHARD SARKER, EPHRATA, PENNSYLVANIA

Nut Ring Loaf

"We make this every year as our main dish for Christmas dinner," says contributor Julie Kauffman. "Our nonvegetarian family and friends always want to try it and end up loving it."

....

1 medium onion, finely chopped
5 stalks celery, finely chopped
1 tablespoon flour
1¼ cup / 300 ml white wine or vegetable broth
In large saucepan sauté onion in 2 tablespoons oil until soft, 4–5 minutes. Add the celery and sauté for 5 minutes. Sprinkle on flour. Cook 1–2 minutes, stirring. Add wine or broth. Cook and stir 1–2 minutes. Set aside.

1½ cup / 350 ml blanched almonds, ground
⅔ cup / 150 ml rolled oats
1 apple, grated
2 eggs
juice of ½ lemon
salt and pepper to taste
Combine in a large bowl. Stir in the onion-celery sauce. Set aside.

1 medium onion, finely chopped
5 cups / 1.25 L mushrooms, finely chopped
1 clove garlic, crushed
1¼ cup / 300 ml walnuts, chopped
In separate saucepan sauté onion in 2 teaspoons oil until soft, 4–5 minutes. Add remaining ingredients and cook 10 minutes, stirring occasionally.

Lightly oil and line a 3½-cup / 850-ml ring mold with parchment paper. Spoon in a third of the creamy almond-apple mixture, add mushroom filling, then cover with remaining almond-apple mixture. Bake at 375° F / 190° C for 50–55 minutes. Cool in pan for 10 minutes. Invert onto a serving dish.

Serves 6–8 Ⓥ
....

JULIE KAUFFMAN AND PAUL HUNT, LANCASTER, PENNSYLVANIA

Sweet Potato Quesadillas

. . . .

1½ cup / 375 ml onion, minced
2 cloves garlic, minced
Sauté in large frypan in 1 tablespoon oil until translucent.

2 teaspoons dried oregano
1½ teaspoon each dried basil, marjoram, chili powder
1½ teaspoon ground cumin (optional)
pinch of ground red pepper, or to taste
Add and cook another minute.

4 cups / 1 L sweet potatoes, cooked and mashed
Add and heat through, frequently stirring to prevent sticking.
Add salt and pepper to taste.

8 flour tortillas
1 cup / 250 ml sharp cheddar cheese, shredded
Spread about ½ cup / 125 ml filling and 2 tablespoons cheese on
half of each tortilla, leaving a ½-inch / 1-cm border on the sides.
Fold tortilla in half. Place on oiled baking sheets. Brush tops
with oil. Bake in preheated oven at 400° F / 200° C until brown,
15–20 minutes. Serve with sour cream and salsa.

Yields 8 quesadillas (V)
. . . .

Variation: Use shredded raw sweet potatoes, sautéed with the
onions and garlic until soft.

. . . .

RANDY AND JUANITA NYCE, PHILADELPHIA, PENNSYLVANIA

Fieldworkers are generally paid piece rate: for example, per bucket of sweet potatoes. They put in long days doing physically demanding labor with no such thing as overtime pay in most states and provinces. In the United States, the average annual income for a farmworker— meaning those who labor in the fields and orchards, as opposed to growers who own the farms—is about $11,000. At least 30 percent of farmworker households live below the poverty line: more than double the poverty rate of all other wage and salary employees.[4]

Farmworker advocates point out that this cheap workforce exists in part because of trade policies that harm the economies of other countries and eliminate small-scale farming opportunities.
—CHW

Black Bean Sweet Potato Burritos

A vegetarian favorite of all ages.

. . . .

3 cups / 750 ml sweet potatoes, peeled and diced
½ onion, chopped
Sauté in large frypan in 1 tablespoon oil just until tender. Add water
or apple juice as needed to prevent sticking.

2 cups / 500 ml cooked black beans
1 teaspoon ground cumin
¾ teaspoon ground cinnamon
½ teaspoon salt
Add and cook until heated through.

8 flour tortillas
1½ cup / 375 ml cheddar cheese, shredded
Divide bean mixture and cheese among the tortillas and roll up.
Place in a 9 x 13-inch / 3.5-L baking pan. Lightly spray with olive
oil if desired. Cover pan with foil and bake at 350° F / 180° C for
20–25 minutes. Or preheat a frypan with a bit of oil and place a
tortilla in pan. Add cheese in center of tortilla and add ¼–½ cup /
60–125 ml bean filling. When the tortilla is crispy, remove and fold
in half. Garnish with sour cream, salsa, and fresh cilantro.

Yields 8 burritos Ⓥ
. . . .

RANDY AND JUANITA NYCE, PHILADELPHIA, PENNSYLVANIA

Healthy eating is important, but who has the time or money to cook? Ask Beverly Gauntlett of Abbotsford, British Columbia, and she'll tell you that not only can you cook delicious meals, you can do so for approximately $1.25 per person per meal. The secret is community.

Through Community Kitchens of the Fraser Valley, participants plan fourteen meals using beef, chicken, pork, and fish, as well as meatless options. Then Gauntlett does all the shopping and divides the bill. The group regathers to "power cook" for six hours, making huge batches of each meal and dividing them into containers to take home for the freezer.

Gauntlett's shopping saves time. Bulk buying saves money. "This program has really restored the family table in homes," says Marilyn Gunn, founder of the Community Kitchen program of Calgary. "Children's health and their capacity to learn have improved, and parents have more energy because they are eating better and so they can cope better. People learn budgeting, cooking, food safety, communication, team building skills, and organizational skills. It benefits people on so many levels."
—Angelika Dawson, Abbotsford, British Columbia

Cheesy Potatoes

This dish, known as Rösti, was first served to contributor Marie Harnish and her husband in Switzerland. "We had driven a long way from Italy to our host family's home and were exhausted. We were so grateful for this warm, cheesy, home-cooked meal. Since then we make this occasionally when our family needs something quick and nourishing to eat."

....

3–4 tablespoons butter
4 cups / 1 L potatoes, shredded
½ teaspoon salt, or more to taste
Melt butter in large frypan. Sauté until potatoes are cooked and slightly browned, stirring occasionally. Press potatoes into pan, allow to cook another minute, then flip and fry the other side.

1–1½ cup / 250–375 ml Colby or cheddar cheese, shredded
While bottom gets crisp, top with cheese. When melted, cut into wedges and serve.

Serves 4 Ⓥ ⒼⒻ
....

MARIE HARNISH, INDIANAPOLIS, INDIANA

Wild Rice Vegetable Bake

1 cup / 250 ml wild rice
Rinse in cold water and strain through fine mesh strainer. Boil gently in 4 cups / 1 L of water for 10 minutes. Drain.

2 cups / 500 ml onion, chopped
Sauté in 2 tablespoons olive oil or butter.

1 cup / 250 ml pearl barley
Place with onions and wild rice in large casserole dish or 9 x 13-inch / 3.5-L baking pan. Stir.

2 cups / 500 ml each sweet potatoes, winter squash, parsnips, peeled and cut in 1-inch / 2.5-cm pieces
1 pound / 500 g mushrooms (optional)
Spread on top of grains. Sprinkle with salt and pepper.

1 cup / 250 ml cider or apple juice
3 cups / 750 ml chicken or vegetable broth
Pour on top. Cover tightly with aluminum foil or lid. Bake at 375° F / 190° C for 1 hour.

Serves 6–8

EVELYN SHELLENBERGER, PAOLI, INDIANA

We tend to think of cheap food as a wise choice—we are getting more for less, so we think. But we should be willing to look beyond price and ask why some food is cheap and other food is expensive. We need to ask who's paying the full cost of our food.
—John Ikerd, professor emeritus of agricultural economics at University of Missouri[5]

Winter Vegetable Crumble

Use whatever root vegetables you have on hand. The nutty sauce and crunchy topping add flavor to this comfort food.

. . . .

⅔ cup / 150 ml rolled oats
½ cup / 125 ml cashews, finely chopped
2 tablespoons whole wheat flour
2 tablespoons oil
1 teaspoon dried rosemary, crushed; or 1 tablespoon fresh
Combine oats, cashews, and flour in a medium bowl. Mix in oil and rosemary with fingers to form a crumble topping. Set aside.

2 pounds / 1 kg root vegetables: carrots, parsnips, rutabaga, turnips, potatoes, scrubbed or peeled and cut into bite-sized pieces
Steam for 10–12 minutes until just tender. Reserve the steaming water for stock. Transfer vegetables to lightly oiled 2-quart / 2-L baking dish.

1 medium onion, finely chopped
2 tablespoons cashews
⅔ cup / 150 ml milk
1¼ cup / 300 ml vegetable broth
In large saucepan sauté onion in 2 teaspoons oil until soft, 4–5 minutes. Add cashews and lightly brown for 3–4 minutes. Stir in milk and vegetable broth.

2 tablespoons flour
1 teaspoon dried rosemary, crushed; or 1 tablespoon fresh
salt and pepper
In a cup mix flour with a little milk to make a smooth paste. Stir into saucepan. Add rosemary. Bring to a boil and simmer until thickened, stirring constantly. Season with salt and pepper. Cool sauce slightly, then purée until smooth. Pour over the steamed vegetables, then sprinkle with oat topping. Bake at 375° F / 190° C for 30 minutes.

Serves 4 Ⓥ
. . . .
JULIE KAUFFMAN, LANCASTER, PENNSYLVANIA

Meltaway Cabbage

With long, slow cooking, a heap of cabbage and chard stems turns meltingly sweet. "During the cold winter months we enjoy this almost weekly," contributor Kirstin Vander Giessen-Reitsma says. "It's best with homemade applesauce."

. . . .

¼ cup / 60 ml butter
Melt in Dutch oven or large soup pot with a heavy bottom.

1 large onion, diced
Add and sauté 10 minutes until very soft.

2 tablespoons paprika
1 medium head cabbage, thinly sliced
stems of 1 bunch Swiss chard, thinly sliced (optional)
2 teaspoons salt
Add paprika and sauté briefly. Add cabbage, chard stems, and salt, stir to coat vegetables with paprika, cover, and cook on very low heat for 1 hour, stirring occasionally, until cabbage is very soft. The longer the cabbage cooks, the sweeter it will be.

1 pound / 500 g egg noodles, spaetzle, or chunky pasta, cooked
Mix into cabbage with pepper to taste. Serve with sour cream.

Serves 6 Ⓥ
. . . .

KIRSTIN VANDER GIESSEN-REITSMA, GRAND RAPIDS, MICHIGAN

A study by the New Economics Foundation in London found that £10 spent at a local food business is worth £25 for the local area, compared with just £14 when the same amount is spent in a supermarket. That is, a pound (or dollar, peso, or rupee) spent locally generates nearly twice as much income for the local economy. The farmer buys a drink at the local pub; the pub owner gets a car tune-up at the local mechanic; the mechanic brings a shirt to the local tailor; the tailor buys some bread at the local bakery; the baker buys wheat for bread and fruit for muffins from the local farmer. When these businesses are not owned locally, money leaves the community at every transaction. —Brian Halweil, senior researcher, Worldwatch Institute[6]

Bounty Rice

"This is a favorite dish at our house," says contributor Janet Regier. "It's a different way to use cabbage, with Italian flavors. I often use leftover rice in this recipe."

. . . .

½–1 pound / 250–500 g ground beef or pork
1 cup / 250 ml onion, chopped
1 cup / 250 ml green pepper, chopped
Sauté in large frypan until meat is browned and vegetables are soft.

4 cups / 1 L canned tomatoes
4 cups / 1 L cabbage, shredded
3 cups / 750 ml cooked rice
1 teaspoon salt
½ teaspoon dried oregano
½ teaspoon dried basil
½ teaspoon garlic powder
Stir in, cover, and continue cooking until cabbage is crisp-tender, 10–15 minutes.

½ cup / 125 ml sour cream
1 cup / 250 ml mozzarella cheese, shredded
Stir in sour cream. Sprinkle cheese on top and cover until cheese is melted. Serve.

Serves 6–8 Ⓖⓕ
. . . .

Baked variation: After all ingredients but mozzarella cheese are mixed together in frypan, pour into greased 2-quart / 2-L casserole and bake at 325° F / 160° C until cabbage is tender and casserole is bubbly, 30–45 minutes. Top with cheese and let melt.

. . . .

Cajun variation: Omit sour cream and add 1 small chopped banana pepper, ¼ teaspoon ground red pepper, and a few drops of hot sauce to the meat mixture.

. . . .

JANET REGIER, NEWTON, KANSAS
REGINA CHRISTMAN MARTIN, BROWNSTOWN, PENNSYLVANIA

Fish Tacos

. . . .

¼ cup / 60 ml plain yogurt
¼ cup / 60 ml mayonnaise
1½ tablespoon lime juice
¼ teaspoon each ground cumin, dried oregano, dried dill
Whisk together in a small bowl. Set aside.

4 teaspoons chili powder
2 teaspoons ground cumin
¼ teaspoon ground red pepper (optional)
Combine in a small bowl.

1½ pound / 750 g mild white fish filets, such as tilapia,
   rockfish, or snapper, rinsed, patted dry, and cut in
   1-inch / 2.5-cm pieces
Dip fish in the spice mixture to lightly coat. Heat 1 tablespoon oil in
large frypan over medium heat. Sauté fish pieces in a single layer
until lightly browned, about 1 minute per side for pieces ½ inch /
1 cm thick. Drain on paper towel. Sprinkle with salt.

8 corn tortillas
2 cups / 500 ml cabbage, thinly sliced
Warm tortillas in microwave under a damp cloth to soften. Fold
¼ cup / 60 ml cabbage, ⅛ of the fish, and 1 tablespoon sauce
inside each tortilla. Top with any of the following: fresh cilantro,
grated carrots, thinly sliced radishes, bean sprouts, onions,
tomatoes, avocados. Serve with a wedge of lime.

Yields 8 small tacos
. . . .

Cilantro cream variation: In place of yogurt-mayonnaise sauce,
purée ¼ cup / 60 ml sour cream, ¼ cup / 60 ml mayonnaise,
tender stems and leaves of ½ bunch cilantro, 1½ tablespoon lime
juice, and 1 clove garlic. May be mixed with cabbage for slaw or
used as a sandwich spread.

. . . .

Grilling variation: Rub spice mixture over whole fish fillets then grill.

. . . .

JOE EBERSOLE, CORVALLIS, OREGON
EMILY SCHACKMANN PLANK, BURBANK, CALIFORNIA
CARMEN ROSE SHENK-MULLETT, CHARLOTTESVILLE, VIRGINIA

As my boys have grown, I've spent more time in my little vegetable plot at the local community garden. It's on the site of a warehouse that burned down years ago—I remember digging piles of brick and glass out of that barren place, hauling in anything that could break down into soil. This year, I let a few of my nonhybrid vegetables go to seed. I gathered up seedpods and flower heads, and in the dark of winter evenings separated out the seeds to save for spring. Their bounty is incredible—one plant alone produces hundreds of seeds, many times more than I could possibly use. I am awash in abundance. The harvest from my garden this year has been rich indeed.
—Pamela Haines, Philadelphia, Pennsylvania

Sausage and Apples

"Easy to prepare and sooooooo good," exclaims one tester. "The combination of apple and onion is delicious."

. . . .

4–6 links sausage, pierced in several places
In wide saucepan lightly coated with oil, brown on all sides on medium-high heat, turning often, 5–7 minutes. Remove from pan; keep warm.

½ cup / 125 ml apple juice
¼ cup / 60 ml apple jelly or hot pepper jelly
2 tablespoons Dijon mustard
Mix together in a small bowl.

1 medium onion, sliced in rings
Add to same saucepan used for sausage. Place on medium heat and stir often until starting to brown. Add more oil if needed.

3 firm apples, cored and sliced in thick wedges
Add and stir until starting to brown. Stir in juice mixture.

1 teaspoon dried basil; or 1 tablespoon fresh, chopped
pinch of pepper
Sprinkle on top. Return sausages to pan, reduce heat to medium-low, cover, and cook until sausages are completely cooked through, about 10 minutes.

Serves 4
. . . .

WENDY JANZEN, WATERLOO, ONTARIO

Marrakesh Lamb Stew

This is a very fragrant stew. Adjust its spiciness by altering the amount of crushed hot chilies.

· ·

1½ pound / 750 g boneless lamb, beef, or venison, chopped in bite-sized pieces
Brown in batches in 1–2 tablespoons oil in soup pot. Set aside.

1 large onion, chopped
2 cloves garlic, minced
Stir into drippings; sauté until translucent and tender. Return meat to pot.

5 medium carrots, chopped
2 cups / 500 ml stewed tomatoes
2 medium turnips or 1 rutabaga, chopped
1 medium potato, chopped
1 cup / 250 ml water, beef broth, or tomato juice
 (if using water, add ½ teaspoon salt)
1 cinnamon stick
1 teaspoon each ground cumin, coriander, cloves, turmeric
¼ teaspoon crushed hot chilies, or more to taste
pinch of ground allspice and ground nutmeg
Add and bring to a boil. Cover; reduce heat. Simmer 40 minutes.

2 cups / 500 ml cooked chickpeas
½ cup / 125 ml pitted prunes, halved
½ cup / 125 ml raisins
Stir in. Cover and cook until vegetables are tender, an additional 10 minutes.

2 tablespoons fresh parsley, chopped (optional)
Stir in. Serve on a bed of couscous or rice. Garnish with 2 tablespoons toasted slivered almonds (optional).

Serves 6
· ·

DIANE JONSON, CARSTAIRS, ALBERTA
JUDY HILDEBRAND, CRYSTAL CITY, MANITOBA

Spicy Baked Apples

A fine dessert that also makes a special breakfast.

. . . .

4 large baking apples
Peel the top third of each apple. Core from the top, making the holes about ¾-inch / 1.75 cm wide.

6 tablespoons maple syrup; or ½ cup / 125 ml brown sugar
1 teaspoon ground cinnamon
1 cup / 250 ml pecans or walnuts, finely chopped (optional)
Whisk together in a small bowl.

½ cup / 125 ml raisins
Stir in. Fill each apple with nut-raisin mixture, mounding it a little on top. Put apples in small baking dish just big enough for apples.

1 cup / 250 ml apple juice or water
⅓ cup / 75 ml maple syrup
2 teaspoons lemon juice (optional)
½ teaspoon ginger root, peeled and minced (optional)
Mix together in a small bowl. Pour over the apples and cover. Bake at 350° F / 180° C just until apples are tender when pricked with the tip of a sharp knife, 40–50 minutes. (Overbaking the apples will cause them to split and lose juice and flavor.) After baking, pour the cooking juices into a saucepan. Boil over high heat until thickened and reduced to about ½ cup / 125 ml. Pour over the apples in the baking dish. Serve each apple in a bowl—with or without whipped cream.

Serves 4 Ⓥ Ⓖⓕ

. . . .

AUDREY METZ, WASHINGTON, DISTRICT OF COLUMBIA
DELORES PLENERT, DAWSON CREEK, BRITISH COLUMBIA

When the holiday season of consumption that began on "black Friday" (the Friday after U.S. Thanksgiving that is supposed to help merchants end the year in the "black") draws to a close, our consumption doesn't stop; it just changes focus. During the holiday season we are encouraged to consume, especially foods, to feel loved. In January we are encouraged to purchase diet foods and exercise equipment; ironically, to assuage our previous overindulgence.
—MBL

Apple Praline Pie

. . . .

3 cups / 750 ml apples, peeled and sliced
⅓ cup / 75 ml sugar
2 tablespoons flour
½ teaspoon ground cinnamon
¼ teaspoon ground nutmeg
Combine in a large bowl, tossing to coat apples.

9-inch / 1-L unbaked pie crust (p. 380)
Place apples in pie crust and bake in preheated oven at 400° F /
200° C for 15 minutes.

½ cup / 125 ml brown sugar
¼ cup / 60 ml milk
3 tablespoons honey
2 tablespoons butter
Combine in saucepan and bring to a boil. Boil 1 minute. Remove
from heat.

½ cup / 125 ml walnuts or pecans, chopped
Add. Remove pie from oven and pour honey-nut mixture over top.
Continue baking at 350° F / 180° C for 30 minutes.

Yields 1 pie Ⓥ
. . . .

MARGARET WYSE, WAXHAW, NORTH CAROLINA
GARY GUTHRIE, NEVADA, IOWA

It was in Bolivia that Gary Guthrie first tasted—really tasted— banana cream pie. He was there with Mennonite Central Committee to do community development, but as much as he taught he learned, including many lessons on hospitality. Food was part of nearly every visit, he recalls. "It was humbling to be a rich North American blessed by the poor of the earth as they shared with me the little food they had." The banana tree growing at his house offered him the chance to develop his own ministry of hospitality. He began making banana cream pies for guests, baking a couple of hundred over his years in Bolivia and El Salvador.

This tradition of hospitality continues on Guthrie's small organic farm in Iowa, which he works mostly by hand—and an 8-horsepower rototiller—in a gesture of solidarity with the majority of the world's farmers. Now he invites the farm's supporters to come out each spring for a garden blessing and potluck. The pies he provides are no longer banana, but pie there is aplenty.
—CHW

Hazelnut Coffee Brownies

. . . .

¾ cup / 175 ml baking cocoa
½ teaspoon baking soda
Combine in a medium bowl.

½ cup / 125 ml strong hazelnut-flavored coffee, boiling
⅓ cup / 75 ml butter, melted
Add and stir until mixture thickens.

2 cups / 500 ml sugar
⅓ cup / 75 ml butter, melted
2 eggs
Add and stir until smooth.

1⅓ cup / 325 ml flour
1 teaspoon vanilla
¼ teaspoon salt
Add and blend completely.

1 (3.5-ounce / 100-g) hazelnut chocolate bar, finely chopped
¾ cup / 175 ml hazelnuts, toasted and chopped (optional)
Stir in. Pour into greased 9 x 13-inch / 3.5-L baking pan. Bake in preheated oven at 350° F / 180° C for 35–40 minutes.

Yields 24 brownies Ⓥ
. . . .

HOLLYE SCHWARTZ, SAN ANTONIO, TEXAS

After Hurricane Mitch hit Central America, I led a learning tour to Nicaragua. We shared disaster funds and wished we could help more but soon had to return home. Shortly afterward I was browsing the Web for Equal Exchange—a fair trade coffee, tea, and cocoa company—and the words *Pueblo Nuevo* caught my eye. An article described Equal Exchange's involvement with a coffee cooperative based in a small Nicaraguan community our group had visited. Its response to the disaster included extending affordable credit to farmers, helping replant trees, and rebuilding processing plants.

As a church we realized the best thing we could do to help the people of Pueblo Nuevo was to buy Equal Exchange coffee blends that include Nicaraguan beans. We began pooling our orders, and the Little Swatara Fair Trade Church Coffee Buying Club was born. Some call fair trade coffee "a cup of justice."
—Sue Wagner Fields, Bernville, Pennsylvania

People have learned so well how to save a nickel here and a dime there, and I think part of the intention has been that those nickels and dimes are being saved in order to give more to people in need. I encourage people to think that when you buy fairly traded foods, you're putting money directly in the pockets of those people in need rather than through charity.
—Karin Kaufman Wall, Newton, Kansas

Apple Cake

This cake can be made with fewer apples, but this amount packs in the nutrients and flavor.

· ·

5 cups / 1.3 L apples, unpeeled and chopped
1⅓ cup / 325 ml sugar (more if apples are very tart)
Combine and let stand while mixing other ingredients.

½ cup / 125 ml oil
2 eggs, slightly beaten
2 teaspoons vanilla
Combine in a separate bowl.

1 cup / 250 ml whole wheat flour
1 cup / 250 ml flour
2 teaspoons baking soda
2 teaspoons ground cinnamon
1 teaspoon salt
1 cup / 250 ml nuts (optional)
Combine in a third bowl. Stir flour mixture into apples alternately with egg mixture. Pour into a greased 9 x 13-inch / 3.5-L baking pan. Bake in preheated oven at 350° F / 180° C, 50–60 minutes (until toothpick inserted in center comes out clean).

⅔ cup / 150 ml brown sugar
¼ cup / 60 ml milk or cream
1 tablespoon flour
While cake bakes, heat to boiling, stirring occasionally. Remove from heat.

⅓ cup / 75 ml powdered sugar
Mix in. Drizzle over hot cake.

Serves 12–16 Ⓥ
· ·

CATHLEEN HOCKMAN-WERT, CORVALLIS, OREGON
DEBRA SEIZER, CANTON, KANSAS
SUSAN LOHRENTZ, SEATTLE, WASHINGTON

Secret Chocolate Cake

Delicious plain, frosted, or served in bowls with applesauce. They'll never know the secret ingredient unless you tell.

. . . .

2 cups / 500 ml beets, cooked, peeled, and chopped
½ cup / 125 ml applesauce
Purée together until smooth. Set aside.

1½ cup / 375 ml sugar
½ cup / 125 ml oil
½ cup / 125 ml plain yogurt
3 eggs
Combine in a large mixing bowl. Beat with electric mixer 2 minutes.

½ cup / 125 ml baking cocoa, sifted
1½ teaspoon vanilla
Add along with puréed beets; beat another 1½ minute.

1½ cup / 375 ml flour
1 cup / 250 ml whole wheat flour
1½ teaspoon baking soda
½ teaspoon salt
1 teaspoon ground cinnamon (optional)
Gradually sift into the batter, mixing it in with a spoon but stirring only until blended.

½ cup / 125 ml chocolate chips and/or nuts, chopped
Stir in. Pour into greased 9 x 13-inch / 3.5-L baking pan. Bake in preheated oven at 350° F / 180° C until knife inserted in center comes out clean, 40–50 minutes. To bake in a bundt pan, pour half of batter into the greased pan, sprinkle chocolate chips evenly on top, then add remaining batter.

Serves 16–24 Ⓥ
. . . .

Summer variation: Substitute 2–3 cups / 500–750 ml shredded raw zucchini or summer squash for the cooked, puréed beets. Use the ground cinnamon and add ½ teaspoon ground allspice.

. . . .

JENNIFER DEGROOT, WINNIPEG, MANITOBA
NANCY K. GAVIN, HUDSON, WISCONSIN
MARY KATHRYN YODER, HARRISONVILLE, MISSOURI

Black Walnut Cake

· ·

2¼ cups / 560 ml flour
1½ cup / 375 ml sugar
3½ teaspoons baking powder
1 teaspoon salt
Blend together in a large bowl.

1 cup / 250 ml milk
½ cup / 125 ml butter, softened
1 teaspoon vanilla
Add and beat with electric mixer 2 minutes.

4 egg whites
Add and beat 2 minutes.

1 cup / 250 ml black walnuts, chopped
Fold in. Pour into two greased and floured 9-inch / 1.5-L round cake pans. Bake in preheated oven at 350° F / 180° C for 35–40 minutes.

Serves 12 Ⓥ
· ·

SARAH MYERS, MOUNT JOY, PENNSYLVANIA

Like coffee, most cocoa beans are grown on small farms, mostly in West Africa, by people with little bargaining power. They earn a pittance for their harvest, about one penny for an average candy bar. One result is that poor families are forced to employ their children rather than sending them to school. In 2002, the International Institute of Tropical Agriculture found that 284,000 West African children on cocoa farms performed hazardous tasks such as using machetes and applying pesticides without adequate protection. Worse, thousands of children are sent to work far from their families, where they are vulnerable to exploitation. UNICEF and the International Labor Organization have reported that trafficking in child slaves is widespread in West Africa. Fair trade organizations like Global Exchange prohibit abusive child labor, provide cocoa famers with significantly higher earnings, and encourage sustainable growing methods.
—CHW

On a field trip, two second-grade classes and I grazed our way through Gathering Together, an organic farm in Philomath, Oregon. My favorite moment of the tour was when farmer John Eveland had us all troop out into the middle of the carrot field. He then invited us to pull out carrots and eat them. Fifty kids lunged at the carrot tops, pulling out gorgeous orange carrots with clods of rich, moist soil clinging to them. Farmer John informed us that he likes to eat dirt, so after a cursory wipe on their pants, all the kids started munching on their lovely and rather dirty carrots. They were delicious!

—Lisa Ebersole, Corvallis, Oregon

Carrot Cookies

. . . .

1 cup / 250 ml butter, softened
¾ cup / 175 ml sugar
Beat together with electric mixer in a medium bowl.

1½ cup / 375 ml raw carrot, shredded
1 egg, beaten
½ teaspoon vanilla
Add and mix well.

2 cups / 500 ml flour
2 teaspoons baking powder
½ teaspoon salt
Sift together into the bowl and stir together. Drop by teaspoons on ungreased baking sheets. Bake in preheated oven at 375° F / 190° C for 10 minutes.

Yields 4–5 dozen Ⓥ

. . . .

Optional frosting: Mix 1 cup / 250 ml powdered sugar and the grated rind of 1 orange with enough orange juice to obtain spreading consistency.

. . . .

JENNIFER DEGROOT, WINNIPEG, MANITOBA

Can sustainably grown, fresh food be made accessible to those outside the middle class? A partnership in Manitoba proves that it can. The West Broadway Good Food Club is made up of mostly low-income Winnipeg residents, many of whom have used food banks and soup kitchens: "food that allows you to survive but doesn't sustain your spirit," explains coordinator Meagan Peasgood. The group didn't just want to eat better food. They wanted to help grow it.

Now during the summer, club members—some of whom have spent their entire lives in the city—spend three or four days a week at Wiens Shared Farm, founded by Dan and Wilma Wiens as the first CSA farm in Canada. After a day of weeding and harvesting, they load up the Veggie Van with fresh, organic food and take it back to the city to sell to neighbors at minimal cost.

The Good Food Club models how healthy economics, healthy relationships, healthy food, and healthy communities are all interconnected, Peasgood notes. The participants' labor offsets the price discounts they receive, Dan Wiens says, making this truly a mutually beneficial program. They also "provide so much through their human presence on the farm; there's a lot of laughter, a lot of discussion, just a warm community spirit."
—CHW

Apple Topping

A delightful topping for pancakes or waffles.

. . . .

½ cup / 125 ml sugar or honey
2 tablespoons butter, melted
2 tablespoons cornstarch
Mix together in a large saucepan.

5 medium apples, peeled and chopped
1¼ cup / 300 ml water or apple juice
¼–½ teaspoon ground cinnamon
Add and cook until apples are soft and mixture thickens.

Yields 6 cups / 1.5 L Ⓥ Ⓖⓕ
. . . .

Peach variation: Substitute 5 medium fresh peaches or 2 cups / 500 ml canned peaches, drained and chopped, for the apples. If using canned peaches, use the juice instead of water. Decrease sugar to 2 tablespoons.

. . . .

SUE WAGNER FIELDS, BALLY, PENNSYLVANIA

Easy Homemade Sauerkraut

"My family really enjoys eating sauerkraut and sausage on mashed potatoes,"
says contributor Christine Burkholder.

. . . .

raw cabbage, shredded
salt
Mix 1 teaspoon salt with every 4 cups / 1 L cabbage in a large
bowl. Pound with fist or potato masher a few minutes, until
cabbage starts to release juices. Pack into a clean quart jar to
within 1 inch / 2 cm of top. Pour in boiling water until the jar is filled
to its neck. Heat the sealing lid in boiling water. Wipe off the rim of
the jar with a clean cloth, put on the hot lid, screw on the ring, and
set the jar in a pan at room temperature. As the cabbage ferments
it may ooze out the top of the jar; hence the need for the pan for at
least a week. The ring will get rusty, as it stays on the jar until the
sauerkraut is used. The flavor will intensify after the second week.

Yields 4 cups / 1 L Ⓥ Ⓖⓕ
. . . .

Sauerkraut and sausage: Brown 1 pound / 500 g ground pork
seasoned with salt, pepper, and sage. Pour sauerkraut over the
meat and add enough water to cover the solids. Boil, uncovered,
until at least half the liquid is evaporated.

. . . .

CHRISTINE BURKHOLDER, LINVILLE, VIRGINIA

The liturgical year begins with Advent—that time of waiting, of remembering past beginnings (advents) and anticipating new beginnings. "Christ has come, Christ is come, and Christ will come." The garden has produced, the garden is producing, and the garden will produce.

Mostly the garden has produced. By now, the end of November, the garden is over. Our last fresh tomatoes, peppers, corn, and beans were the end of September—or, with luck and protection from early frosts, the end of October.

But the garden is still producing. The hardy kale is still green and tastier than ever thanks to mild frosts. Such a hopeful vegetable, hardy kale is full of nutrition. Covered with snow, it still thrives, giving us fresh greens into January.

The garden will produce. Amid the dark of winter, on the shortest, coldest day of the year, when hope wanes and the garden seems dead, the seed catalogs arrive. They herald good tidings of hope for a new garden. Pulling up a chair beside the woodstove, seed catalogs in hand, I light the Advent candles and anticipate the advent of both Christ and garden.
—MBL

Pickled Red Beets

. . . .

1 gallon / 4 L beets of similar size
Scrub beets. Leave on tails and 2–3 inches / 5–8 cm of tops. Place beets in large soup pot. Add water to halfway up beets. Boil until fork-tender, 1–2 hours. Drain and set aside beet juice. Run cold water over hot beets while sliding off peels with hands. Slice or dice beets as preferred.

3 cups / 750 ml white vinegar
2½ cups / 625 ml brown sugar
2 cups / 500 ml beet juice (from cooking)
1 cinnamon stick
6 whole cloves
1½ teaspoon salt
Combine in a large soup pot. Add sliced or diced beets and bring to a boil. Boil 3–5 minutes. Cool. Beets may be kept, covered and refrigerated, for 4–6 weeks. Or place hot beets and liquid into hot canning jars and seal with sterilized lids and rings. Process either pint- or quart-sized jars in boiling water bath for 30 minutes.

Yields 24 cups / 6 L Ⓥ Ⓖⓕ

. . . .

Pickled eggs: Eat the pickled beets and reserve the pickled juice. Hard-cook several eggs. (To hard-cook eggs with minimal use of energy, boil covered with water for 3 minutes, remove from heat, cover saucepan, and rest for 20 minutes.) Immerse and marinate peeled eggs in beet juice for 24 hours. Remove and eat cold with salt and pepper. Pickled eggs will not keep as long as the beets, so don't store them together.

. . . .

MARGARET HIGH, LANCASTER, PENNSYLVANIA

Provider God,

Transform this chore, this reluctant shopper.
Journey with me on this expedition of privilege.

I stroll past the breads cooling on the trolley;
    yeast-smells proclaim their rising
        and invite me to taste
            and see that they are good.
My hand hovers over the carrots, parsnips, beets . . .

Thank you for signs of your presence,
    for foods and peoples rooted in the soil.
Bless me as I choose.

—RUTH PRESTON SCHILK, LETHBRIDGE, ALBERTA

May there be abundance of grain in the land;
may it wave on the tops of the mountains.
(Psalm 72:16)

Behind the scent of freshly baked bread is the story of grain planted and harvested, flour mixed and kneaded, yeast rising, and warm dough baking until finally the bread is shared around the tables of spring, summer, autumn, and winter. All Seasons invites us to explore the story behind our foods and consider how our food choices affect our neighbors near and far.

all seasons

Breads and Breakfast

Soups

Main Dishes

Desserts

Extras

dairy

dried beans

dried fruits

meats

nuts

seeds

tofu / tempeh

whole grains

Invitations to Action

Get to know a farmer. Visit a farm.

If you eat meat, buy it directly from a farmer. Choose meat, milk, and eggs from free-range, grassfed animals.

Encourage your grocery store to carry locally grown food. Do the same at your cafeteria at school or work. Consumer demand for local foods helps create new markets for family farmers.

consider

Try shopping at a farmers' market. The money you spend directly supports a farming family. Be aware that not all farmers' market stands sell local food. Ask sellers where their foods are grown.

Befriend migrant workers. Promote fair wages and fair immigration laws.

Join a Community Supported Agriculture (CSA) farm. If your household is small, team up with a friend to purchase a share.

your neighbors

Naan Bread

. . . .

¼ cup / 60 ml water
1 tablespoon active dry yeast
1 tablespoon sugar
Mix in a small bowl until dissolved.

1 cup / 250 ml lukewarm water
¼ cup / 60 ml plain yogurt
1 beaten egg
2 tablespoons oil
2 teaspoons salt
Mix in a separate bowl. Stir in yeast mixture.

5+ cups / 1.3+ L bread flour (up to half whole wheat)
Stir in enough flour to make a soft dough. Knead 5–10 minutes.
Place in greased bowl. Turn to grease both sides. Cover with damp
cloth and let rise 1 hour. Separate dough into golf ball–sized balls.
Roll each to ¹⁄₁₆-inch / 3-mm thickness (they cook best when thin).
Preheat frypan on stove to medium-high heat. Add ½ teaspoon
butter to frypan and allow to melt. Place 1 round of dough at a
time in frypan. Cook on each side until lightly browned and puffy
(approx. 2–3 minutes per side). Wrap in a towel to keep warm while
cooking the remaining breads.

Serves 8 Ⓥ
. . . .

Alternative directions: Preheat dry heavy frypan (cast iron
preferred) to medium-high heat. Turn on oven broiler. Slap flattened
dough onto hot frypan and cook on one side until lightly browned.
Place cooked side down on baking sheet and place under the
broiler, 4 inches / 10 cm from heat. Broil until dough puffs and
forms a few brown spots, 30–60 seconds (watch closely to avoid
burning). Remove and brush with a little butter.

. . . .

HANNAH AND MARC GASCHO REMPEL, CORVALLIS, OREGON
REBECCA WYSE, ANN ARBOR, MICHIGAN

Grilled Bread

"After flipping on the grill, bread can be topped with cheese and pizza toppings, but it is also good just as it is," says contributor Rebecca Horst. "Our young adult sons ask for this with birthday meals and like to take dough to cookouts with their friends."

. . . .

1¼ cup / 300 ml warm water
1 teaspoon active dry yeast
Combine in a mixing bowl, stirring until dissolved.

1½ cup / 375 ml bread flour
1½ cup / 375 ml whole wheat bread flour
2 tablespoons olive oil
1 teaspoon salt
Add and stir until a stiff dough forms, adding more water or flour as needed. On a floured surface, knead 10 minutes or until smooth. Place in a bowl greased with olive oil, turn to grease both sides, cover with a damp cloth, and let rise until doubled in bulk, 1–2 hours. Rising time can be cut shorter or dough may rise in refrigerator 6–8 hours.

Start a medium hot charcoal or wood fire or preheat a gas grill to the maximum. Divide dough into equal pieces and form into flat rounds. Let the rounds rest a few minutes. Roll or lightly press as thin as desired, lightly flouring the work surface and dough as necessary. Brush tops of several rounds with olive oil. Place on hot grill, oiled side down. Brush top lightly with oil. Move bread rounds around the grill to avoid burning the bottom and cook 1–6 minutes, depending on grill temperature. Turn and brush again with oil.

1 tablespoon or more fresh herbs, minced;
**   or 1 teaspoon or more dried**
1 teaspoon garlic, minced
½ teaspoon pepper
Sprinkle on top and grill until crisp and brown. Serve immediately or at room temperature.

Serves 6 Ⓥ

. . . .

REBECCA HORST, GOSHEN, INDIANA

Whole Wheat Dinner Rolls

. . . .

2 cups / 500 ml milk, scalded and cooled until warm
2 tablespoons active dry yeast
½ cup / 125 ml sugar; or ⅓ cup / 75 ml honey
Dissolve yeast in the warm milk; add sugar or honey and let stand
until bubbly, 5 minutes.

2 eggs, beaten
3 tablespoons oil
2 teaspoons salt
Add to yeast mixture.

7–8 cups / 1.8–2 L whole wheat bread flour or one of the
variations below
Add enough flour to make a soft dough. Knead 8–10 minutes.
Place in a greased bowl, turn to grease both sides, cover with a
damp cloth, and let rise until doubled in bulk, about 1 hour. Punch
down. Divide into 24 pieces for rolls or in half for bread. Let rest
5–10 minutes. Shape into rolls, loaves, or a combination. Place in
greased pans. Let rise until double, about 45 minutes. Bake rolls in
preheated oven at 400° F / 200 C for 10–12 minutes. Bake loaves
in preheated oven at 350° F / 180° C for 30–35 minutes. For a soft
crust, brush top with milk after removing from oven.

Yields 24 rolls or 2 loaves Ⓥ
. . . .

Variation 1:

4 cups / 1 L whole wheat bread flour
3–4 cups / 750 ml–1 L bread flour

. . . .

Variation 2:

4–5 cups / 1–1.3 L bread flour
2 cups / 500 ml whole wheat bread flour
1 cup / 250 ml cracked wheat or bulgur, or substitute up to
half with rolled oats
Use uncooked bulgur or mix with boiling water, cover, and let stand
15 minutes. Drain excess liquid before adding to bread dough.

. . . .

JUDY HILDEBRAND, CRYSTAL CITY, MANITOBA
CORA KURTZ, GAINESVILLE, FLORIDA
JUDITH UNRUH, HILLSBORO, KANSAS

When you woke up this morning, was there any question in your mind as to whether you and your family would have enough nutritious food today? Food security is a growing concern for all populations across the United States and Canada because of our reliance on foods produced far away. This reliance means increased dependency on fossil fuels for transport and vulnerability to a failure of delivery, whether caused by extreme weather or political unrest. Importing countries also have less control over food quality and production methods. Wherever you live, worldwide, a key to food security is locally produced food.
—CHW

Seeded French Bread

Tie a bow around a loaf for a lovely gift.

. . . .

4 cups / 1 L whole wheat bread flour
2 cups / 500 ml bread flour
2 tablespoons active dry yeast
2 tablespoons sugar
1 teaspoon salt
Mix together in a large mixing bowl.

2½ cups / 625 ml hot water
2 tablespoons olive oil
Gradually add. Mix well. Add more flour if needed to make a soft dough. Knead 10 minutes or until smooth and elastic. Place in a greased bowl, turn to grease both sides, cover with a damp cloth, and let rise until doubled in bulk. Punch down and let rest for 20 minutes. Divide into 3 parts; shape each into a rectangular loaf. Place on greased baking sheet that has been sprinkled with cornmeal. Make 4–5 diagonal slices on the top of each loaf.

1 egg
2 tablespoons water
Beat together in a small bowl. Brush on the loaves.

1–2 tablespoons fennel seeds, sesame seeds,
  or poppy seeds
Sprinkle over each loaf. Let rise until double. Bake in preheated oven at 400° F / 200° C for 20 minutes.

Yields 3 loaves Ⓥ
. . . .
JOCELE MEYER, FRESNO, OHIO

Italian Parmesan Bread

. . . .

2 cups / 500 ml warm water
2 tablespoons active dry yeast
Combine in mixing bowl, stirring until dissolved.

3 cups / 750 ml whole wheat bread flour
2 cups / 500 ml bread flour
½ cup / 125 ml butter, melted, or oil
2 eggs
2 tablespoons sugar
1 tablespoon onion flakes; or 2 teaspoons onion powder
2 teaspoons salt
1 teaspoon garlic powder
Add and mix well.

1 cup / 250 ml Parmesan cheese, grated
Add with enough additional flour to make a soft dough. Knead
8–10 minutes, until smooth and elastic. Place in greased bowl, turn
to grease both sides, cover with a damp cloth, and let rise 1 hour.
Divide in half and divide each half into thirds. Roll into 15-inch /
37-cm ropes. Braid loosely into 2 braids and tuck ends under.
Place on greased baking sheets, cover, and let rise 30 minutes.
(Instead of braids, dough may also be shaped into 3 loaves and
placed in greased 8 x 4-inch / 1.5-L pans.) Bake in preheated oven
at 350° F / 180° C until golden brown, 35 minutes.

Yields 2–3 loaves Ⓥ

. . . .

BARBARA WIEBE, BRUNKILD, MANITOBA

**Relying only on supermarkets,
our food security is quite risky.
Most urban centers have only
enough fresh food to last for
three days. A garden, root cellar,
pantry shelves, and freezer hold
enough for six to twelve months.
—MBL**

Wild Rice Bread

. . . .

1 cup / 250 ml water
½ cup / 125 ml wild rice
½ teaspoon oil
Cook together until tender, 30 minutes. Cool to lukewarm.

¼ cup / 60 ml warm water
2 tablespoons molasses
1 tablespoon active dry yeast
Combine in a mixing bowl, stirring until dissolved. Add cooled rice.

2½–3 cups / 625–750 ml bread flour
1½ cup / 375 ml whole wheat bread flour
1 cup / 250 ml warm water
2 tablespoons oil
1 tablespoon salt
¼ teaspoon ground ginger
Add, stirring in enough flour to make a stiff, smooth dough. Knead about 10 minutes. Place in a greased bowl, turn to grease both sides, cover with a damp cloth, and let rise until doubled in bulk, about 1–1½ hour. Punch down, divide in half, shape into loaves, and place in greased loaf pans. Let rise again, about 1 hour. Bake in preheated oven at 375° F / 190° C for 30 minutes.

Yields 2 loaves Ⓥ
. . . .

PHYLLIS LIND, SALEM, OREGON

"Marta, a peasant leader from Nicaragua and my breakfast guest, smiles and tells me she cannot see why we bother to eat toast because it really has no taste. I laugh and respond with a similar comment on tortillas. We both enjoy the moment," says Nettie Wiebe, Delisle, Saskatchewan, a leader of Via Campesina, a global coalition of small-scale farmers.

"As farmers, mothers, cooks, and eaters, we both recognize the import of these observations. The food we grow does not only have to be agriculturally appropriate: right for our climate and soil conditions. It must also be culturally appropriate. We have to be able to retain our identity and taste preferences while we meet our nutritional needs."

The World Bank defines food security as "access by all people at all times to enough food for an active, healthy life." *Access* here encompasses two things: that enough culturally appropriate food is available to be eaten and that the eaters can obtain it while maintaining their dignity.
—CHW

Whole Wheat Flax Bread

Flax is grown on the Canadian prairies and is prized for its high amounts of omega-3 fatty acids, along with other nutrients.

. . . .

3 cups / 750 ml warm water
2 tablespoons active dry yeast
Combine in a mixing bowl and stir until dissolved. Set aside until bubbly, 5 minutes.

3 cups / 750 ml whole wheat bread flour
3 tablespoons honey
3 tablespoons oil
Add and stir until smooth.

2–3 cups / 500–750 ml bread flour
1½ cup / 375 ml flaxseed meal
⅓ cup / 75 ml raw sunflower seeds
2 tablespoons poppy seeds
2 teaspoons salt
⅓ cup / 75 ml flaxseeds (optional)
Add, stirring in enough flour to make a stiff, smooth dough. Knead about 10 minutes. Place in a greased bowl, turn to grease both sides, cover with a damp cloth, and let rise until doubled in bulk, about 1–1½ hour. Punch down, divide in half, let rest 5 minutes, shape into loaves and place in greased loaf pans or shape into round loaves, and place on a greased baking sheet sprinkled with cornmeal. Cover and let rise again, about 1 hour. Bake in preheated oven at 375° F / 190° C for 30 minutes.

Yields 2 loaves (V)
. . . .

KEVIN PRIER, EUGENE, OREGON
TONYA RAMER WENGER, MADISON, WISCONSIN
HELGA GUENTER, WINNIPEG, MANITOBA

Seeded Sour Rye Bread

"The flavor of this bread is best when you let the sponge set overnight," notes contributor Jeanne Heyerly. *"It makes wonderful Reuben sandwiches and is also very good toasted."*

. . . .

1 cup / 250 ml warm water
1 tablespoon active dry yeast
Mix in a large bowl and let stand 3–5 minutes.

1 cup / 250 ml coarsely ground rye flour
¼ cup / 60 ml bread flour
**1 tablespoon caraway seed, or substitute up to half
    fennel seed**
Add and stir. Cover with a tight lid or plastic wrap and let stand at least 2 hours or overnight.

¾ cup / 175 ml warm water
2½ teaspoons salt
2 teaspoons sugar
3 cups / 750 ml bread flour
1 egg white, beaten
Stir down the yeast sponge and add remaining ingredients. Knead for about 5 minutes. Place in a greased bowl, turn to grease both sides, cover with a damp cloth, and let rise until doubled in bulk, about 1 hour. Punch down and shape into 1 large loaf or two to three small ones. Let rise until almost doubled. Brush loaf with beaten egg white before baking and again after baking 20 minutes. Bake in preheated oven at 375° F / 190° C for 30–35 minutes.

Yields 1 large loaf Ⓥ
. . . .

JEANNE HEYERLY, CHENOA, ILLINOIS

Would an efficient food system ship vegetables thousands of kilometers by ship, truck, and plane when much of that food could be grown locally? Would an efficient system transport lamb meat from New Zealand to Toronto while it simultaneously bankrupts Ontario lamb farmers? A food system that ships wheat from Saskatoon to Montreal to make flour for bread and bagels and then makes bagels in Montreal and ships them back to Saskatoon: Could anyone call this system efficient? Wouldn't an efficient system just fax the Montreal recipe to Saskatoon and make the bagels there?
—National Farmers Union (Canada)[1]

Cinnamon Bread

"This was the first bread I ever made; my sister gave the recipe to me,"
says contributor Jill Heatwole. One tester commented, "I'll make this again—
just to smell it baking!" Try it with apple butter.

. . . .

¼ cup / 60 ml warm water
1 tablespoon dry active yeast
Combine in a small bowl and stir to dissolve.

2 cups / 500 ml whole wheat bread flour
1 cup / 250 ml milk, scalded
¾ cup / 175 ml orange juice
½ cup / 125 ml sugar
¼ cup / 60 ml oil or butter, melted
1 egg
1 tablespoon orange peel, grated
1½ teaspoon salt
Combine in a large mixing bowl and mix well. When cooled to
lukewarm, add yeast mixture and mix.

4½–5½ cups / 1.1–1.3 L bread flour
Add enough flour to make a soft dough. Knead 8–10 minutes
until smooth. Place in a greased bowl, turn to grease both sides,
cover with a damp cloth, and let rise until doubled in bulk, about
1¼ hour. Punch down and divide in half. Roll or stretch each
portion to a rectangle measuring 15 x 7 inches / 38 x 18 cm.

⅓ cup / 75 ml sugar
1 tablespoon ground cinnamon
Combine and divide in two parts. Sprinkle evenly on the two
rectangles of dough. Roll up, jelly-roll fashion, from short end and
place in greased 9 x 5-inch / 2-L loaf pans. Let rise until doubled.
Bake in preheated oven at 350° F / 180° C for about 30 minutes.
Leave in pans 5 minutes then remove and cool on wire rack.

Yields 2 loaves Ⓥ
. . . .

JILL HEATWOLE, PITTSVILLE, MARYLAND

Everyday Oatmeal Bread

A moist, all-purpose bread with a smooth texture and distinctive flavor from the molasses.

. . . .

1½ cup / 375 ml boiling water
1 cup / 250 ml rolled oats
Combine and let stand 30 minutes.

¾ cup / 175 ml molasses
3 tablespoons butter or oil
2 teaspoons salt
Stir into oatmeal.

2 cups / 500 ml lukewarm water
1 tablespoon active dry yeast
Mix in a large bowl until dissolved. Add oatmeal mixture.

6 cups / 1.5 L bread flour
2 cups / 500 ml whole wheat bread flour
Work in flour to make a medium-soft dough. Add more flour as needed. Turn onto floured surface and knead 8–10 minutes until smooth. Place in greased bowl and turn to grease both sides. Cover with a damp cloth and let rise until doubled, about 1 hour. Punch down. Divide and shape into 2 loaves. Place in greased 9 x 5-inch / 2-L loaf pans. Cover and let rise in warm place until double, about 45 minutes. Bake in preheated oven at 400° F / 200° C for 5 minutes, then lower heat to 350° F / 180° C and bake until loaves sound hollow when tapped, 35–40 minutes. Brush tops with milk for soft crust.

Yields 2 loaves Ⓥ
. . . .

JANET STEINER, WASHINGTON, DISTRICT OF COLUMBIA

Oat Bran Muffins

Tried and true. Vary with different dried fruits.

. . . .

⅔ cup / 150 ml brown sugar
⅓ cup / 75 ml oil
1 cup / 250 ml buttermilk or milk
1 egg
2 tablespoons molasses
Combine.

1½ cup / 350 ml oat bran or wheat bran
1 cup / 250 ml dried fruit such as raisins, chopped apples,
    or cranberries
⅔ cup / 150 ml flour
½ cup / 125 ml raw or toasted wheat germ
¼ cup / 60 ml sesame seeds
¼ cup / 60 ml flaxseed meal
1 teaspoon baking soda
½ teaspoon salt
½ teaspoon cinnamon
Mix together, then stir into wet mixture. Fill greased muffin tins
about three-quarters full. Bake in preheated oven at 400° F / 200°
C for 18–20 minutes.

Yields 12 muffins Ⓥ
. . . .

IRMA PETERS, RANDOLPH, MANITOBA
JUDITH REMPEL SMUCKER, AKRON, PENNSYLVANIA

In *Plenty: One Man, One Woman, and a Raucous Year of Eating Locally*, Alisa Smith and J. B. MacKinnon describe their experiment with only eating foods produced within a one-hundred-mile radius of their British Columbia home. The greatest challenge they faced was their inability to find locally grown grains—no wheat, oats, rice, barley.

Farther south, eastern Oregon produces a lot of soft white wheat, the kind used in noodles and quick breads. But most of it is exported to Asia. Inspired by the one-hundred-mile diet, a group of citizens in western Oregon's Willamette Valley formed a partnership with local farmers to try growing hard red wheat—the kind preferred for yeast breads—for local consumption. By the second year, three thousand pounds were harvested.
—CHW

Baked Oatmeal

This recipe can be prepared quickly in the morning by mixing the dry ingredients and wet ingredients separately the night before. Combine and pop in the oven as soon as you get up. Leftovers keep well in the refrigerator and can be reheated in the microwave in individual bowls.

. . . .

2 cups / 500 ml rolled oats
⅓ cup / 75 ml brown sugar
1 teaspoon baking powder
⅓ cup / 75 ml raisins or other chopped dried fruit (optional)
3 tablespoons chopped walnuts (optional)
Combine in a medium bowl.

1 cup / 250 ml milk
½ cup / 125 ml applesauce
2 tablespoons oil
1 egg, beaten
Combine in a separate bowl. Add to oat mixture; stir well. Pour into a greased 8 x 8-inch / 2-L baking pan. Bake in preheated oven at 350° F / 180° C for 25 minutes. Serve warm with milk.

Serves 3–4 Ⓥ
. . . .

KIM BURKHOLDER, SANTA FE, NEW MEXICO
PHYLLIS I. LIND, LEBANON, OREGON
SARA WEAVER, COLUMBIANA, OHIO

We've come a long way . . . or have we? I've been fortunate to have several of my grandmother's cookbooks and scrapbooks of recipes. In her copy of the original *My Better Homes and Gardens Cookbook* (1930), I found some interesting and still relevant data: "We've been confronted with a good many food fads and fallacies." The book goes on to list several of these: "Fletcherism," diets for reducing or gaining, vegetable diets, fiber diets, meat or non-meat diets. And so it goes. Today I could add any of several trendy diets. Then as now, "in the face of such contradictory theories many homemakers have been wondering just what to do. They are asking for a few simple rules." The book follows with ten rules, all of which still have some relevance. These three seem to be especially relevant today: Serve simple meals. Serve a variety of foods. Keep the seasons of the year.
—MBL

Mostly Oats Granola

. . . .

6 cups / 1.5 L rolled oats
1 cup / 250 ml shredded coconut
1 cup / 250 ml raw wheat germ
¾ cup / 175 ml peanuts or other nuts
½ cup / 125 ml raw sunflower seeds
½ cup / 125 ml sesame seeds (optional)
Combine in a large bowl.

½ cup / 125 ml honey
⅓ cup / 75 ml oil
⅓ cup / 75 ml water
1 teaspoon vanilla
Mix together and pour over oat mixture. Stir well. Spread in a thin layer on baking sheets. Bake in preheated oven at 325° F / 160° C for 10 minutes. Stir and bake another 5 minutes. Stir again and bake 3–5 minutes. Watch carefully to prevent burning. Cool.

1 cup / 250 ml raisins or dried cranberries
Add and store In airtight containers.

Yields 11 cups / 2.7 L (V)
. . . .

JUDY HILDEBRAND, CRYSTAL CITY, MANITOBA
MARION S. YODER, SARASOTA, FLORIDA

Much of the food in Canada and the United States today is produced on large-scale farms owned by businesses rather than families, and these agribusinesses own much more than the farm. They own the entire food-production chain: seeds, machinery, fertilizer, pesticides, farm finance, grain collection and milling, livestock feed processing, livestock production, slaughtering, and processed food brands with the names we recognize on grocery shelves.

Agribusinesses determine how much individual farmers have to pay for essential farm inputs, such as seed and fertilizer, and set the prices they get for their crops. The results: strong profit for agribusinesses and disappearing profit margins for farmers. In 1910 American farmers received forty cents of every dollar spent on food in the United States; in 1997, they received seven cents. In Canada, farmers retained (in net income) about fifty cents of every dollar they generated in the 1940s; in 2013, they retained about twelve to sixteen cents per dollar.[2] —CHW

Chunky Crunchy Granola

Not too sweet, this granola is good with yogurt, milk, or fresh fruit.

. . . .

3 cups / 750 ml rolled oats
1 cup / 250 ml whole wheat flour
¼ cup / 60 ml brown sugar
1½ teaspoon ground cinnamon
½ teaspoon salt
¼ teaspoon ground ginger
Mix together in a large bowl. Make a well in the center.

¼ cup / 60 ml oil
¼ cup / 60 ml honey
¼ cup / 60 ml milk
1½ cup / 375 ml raisins, other dried fruit, or nuts (optional)
Pour into the well. Mix thoroughly, making sure all loose flour has
been incorporated (add another tablespoon of milk if necessary).
Spread in 9 x 13-inch / 3.5-L pan and bake in preheated oven at
300° F / 150° C, stirring every 10 minutes, until light brown, 50–60
minutes. Store in airtight container up to a week; also freezes well.

Yields 5–6 cups / 1.3–1.5 L Ⓥ
. . . .

KATHRYN STUTZMAN, GOSHEN, INDIANA

Hearty Oatmeal Pancakes

You'll need to soak the oats overnight, so while you're in the kitchen, mix the dry ingredients together also to save time in the morning.

. . . .

2 cups / 500 ml rolled oats
2 cups / 500 ml buttermilk or plain yogurt
The night before using, mix together in a large bowl. Cover and refrigerate overnight.

2 eggs, lightly beaten
¼ cup / 60 ml oil
In the morning, stir into oat mixture.

½ cup / 125 ml flour
2 tablespoons sugar
1 teaspoon baking powder
1 teaspoon baking soda
½ teaspoon ground cinnamon
¼ teaspoon salt
In a small bowl mix together then add to batter and mix briefly. Fry in a hot, greased frypan.

Serves 3–4 (v)
. . . .

Variation: Stir in blueberries or shredded apples.

. . . .

NAOMI FAST, HESSTON, KANSAS
SUSAN MILLER HUYARD, ANCHORAGE, ALASKA
BONITA SUTER, RED WING, MINNESOTA

One common perception is that farmers today must "get bigger or get out": in order to compete, they must become as economically efficient as possible. That is thought to mean having bigger farms, more powerful machinery, and fewer types of crops.

A growing number of studies, however, show that small farms are more productive than large ones, yielding as much as four to five times greater output per acre. The difference is largely attributed to the kinds of crops grown. A thousand-acre farm that grows only corn and soybeans may produce more corn per acre than a small farm where corn is grown with other crops. But the total amount of food will be more on the small farm, whether judged by volume, weight, calories, or cash value.[3]
—CHW

Here are three good reasons to support local farmers.

Good food: We all need to eat. Fresh food tastes better and retains more of its nutrients.

Good for the environment: When farming is spread out on small, diversified farms rather than concentrated in huge industrial facilities, it tends to have a lower impact on the environment. Less packaging may be needed, so less waste ends up in landfills. Foods sold fresh soon after they're harvested require less processing and refrigeration and thus use less energy. Eating locally produced foods also reduces the use of transportation powered by fossil fuels; those emissions release carbon dioxide into the atmosphere, which contributes to climate change.

Good for communities: In areas with large industrial farms, small towns tend to die off. Skilled jobs are reduced, machines do more work, and low-wage positions increase while corporate profits are pocketed by distant shareholders. Local farmers, in contrast, reinvest in local businesses, hire local labor, and contribute to the civic strength of their communities. The results: higher employment and a more vibrant social fabric.
—CHW

Cornmeal Wheat Pancakes

Delicious with creamed chicken gravy or maple syrup.

. . . .

1 cup / 250 ml boiling water
¾ cup / 175 ml cornmeal
Stir together until thick. (Cold water and cornmeal may also be cooked together in the microwave 3–5 minutes, until thick.)

1–1¼ cup / 250–300 ml buttermilk
2 eggs
1 tablespoon honey or molasses
Beat into cornmeal.

1½ cup / 375 ml whole wheat flour
1 tablespoon baking powder
1½ teaspoon salt
¼ teaspoon baking soda
Sift together and stir into cornmeal. Do not beat. Fry by the spoonful on greased medium-hot frypan.

Serves 4 Ⓥ
. . . .

Variation: Add ½ cup / 125 ml cooked corn to batter.

. . . .

ARDIS DILLER, BELLEVILLE, PENNSYLVANIA

Buckwheat Pancakes

"Light, fluffy buckwheat pancakes were often a Saturday brunch treat during my childhood," says contributor Miriam Huebert-Stauffer. "Serve with syrup, sausage gravy, head cheese, jam, or applesauce."

. . . .

¾ cup / 175 ml flour
¾ cup / 175 ml buckwheat flour
3 tablespoons sugar
3½ teaspoons baking powder
¾ teaspoon salt
Sift into a mixing bowl.

1 egg, well beaten
1 cup / 250 ml milk
3 tablespoons oil
1 tablespoon molasses
Combine separately and pour into flour mixture. Stir just enough to moisten dry ingredients. Do not beat. Fry in a hot, greased frypan.

Serves 4 Ⓥ
. . . .

MIRIAM HUEBERT-STAUFFER, CANTON, KANSAS

Whole Wheat Waffles

Excellent topped with vanilla yogurt and fresh fruit.

. . . .

2 eggs, beaten
2 cups / 500 ml buttermilk or plain yogurt
Combine in a large bowl.

1 cup / 250 ml whole wheat flour
1 cup / 250 ml flour
2 teaspoons baking powder
1 teaspoon baking soda
½ teaspoon salt
Combine in a small bowl then stir into egg mixture.

¼ cup / 60 ml oil
Add and stir just until blended; do not overmix or the waffles will get tough. Bake in a hot waffle iron.

Serves 3–4 Ⓥ
. . . .

VALERIE BAER, BAINBRIDGE, PENNSYLVANIA

Ethiopian Lentil Bowl

Keep colds away with lentil soup! A dish somewhere between a thick soup and a dahl, this recipe came from the Tayeeb Foods and Café in Coralville, Iowa, a business owned by a family from Sudan, with the disclaimer "This is not a substitute for a visit with a qualified health professional." "It is absolutely delicious," says contributor Nancy Halder, "but not for those fearful of garlic."

. . . .

2 cups / 500 ml dried red lentils, sorted and rinsed
Cover with water and soak 30 minutes. Drain.

2 large onions, finely chopped
1 head garlic, peeled and mashed
In a soup pot sauté in 3 tablespoons oil until golden.

3 tablespoons tomato paste
½ teaspoon paprika
1 teaspoon salt
½ teaspoon ground ginger
¼ teaspoon pepper
3 cups / 750 ml water
Mix in tomato paste and paprika. Add remaining seasonings and half the water. Stir well and then add the rest of the water. Stir again, cover, and bring to boil. When the water boils, add the lentils, lower the heat, and cook until lentils have softened, 20–30 minutes.

¼ cup / 60 ml lemon or lime juice
Add and serve hot.

Serves 8 Ⓥ Ⓖⓕ
. . . .

NANCY HALDER, PARNELL, IOWA

My head bent over a bowl of steaming soup, my prayer seems to be incense floating up to heaven. I think God likes soup.
—MBL

Hearty Lentil Stew

Love onions? Double the amount listed in this earthy stew.

. . . .

4 cups / 1 L water
1 cup / 250 ml dried lentils
1 cup / 250 ml fresh or canned tomatoes, chopped
4 large carrots, chopped
2 onions, chopped
1 teaspoon dried thyme
½ teaspoon dried marjoram
2 tablespoons dry sherry (optional)
Cook together until lentils and carrots are soft, 40–45 minutes.

¼ cup / 60 ml fresh parsley, chopped
2–3 teaspoons salt
Stir in parsley with salt to taste. Heat another minute and serve, garnished with grated Swiss or Gruyere cheese (optional).

Serves 6 Ⓥ Ⓖⓕ

. . . .

ELLEN MILLER, WATERLOO, IOWA

Taco Soup

Simple to double or triple to serve a crowd. Cornbread is a natural accompaniment.

. . . .

1 pound / 500 g ground beef, venison, or turkey
1 small onion, chopped
Brown in a soup pot.

6 cups / 1.5 L tomato juice
2 cups / 500 ml corn
2 cups / 500 ml cooked kidney beans
1–2 tablespoons chili powder
1 tablespoon sugar, or to taste
Add and heat to boiling. Simmer 10 minutes. Or place everything in a slow cooker and cook on low for 2–4 hours. Serve over corn chips with sour cream and/or grated cheese (optional).

Serves 6 Ⓖⓕ

. . . .

DONNA GOCKLEY, PHILADELPHIA, NEW YORK

Vegetarian Chili

....

2 pounds / 1 kg any combination of dried beans such as pink, pinto, navy, kidney, soy, black, or chickpeas
Rinse and soak in water overnight. Drain water. Cook in fresh water until soft, 45–60 minutes or longer, depending on the beans used.

1 cup / 250 ml red sweet pepper, chopped
1 cup / 250 ml green pepper, chopped
1 onion, chopped
3 cloves garlic, minced
In a large soup pot, sauté in 1 tablespoon oil.

8 cups / 2 L tomatoes, chopped
1 tablespoon salt
1 tablespoon honey, molasses, or sugar
Add and heat to boiling. Add beans and one of the seasoning options below. Simmer for 45 minutes. Serve with cornbread or rice.

Yields 5 quarts / 5 L Ⓥ
....

Hominy option:

3½ cups / 875 ml hominy (four 15-ounce / 450-g cans)
1 tablespoon ground cumin
1 tablespoon ground coriander
1 tablespoon dried oregano
1 teaspoon crushed hot chilies
1 cup / 250 ml bulgur (optional, for thicker chili)
½ cup / 125 ml fresh cilantro, chopped; wait to add until the last 5 minutes
....

Winter squash option:

1 butternut squash, peeled, seeded, and chopped into ½-inch / 1-cm cubes
1 chipotle pepper or jalapeño pepper, minced, seeds removed
1 tablespoon chili powder
1 teaspoon ground cumin
....

AUDREY HESS, GETTYSBURG, PENNSYLVANIA
KARIN SHANK, RALEIGH, NORTH CAROLINA
LINDA NAFZIGER-MEISER, BOISE, IDAHO

Slow Cooker Chili

. . . .

1 pound / 500 g ground beef, venison, or turkey
Brown in a large frypan.

1 onion, chopped
1–2 cloves garlic, minced
1 cup / 250 ml green pepper, chopped
1 cup / 250 ml celery, chopped (optional)
Add and sauté for 3–5 minutes. Place in a slow cooker.

4 cups / 1 L cooked kidney beans or pinto beans
4 cups / 1 L tomatoes, chopped, or tomato juice
1–2 tablespoons chili powder
1 tablespoon sugar, honey, or molasses
1 teaspoon salt or seasoned salt
1 cup / 250 ml corn (optional)
1 cup / 250 ml mushrooms, chopped (optional)
1 tablespoon Worcestershire sauce (optional)
1 hot chili pepper, minced (optional)
Add (except mushrooms if using) and cook on high for 15 minutes then on low for 8–10 hours. Add the mushrooms, if desired, during the last hour. Serve as a soup or over rice or pasta.

Yields 8 cups / 2 L
. . . .

ARDIS DILLER, BELLEVILLE, PENNSYLVANIA
SHELAH NYVELDT, BAINBRIDGE, PENNSYLVANIA
MARIE MOYER, LETHBRIDGE, ALBERTA

When I began a serious venture in organic farming and market gardening following twenty-five years in smaller-scale farming, I thought I knew what to expect. Long days of physical work. Struggles with controlling insects and diseases. The fulfillment of working alongside family members. And all of this is true. But one unexpected benefit of this work has been the building of relationships, particularly through our farmers' market sales.

There's Ruth, who asks us each week to hold a quart of ground cherries for her, who checks on how our children are doing, who even called us once just to tell us how good our pasture-raised chicken was. Michael, who eagerly waited for our tomatoes to ripen, then brought us a jar of his delicious marinara sauce. Renate, whose sense of adventure makes our experiments with produce worthwhile: "I love to try new things." And many others whom we've come to know as more than just buying customers.
—Ron Meyer, Strawberry Hill Farm, Fresno, Ohio

White Chili

A wonderful, quick dinner with corn muffins and tossed salad. Freezes well.

. . . .

½ medium onion, chopped
½ cup / 125 ml green pepper, chopped
3 stalks celery, chopped
¼ cup / 60 ml mild green chilies
2 cloves garlic, minced
In a large frypan, sauté in 1 tablespoon oil until just tender.
Set aside.

2 tablespoons butter
2 tablespoons flour
2 cups / 500 ml chicken broth
½ cup / 125 ml milk
In a soup pot, melt butter, blend in flour, and cook briefly. Stir in
broth and milk. Cook over medium high heat, stirring constantly,
until sauce thickens.

2 cups / 500 ml cooked navy beans
2 cups / 500 ml corn
1 cup / 250 ml cooked chicken or turkey, chopped
¼ cup / 60 ml sour cream
1 teaspoon poultry seasoning
1 teaspoon ground cumin
Add to soup pot with sautéed vegetables and heat through.
Season to taste with chopped fresh cilantro, salt, and pepper.
Garnish with shredded cheese (optional).

Serves 4
. . . .

LORIE MILLER, INDIANAPOLIS, INDIANA

Most of us like to eat meat, but few of us like to think about where it comes from. When we do, we prefer to imagine a storybook landscape of green pastures and sunny skies. This is not where most meat on Canadian and U.S. plates comes from. Worldwide, some 43 percent of beef comes from feedlots, and 50 percent of pork and 74 percent of poultry are raised on large-scale industrial farms.[4] In facilities known as "concentrated animal feeding operations" (CAFOs), thousands of animals are squeezed into tight spaces. A chicken may have little more floor space than the size of this cookbook in which to move. In such stressful conditions, animals often become unnaturally aggressive. They are routinely fed hormones and drugs to make them grow faster and to prevent outbreaks of disease.
—CHW

Sandwich Tofu

*The prepared tofu, cut into smaller pieces, may also
serve as a quick addition to stir-fried vegetables.*

. . . .

2 cloves garlic, minced
½-inch / 1-cm piece of ginger root, peeled and minced
In a frypan sauté very lightly in 1 tablespoon olive oil for 1 minute.

**1 block extra firm tofu, cut in ⅛ to ¼-inch / 3- to 5-mm
    slices**
Add and sauté until lightly browned.

3 tablespoons tamari or soy sauce
Add and shake the pan until all the tofu comes into contact with the
tamari. Cook about 2 minutes then turn the slices over. Brown the
tofu as desired (some like it a bit crisp, others softer). When cool,
this makes a great sandwich filler with any variety of trimmings,
such as lettuce and mustard or mayonnaise (pictured on p. 259).
Keeps well in the refrigerator for a couple of days.

Yields 4 sandwiches Ⓥ

. . . .

ANNE LINDSEY, WINNIPEG, MANITOBA

Tofu Bites

. . . .

¼ cup / 60 ml nutritional yeast
1 block firm tofu, cut in ¼-inch / 5-mm thick slices
Place nutritional yeast in a large shallow dish. Heat 2 teaspoons oil
in an electric frypan or large frypan to about 350° F / 180° C. Blot
tofu on a paper towel, then bread tofu in yeast and place in hot
oil. Fry each side about 1 minute. Drain. Serve immediately with
tamari, soy sauce, or the dipping sauce below. May also be served
with stir-fried vegetables.

Serves 4 Ⓥ

. . . .

Dipping sauce: Combine ¼ cup / 60 ml low-sodium soy sauce,
2 cloves minced garlic, 2 tablespoons red wine vinegar, 2 teaspoons
ground ginger, 2 teaspoons brown sugar, and 1 teaspoon sesame oil.

. . . .

CHARLOTTE WOOD-HARINGTON, CHICAGO, ILLINOIS
MARIA HERMANN, LANCASTER, PENNSYLVANIA

Taco Filling

"I prefer to include rice in my taco filling," says contributor Marie Moyer. "Considering how many people in the world are malnourished from too little or too much meat, we try not to overdo the meat."

. . . .

1 pound / 500 g ground meat;
    or 2 cups / 500 ml kidney beans, cooked
¾ cup / 175 ml onion, chopped
½ cup / 125 ml green pepper, chopped
1 carrot, shredded (optional)
In a large frypan, sauté until onions are clear and meat is browned. If using beans, drain them, reserving the liquid, and set aside.

3 cloves garlic, or to taste, crushed
1 tablespoon fresh cilantro, chopped; or 1 teaspoon dried
1 tablespoon fresh parsley, chopped; or 1 teaspoon dried
2 teaspoons chili powder
2 teaspoons lime juice
1 teaspoon ground cumin
½ teaspoon salt
dash of chipotle pepper or other hot chili pepper (optional)
Add and sauté until garlic is cooked. If using beans, add to the mixture with enough liquid so that it can simmer without getting dried out. If using meat, add liquid if needed so that it can stew a little, allowing the flavors to blend.

¾ cup / 175 ml cooked rice
Add and stir well. Use mixture to top tortilla chips or to fill taco shells or tortillas. Garnish with any of the following: grated sharp cheese, chopped tomatoes, chopped onions, sliced jalapeño peppers, olives, shredded lettuce or spinach, fresh cilantro, chopped avocado, guacamole, salsa, sour cream, or plain yogurt.

Serves 3–4 (Gf)
. . . .

MARIE MOYER, LETHBRIDGE, ALBERTA
PILY HENDERSON, DAVIS, WEST VIRGINIA

Cows in feedlots eat grains like corn, soybean meal, and barley, which mostly are grown on large industrial farms fueled by petroleum. By one estimate, it takes 5 pounds / 2.5 kg of grain and 1 quart / 1 L of gasoline to produce 1 pound / 500 g of beef in a conventional feedlot system.[5] Pasture-raised cows, in contrast, convert grass—produced through the energy of the sun—into a food that human bodies can use. This process uses fewer or no chemical fertilizers and pesticides, requires less machinery and water, and produces less soil erosion and pollution—while utilizing land that may be fine for grazing but not suitable for long-term cultivation. Grassfed meats are often sold in farmers' markets and through natural foods stores.
—CHW

Black Bean and Rice Skillet

A favorite meatless entree.

. . . .

1 medium onion, chopped
1 small green or red sweet pepper, chopped
In a frypan, sauté in 1 tablespoon oil until soft, 5 minutes.

2 cups / 500 ml cooked black beans
1½ cup / 375 ml chicken or vegetable broth
½ cup / 125 ml uncooked rice
¼ teaspoon crushed hot chilies
¼ teaspoon dried thyme
2 cloves garlic, minced
1 bay leaf
Add and bring to a boil, reduce heat, and simmer covered until rice is done: 20 minutes for white rice, 40 for brown rice. Remove from heat. Remove bay leaf.

½ cup / 125 ml sharp cheddar cheese, shredded
Sprinkle on top and serve.

Serves 4
. . . .

RAMONA HARTZLER, NORTH LAWRENCE, OHIO
HELEN BROWN, HUNTINGTON, WEST VIRGINIA

Chipotle Pinto Beans

"I grew up in San Antonio, Texas, where winters were generally mild enough that central heat was uncommon," writes contributor Donna Forsman. "Instead, on chilly days, my grandmother, Hattie Bierschwale, would simmer a pot of pinto beans throughout the day, adding warmth to the kitchen. My only modification to her recipe is a brief visit to the cooking pot by a chipotle (smoked jalapeño) pepper. In Mexico, this method of seasoning is called 'walking the chili' through the soup."

. . . .

1 pound / 500 g dried pinto beans, sorted and rinsed
Soak overnight. Drain. Add fresh water to cover beans. Cover and bring to a boil. Simmer, covered, 10 minutes.

2 cups / 500 ml tomatoes, chopped
1 cup / 250 ml onion, chopped
1 tablespoon garlic, chopped
2 teaspoons ground cumin
1 teaspoon chili powder
1 whole chipotle pepper in adobo sauce
1 ham hock (optional)
Add, cover, and bring to a boil. Remove chipotle pepper and reserve. Lower heat and simmer until beans are tender, stirring frequently and adding more water if necessary to prevent scorching. Salt to taste and return chipotle pepper to pot if a hotter stew is desired. Serve in soup bowls over freshly baked cornbread or with warm, buttered flour tortillas.

Serves 8 Ⓥ

. . . .

DONNA FORSMAN, ANNANDALE, VIRGINIA

Recently I found some dried beans that my mother had saved from her garden. My mother has been dead almost twenty years. So finding the seeds was a special moment flooded with lots of warm memories. I wanted to just hold on to the seeds but instead I planted a few in my garden. I now have lots of beans from my mother and will continue to have for many years.
—MBL

For me, what's most difficult is being away from my family. I think about my family all the time, so far away. I wonder how they are. Are they satisfied? Content? Happy? Are they sad because I'm not there with them? I think about how we live back home, with the whole family together—all fifteen of us. Then I think about my life in the United States, wandering around, on the other side of the border, alone. . . . This season went well, and now I'm leaving, going back to Mexico to see my family. When you go home, you return a bit like a hero. You feel more of a man. When you return, you're one of those people who've been to el Norte. You know what it's all about. . . . Still, it's difficult to tell someone back home the truth, to explain what life is really like here, and why they should stay in school.
—Salvador Moreno, who first came to the United States at age fifteen[6]

Turkey Lentil Pilaf

A Middle Eastern–style dish. Try it using leftover cooked poultry.

. . . .

1 pound / 500 g ground turkey or chopped chicken
In a large frypan, cook over medium heat until all pink color has disappeared, 5 minutes, stirring to break ground meat into crumbles.

1 cup / 250 ml onion, chopped
2–3 cloves garlic, minced
Add and cook until tender, 5 minutes.

3 tablespoons fresh mint, chopped; or 1 tablespoon dried
1½ teaspoon ground cinnamon
½ teaspoon peppercorns, crushed; or ¼ teaspoon pepper
Add and cook 2 minutes.

1 cup / 250 ml dried lentils, sorted, rinsed, and drained
¾ cup / 175 ml uncooked brown rice
2 cups / 500 ml turkey, chicken, or vegetable broth
1 large fresh tomato, chopped; or ½ cup / 125 ml tomato
    sauce
Add and cover. Bring to a boil, reduce heat, and simmer until rice is cooked, 45–50 minutes. Optional garnish: Mix together ½ cup / 125 ml crumbled feta cheese, 1 large firm tomato, chopped, and 3 tablespoons chopped fresh mint or 1 tablespoon dried mint. Sprinkle over each serving.

Serves 6
. . . .

DIANE JONSON, CARSTAIRS, ALBERTA

At Longview Farm near Fiske, Saskatchewan, Bob and Charlene Siemens have been phasing out grain and raising beef cattle instead. This is sandy land, and during the dry 1980s, it became clear that wind damage was worsened by the heavy machinery and soil disruption necessary for grain agriculture. The Siemens began seeding more and more acreage with grass.

With careful management their one hundred cows can graze ten months out of the year. The cows provide natural fertilizer, and their hooves break up the sod to allow the grass seed to take root. "We strive to leave the land better than when we got it," Charlene says. "We try to keep the big picture in mind." —adapted from *Timbrel* magazine[7]

Oven-Barbecued Chicken

Tender and easy—a sure winner with guests.

. . . .

3–4 pounds / 1.5–2 kg chicken pieces
In a large frypan, fry in small amount of oil until brown. Drain off fat; reserve. Place chicken pieces in 9 x 13-inch / 3.5-L baking dish.

⅓ cup / 75 ml onion, chopped
In frypan, sauté in reserved fat, until tender.

¾ cup / 175 ml ketchup
½ cup / 125 ml water
⅓ cup / 75 ml vinegar
3 tablespoons brown sugar
1 tablespoon Worcestershire sauce
2 teaspoons prepared mustard
¼ teaspoon salt
⅛ teaspoon pepper
Stir in and simmer uncovered for 15 minutes. Pour over chicken. Bake at 350° F / 180° C until chicken is no longer pink, 45–60 minutes, basting occasionally.

Serves 8–10
. . . .

KAY SHUE, DALTON, OHIO

Middle Eastern Meat Loaf

The traditional accompaniment for this savory spiced meat loaf, kofta, *would be a salad of tomatoes, onion, cucumbers, and generous amounts of parsley, tossed with lemon juice, olive oil, and salt. Kofta and salad in pita bread also makes a great sandwich.*

. . . .

1 medium onion, chopped
½ cup / 125 ml fresh parsley, chopped (can include stems)
Place in food processor or put through meat grinder.

1 pound / 500 g ground beef or mutton
1 teaspoon ground cinnamon
1 teaspoon salt, or to taste
½ teaspoon ground nutmeg
½ teaspoon ground allspice
½ teaspoon ground coriander
½ teaspoon pepper
Add and process in batches, if necessary. Meat is ready to use immediately but chilling mixture in refrigerator for several hours will improve flavor. Press meat mixture into bottom of 9 x 9-inch / 2.5-L pan. Bake at 350° F / 180° C about 1 hour. Allow to cool 5 minutes, cut in squares, and serve on a bed of chopped parsley.

Serves 4 Ⓖⓕ
. . . .

Potato-tomato variation: Arrange ¼-inch / 5-mm slices of potatoes (parboiled 12 minutes) and tomatoes on top of the meat after 15 minutes of baking. Continue baking according to recipe.

. . . .

To grill: Press a handful of meat around a skewer, forming sausage-shaped cylinders. Grill (gas grill preheated on low), turning occasionally, until golden brown, about 30-40 minutes.

. . . .

To panfry: Form into patties or sausage-shaped cylinders and coat with bread crumbs. Fry in a small amount of oil in nonstick pan until brown and cooked through.

. . . .

LINDA HERR, CAIRO, EGYPT
SAMIRA MUSLEH, ABBOTSFORD, BRITISH COLUMBIA

Venison Meatballs

. . . .

2 pounds / 1 kg ground venison or ground beef
2 eggs, beaten
1 cup / 250 ml bread crumbs, cracker crumbs, or
**   rolled oats**
1 cup / 250 ml milk or broth
½ cup / 125 ml onion, minced
1 clove garlic, minced
1 teaspoon each salt and pepper
1 teaspoon chili powder or crushed hot chilies
Mix thoroughly and form into 1-inch / 2.5-cm or larger balls.
Place in a shallow baking pan.

1 cup / 250 ml ketchup
½ cup / 125 ml brown sugar
¼ cup / 60 ml onion, chopped
1 tablespoon Worcestershire sauce
1 clove garlic, minced
Combine and pour sauce over meatballs. Bake at 350° F / 180° C
for 45 minutes.

Serves 8–10
. . . .

Fresh herb variation: Add ¾ cup / 175 ml chopped fresh parsley,
2 tablespoons minced fresh oregano, 2 tablespoons minced fresh
basil, and ¾ cup / 175 ml grated Parmesan cheese to the meat
mixture. Form into balls, place in shallow baking pan and pour
1 cup / 250 ml beef broth on top. Bake at 450° F / 230° C until
meatballs are thoroughly cooked, 20 minutes. Pairs well with
roasted winter vegetables, as shown (recipe on p. 307).

. . . .

MARY ELLEN LEHMAN, BOSWELL, PENNSYLVANIA
LINDA GEISSINGER, MIFFLINTOWN, PENNSYLVANIA

The garden harvest is over;
however, unless you are a
vegetarian, one more harvest
awaits: meat. Traditionally,
hunting was part of life, part of
the harvest. Today, it has become
a sport. Harvest or sport, let's
take only what we need and use
it wisely with gratitude.

Have more than you need?
Some areas have wonderful
programs in which hunters can
donate their excess harvest to
local food banks.
—MBL

Grilled Venison

. . . .

1 cup / 250 ml oil
¾ cup / 175 ml soy sauce
½ cup / 125 ml wine vinegar
⅓ cup / 75 ml lemon juice
¼ cup / 60 ml Worcestershire sauce
2 tablespoons prepared mustard
2 teaspoons fresh parsley, chopped
2 teaspoons each salt and pepper
2 cloves garlic, minced
Mix together in a casserole dish. Remove and set aside some of this marinade to use for basting.

2 pounds / 1 kg venison or beef tenderloin, sliced about
    ½ inch / 1 cm thick
Add to marinade. Refrigerate for several hours or overnight. Grill to desired doneness, brushing occasionally with reserved marinade.

Serves 8
. . . .

MARY BETH LIND, HARMAN, WEST VIRGINIA
KATRINE ROSE, WOODBRIDGE, VIRGINIA

Venison Roast

Testers suggest marinating the roast in wine vinegar or cider for a few hours before roasting. The cooked meat is good cooled and thinly sliced for sandwiches.

. . . .

2–2½ pounds / 1–1.25 kg venison or beef roast
Place in a roasting pan.

½ cup / 125 ml soy sauce
¼ cup / 60 ml water
¼ cup / 60 ml fresh lemon juice
2 cloves garlic, minced
½ teaspoon ground ginger
Mix together and pour over roast. Cover. Bake at 275° F / 140° C for 4–5 hours. Turn roast for last hour.

Serves 6–8
. . . .

MARY ELLEN LEHMAN, BOSWELL, PENNSYLVANIA

Chipotle Carnitas

Pork shoulder tends to have fat layered with the muscle, and the meat can be tough. A friend from Mexico taught contributor Pat Kight this method of slowly simmering the meat in liquid, thereby rendering out most of the fat. Delicious over rice or tucked into tortillas.

. . . .

**2–3 pounds / 1–1.5 kg boneless pork shoulder,
cut in 1-inch / 2.5-cm cubes; do not trim away the fat**
6 cups / 1.5 L water
2 cloves garlic, peeled and crushed
1 tablespoon salt
1 teaspoon cumin seeds
a few black peppercorns
Combine in a large heavy soup pot or Dutch oven and bring to a boil. Reduce heat to low and simmer uncovered, stirring occasionally, until all the water evaporates (at least 2 hours). Increase heat to medium and allow pork to brown until edges are slightly crisp. Remove from heat and use a slotted spoon to transfer pork to a bowl, draining off any remaining melted fat.

1 large or 2 small dried chipotle chilies
2 large mild dried chilies such as ancho or paprika
2 cups / 500 ml water
1 small onion, chopped
2 cloves garlic, peeled and crushed
While pork simmers, remove stems and seeds from chilies. In a nonreactive saucepan, bring water, chilies, onion, and garlic to a boil; reduce heat and simmer until chilies are soft, 30 minutes. With a slotted spoon transfer to food processor or blender; reserve liquid.

1 tablespoon cumin seeds, toasted
1 tablespoon unsweetened cocoa
Grind together in coffee grinder or with mortar and pestle.

juice of two limes
½ teaspoon salt
Squeeze limes into a measuring cup and add cooking liquid to make 1 cup / 250 ml. Add to food processor or blender with spice blend. Purée smooth. Add salt to taste. If sauce is too thin, return to saucepan (after discarding remaining cooking liquid) and simmer until reduced. To serve, mix about a third of the sauce into the meat with more added to individual servings to taste.

Serves 8–12

. . . .

PAT KIGHT, ALBANY, OREGON

Looking at glistening piles of fruits and vegetables in supermarket produce departments, it's easy to forget that most were picked and packed by human hands. In the best cases farmworkers in Canada and the United States are treated humanely, sometimes working side by side with growers. In the worst cases workers in labor camps are kept in perpetual debt and virtual slavery. Most are somewhere in between, receiving no sick leave, vacation, or pension, lacking adequate healthcare, and vulnerable to mistreatment. —CHW

Pork Apricot Skillet

. . . .

8 ounces / 250 g dried apricots
1½ cup / 375 ml boiling water
Pour boiling water over apricots; soak while preparing pork.

2 pounds / 1 kg boneless pork tenderloin roast, cubed
1 small onion, chopped
Brown in a large frypan in 1 tablespoon oil over medium heat.

1–2 tablespoons soy sauce
¼ teaspoon pepper
Add with apricots and ½ cup / 125 ml soaking liquid. Cover frypan, lower heat, and simmer for 45 minutes, adding more liquid to prevent sticking as needed. Serve over rice.

Serves 10 or more
. . . .

Variation: Add broccoli to the frypan in the last 5 minutes of cooking.

. . . .

TRUMAN AND BETTY KENNEDY, REEDLEY, CALIFORNIA

Sunflower Chip Cookies

"My family loved these cookies," said one tester. "The first bite is a little bit of a surprise when one is used to eating the chocolate chip cookie recipe found on the back of the chocolate chip bag. I was so pleased to find that my entire family liked this healthier version."

. . . .

¾ cup / 175 ml whole wheat flour
½ cup / 125 ml wheat germ
2 tablespoons dry milk powder
½ teaspoon baking soda
Mix together and set aside.

½ cup / 125 ml butter, softened
½ cup / 125 ml brown sugar
1 egg
½ teaspoon vanilla
Cream together butter and brown sugar until light and fluffy.
Mix in egg and vanilla. Stir in dry ingredients.

1 cup / 250 ml chocolate chips and/or raisins
½ cup / 125 ml roasted sunflower seeds
½ cup / 125 ml chopped peanuts
Stir in and drop by rounded teaspoons on greased baking sheets.
Bake in preheated oven at 350° F / 180° C for 8–12 minutes.

Yields 3 dozen Ⓥ

. . . .

PHYLLIS I. LIND, LEBANON, OREGON

Oatmeal Fruit Cookies

. . . .

½ cup / 125 ml butter, softened
½ cup / 125 ml oil
1 cup / 250 ml sugar
2 tablespoons mild molasses or honey
In a large bowl cream together with an electric mixer until light
and fluffy, scraping bowl frequently.

1 egg
2 teaspoons vanilla
Beat in.

2½ cups / 625 ml rolled oats
1½ cup / 375 ml whole wheat flour
1–1½ cup / 250–375 ml diced dried fruit: cherries,
**   blueberries, apricots, raisins, cranberries, currants**
1 cup / 250 ml grated coconut or nuts, chopped
1 teaspoon baking soda
Combine separately. Add dry mixture to the creamed mixture in
about 3 additions, stirring just until thoroughly mixed. Add a little
extra flour if mixture seems too wet. Drop by rounded teaspoons
on greased baking sheets.

Yields 4 dozen Ⓥ
. . . .

For chewy cookies: Bake in preheated oven at 325° F / 160° C
until just set (edges spring back when touched gently but centers
still leave an imprint), 18–20 minutes. Immediately remove from
pans and place directly onto clean countertop or table surface. As
soon as cookies are cool put into airtight containers.

. . . .

For crisp cookies: Bake in preheated oven at 375° F / 190° C
until centers spring back, 11–13 minutes. Watch carefully to avoid
burning. Cool on a wire rack.

. . . .

LINDA NAFZIGER-MEISER, BOISE, IDAHO
KAREN REMPEL ARTHUR, WAINFLEET, ONTARIO

Shortcake or Scones

....

2 cups / 500 ml flour or whole wheat pastry flour
½ cup / 125 ml sugar
1 teaspoon baking powder
½ teaspoon salt
½ teaspoon baking soda
In a large bowl, mix together.

2 tablespoons butter, chilled
Cut in with pastry blender until crumbly.

1 cup / 250 ml plain yogurt
1 egg
Combine then add to dry ingredients. Mix briefly. Pour into a greased 8 x 8-inch / 2-L baking pan. Bake in preheated oven at 350° F / 180° C for 30 minutes; or drop by spoonfuls onto greased baking sheets and bake in preheated oven at 400° F / 200° C for 12–15 minutes. Serve warm with sliced fresh fruit and milk.

Serves 6–8 Ⓥ
....

Variation: Stir in 1 cup / 250 ml chopped dried fruit, such as apricots, peaches, or cherries.

....

JEAN SHENK, MOUNT JOY, PENNSYLVANIA
LOIS NAFZIGER, GOSHEN, INDIANA
DOROTHY MACBRIDE, WATERLOO, ONTARIO

Eating is a moral act, and sometimes a religious act. Just as I believe that bread and wine are transformed in the Eucharist, so we may be transformed—transformed into people of compassion, people who see what others overlook, people who can begin to trace the vague outlines of the prophetic vision of the reign of God where justice and mercy embrace and a grand table is set. Where bankers sit next to farmers, border guards converse with the undocumented, and ranchers share toasts with environmentalists. Where work gloves lie next to linen napkins, hands are scrubbed, feet are washed, thirst is quenched, hunger satisfied, and there's no hint of injustice anywhere!
—David Andrews, executive director, National Catholic Rural Life Conference[8]

Pie Crust

The trick to a good pie crust is keeping the fat cold and using only a minimal amount of cold water.

. . . .

1 egg, slightly beaten
5 tablespoons cold water
1 tablespoon apple cider vinegar
Combine thoroughly in a small bowl. Set aside.

2 cups / 500 ml flour
1 cup / 250 ml whole wheat pastry flour
1 cup / 250 ml butter, chilled
1 teaspoon salt
Quickly cut together with a pastry blender until chunks of butter are nearly pea-sized. (If you can't get them that small, use your clean fingers to mash them as fast as you can so the butter doesn't get too warm.)

Mix wet ingredients into dry ingredients with a fork, adding more water by the tablespoon if needed, until dough forms a ball. Cut into 3 equal pieces; chill for 20–30 minutes. Remove one ball at a time from the refrigerator, place on floured surface and roll out gently (adding flour as needed to prevent sticking) to circle slightly larger than 9-inch / 1-L pie pan. Fold carefully in half, then in half again, and place point of crust in center of pie plate, opening crust to fill pan. Ease sides in, trim excess crust to edge of pan. Flute edge of crust with fingers or press with fork. Add filling of choice and bake according to recipe; or prick crust several times with fork and bake in preheated oven at 400° F / 200° C until golden brown, 10–12 minutes.

Yields 3 single crusts Ⓥ
. . . .
KRISTIN SHANK ZEHR, HARRISONBURG, VIRGINIA

Shortbread Tart Crust

· ·

**1 cup / 250 ml flour (may use up to ⅓ cup / 75 ml whole
 wheat pastry flour)**
⅓ cup / 75 ml butter
2 tablespoons powdered sugar
In a mixing bowl, mix together until crumbly, with no pieces bigger
than a pea. Press into a 9-inch / 1-L pie pan or tart pan. Bake in
preheated oven at 425° F / 220° C until golden, 10–12 minutes.
Cool.

Fill with favorite berry or other fruit filling (see Strawberry Pie, p. 97,
or Plum Tart, p. 183).

Yields 1 tart Ⓥ

· ·

DONNA FORSMAN, ANNANDALE, VIRGINIA
JILL HEATWOLE, PITTSVILLE, MARYLAND

Chilled Berry Sauce

*Delicious served with plain or vanilla yogurt and granola for breakfast or
layered in a parfait for dessert. Other frozen fruits can be used.*

· ·

1 cup / 250 ml grape juice
3 tablespoons sugar or maple syrup
2 tablespoons cornstarch
Combine in a saucepan. Heat slowly, stirring constantly until clear.
Remove from heat.

4 cups / 1 L frozen strawberries
2 cups / 500 ml frozen raspberries
½ teaspoon vanilla
Stir in and chill.

Serves 4–6 Ⓥ Ⓖ🇫

· ·

MARY BETH LIND, HARMAN, WEST VIRGINIA

Sherbet

Servings can be small; the flavor is wonderful!

. . . .

2 cups / 500 ml fruit such as berries, peaches, apricots
Purée and strain through a fine-mesh sieve for a smoother sherbet (optional). Refrigerate.

¾ cup / 175 ml water
½ cup / 125 ml sugar; or ⅜ cup / 90 ml honey
Combine in a small saucepan and bring to a boil, stirring occasionally. Cook over medium-high heat until the syrup reaches 240° F / 115° C on a candy thermometer, about 5 minutes.

2 egg whites (at room temperature)
Beat with an electric mixer until soft peaks form. Return the syrup to the heat until it boils. Gradually pour the syrup into the egg whites, but not on the beaters. Beat constantly until egg whites are cool and stiff, about 5 minutes. Fold fruit into egg whites and freeze in a metal pan. When solid, process in a food processor until smooth. Refreeze.

Yields 4 cups / 1 L
. . . .

JULIE BERGEN, SASKATOON, SASKATCHEWAN

As a leader in Via Campesina, a global movement of peasant, small-scale farmers' and indigenous peoples' organizations, I have worked with rural leaders from many parts of the world. Agriculture everywhere is being reordered through trade agreements and financial instruments. Peasants in poorer countries are under pressure to use their best land for raising specialty crops for export. Others are simply displaced as their local markets for staple foods are taken over by cheaper imports from industrialized countries. This destroys traditional food cultures and undermines the autonomy and food security of peoples.

Genuine food security requires food sovereignty. Food security can only be achieved if food production is broadly based, environmentally sustainable, and locally controlled. This means that peasants must have access to land, seed, and water and that the rights of people to produce their own food must be protected. Food sovereignty treats food as the basis of life and culture, not just another commodity.
—Nettie Wiebe, Delisle, Saskatchewan

Scandinavian Sweet Soup

"In my home community of Adams, Minnesota, this is prepared mainly in the fall and winter and is especially eaten at holidays," says contributor Al Mortenson. Testers loved it as a side dish compote and as a dessert.

. . . .

4½ cups / 1.1 L water
3 cups / 750 ml mixed dried fruit such as currants, raisins,
    prunes, pears, apricots, peaches, apples
¾ cup / 175 ml sugar
½ medium orange, sliced; peeling is optional
1½ tablespoon quick-cooking tapioca
½ teaspoon ground cinnamon
¼ teaspoon salt and dash of ground nutmeg and cloves
Mix together in a large saucepan. Bring to a boil, cover, and simmer until fruits are tender, about 35 minutes. Serve hot or cold.

Serves 8–12 Ⓥ Ⓖⓕ
. . . .

AL MORTENSON, LOUISVILLE, KENTUCKY

Fruit Smoothie

"This is based on the many licuados *we drank in Central America, where fresh fruit was always in season," says contributor Jenn Esbenshade. "We continue to enjoy experimenting with various fruits and some spices (like berries with cinnamon). This recipe leaves plenty of room for personal adaptations."*

. . . .

2 cups / 500 ml fruit such as berries, melon, peaches
Purée in a blender.

1½ cup / 375 ml plain yogurt
1 cup / 250 ml milk
2–4 tablespoons honey or sugar, to taste
Add and blend until smooth. Yogurt may be replaced by milk for a thinner smoothie.

Yields 4 (10-ounce / 300-g) smoothies Ⓥ ⓖⓕ
. . . .

Tofu variation: Replace the plain yogurt with ¾ cup / 175 ml vanilla yogurt and ¾ cup / 175 ml silken tofu. Instead of milk, use 1 cup / 250 ml orange juice.

. . . .

JENN ESBENSHADE, NEW HOLLAND, PENNSYLVANIA
NATHAN LEWANDOWSKI, ATHENS, OHIO
SHARON SWARTZENTRUBER, MARION, PENNSYLVANIA

Sweetened Condensed Milk

. . . .

1 cup / 250 ml dry milk powder
⅔ cup / 150 ml sugar
⅓ cup / 75 ml boiling water
3 tablespoons butter or oil (optional)
Combine in blender and blend until smooth. Refrigerate 24 hours to thicken. Yields the equivalent of one can.

Yields about 1¼ cup / 300 ml Ⓥ
. . . .

AMY DUECKMAN, ABBOTSFORD, BRITISH COLUMBIA

Easy Dependable Yogurt

"I was motivated to find a yogurt recipe because I got so tired of all those unrecyclable individual yogurt containers, and because I wanted to use local milk, honey, and fruit," says contributor Sue Wagner Fields.

. . . .

Special equipment needed:
1 (8-cup / 2-L) wide-mouthed thermos or 2 (4-cup / 1-L) wide-mouthed thermoses; cooking thermometer

8 cups / 2 L raw or store-bought fresh milk
Put in a saucepan and scald by heating until tiny bubbles form around the edges of the milk; do not boil. Pour into another container to cool. Insert the cooking thermometer. Fill the thermos with hot water, and put the top back on. Allow the milk to cool to 105–110° F / 40–45° C.

¼ cup / 60 ml yogurt starter (see below)
Once milk reaches 105–110° F / 40–45° C, stir in yogurt starter. Empty the thermos, pour in the milk mixture, and screw on the lid. (Do not move the thermos much while incubating.) After 4–6 hours, pour the yogurt into a bowl.

⅜–½ cup / 90–125 ml honey or sugar or combination
1 teaspoon vanilla
fresh peaches or berries (optional)
Fold in. Finished yogurt should not be stirred vigorously. If you forget about the yogurt and leave it in the thermos too long, pour off the water that forms and add additional sweetener.

Yields 8 cups / 2 L Ⓥ Ⓖⓕ
. . . .

Yogurt starter is plain yogurt with active cultures, either purchased or saved from your last batch before adding the sugar or honey. What I have found easiest is to purchase a large container of plain yogurt and freeze it in ice cube trays, 2 or 4 tablespoons per section. When frozen, remove from trays and put cubes into a freezer bag. When needed, just thaw desired number of cubes. Even if you prefer to save your own starter, every once in a while it is best to start over with purchased yogurt, as what is saved from the last batch won't coagulate as well over time. Milk or yogurt starters that are not fresh will take longer to gel. Starter that is frozen when fresh and used the same day it is thawed works fine.

. . . .

Yogurt cheese: Place yogurt in a strainer lined with cheesecloth and drain for 1 hour. Use the whey, the drained liquid, in bread baking. The drained, thickened yogurt is "yogurt cheese." It can replace cream cheese in some recipes.

. . . .

SUE WAGNER FIELDS, BERNVILLE, PENNSYLVANIA

Cream Soup Substitute

At last: a low-fat substitute for canned cream soups in casseroles or soups.

. . . .

2 cups / 500 ml dry milk powder
¾ cup / 175 ml cornstarch
¼ cup / 60 ml chicken or beef bouillon granules
1 teaspoon dried basil
½ teaspoon pepper
2 teaspoons dried minced onion (optional)
Mix together and store in a covered container in refrigerator. To use combine 1¼ cup / 300 ml cold water with ⅓ cup / 75 ml of the mix in a small saucepan. Cook, stirring constantly, until thickened. Substitute this sauce for a 10-ounce / 300-g can of condensed creamed soup. Add herbs such as thyme or dill or ¼ cup / 60 ml minced fresh onion when preparing (optional).

Yields 8 cups / 2 L

. . . .

JOCELE MEYER, FRESNO, OHIO

Flavored Butters

. . . .

Herbed butter:

½ cup / 125 ml butter, softened
1 shallot or ¼ cup / 60 ml chives, minced
1 clove garlic, minced
2 tablespoons fresh basil, parsley, or dill, minced
1 teaspoon lemon or lime juice (optional)
Mix and form into ball or fill a small bowl.

Yields ½ cup / 125 ml Ⓥ ⒼⒻ

. . . .

Lemon butter:

½ cup / 125 ml butter, melted
3 tablespoons lemon juice
2 teaspoons lemon rind, grated
Combine in blender and blend until smooth and fluffy. Use to dress up grilled or baked fish, steamed asparagus, broccoli, carrots, brussels sprouts, or other vegetables.

Yields ½ cup / 125 ml Ⓥ ⒼⒻ

. . . .

Maple butter:

2 cups / 500 ml maple syrup
1 cup / 250 ml butter, softened
Heat maple syrup to 232–234° F / 111–112° C using a candy thermometer. Cool to 80–100° F / 27–38° C. Beat with an electric mixer until it becomes lighter in color, about 2 minutes. Add softened butter and beat until mixture is buttery in texture, about 1½ minute. Store in the refrigerator.

Yields 2 cups / 500 ml Ⓥ ⒼⒻ

. . . .

Healthy butter:

¾ cup / 175 ml oil
¼ cup / 60 ml water
1 cup / 250 ml butter, softened
Combine oil and water in blender. Gradually add softened butter;
blend until smooth. Place in containers and store in the refrigerator.
Blended butter will be soft and spreadable straight out of the
refrigerator.

Yields 2 cups / 500 ml Ⓥ ⒼⒻ

BERNITA BOYTS, SHAWNEE MISSION, KANSAS
MARY BETH LIND, HARMAN, WEST VIRGINIA
RUTH STAUFFER, NICHOLVILLE, NEW YORK

White Sauce

A good base for cheese sauce, mushroom sauce, mustard sauce, and so forth.

2 tablespoons butter or oil
2 tablespoons whole wheat flour (pastry flour recommended)
Heat butter or oil in small saucepan. Add flour and cook over
medium heat, stirring constantly for 3 minutes. Remove from heat.

1 cup / 250 ml milk
¼ teaspoon salt
pinch of ground nutmeg
Add and return to heat. Bring to a boil, stirring constantly until
thickened. For a thicker sauce, increase flour to ¼ cup / 60 ml. For
a thinner sauce, decrease flour and oil to 1 tablespoon each.

Yields 1 cup / 250 ml Ⓥ

Cheese sauce: After sauce thickens, add ¼ teaspoon dry
mustard and 1 cup / 250 ml shredded cheddar cheese. Stir until
cheese melts.

MARY BETH LIND, HARMAN, WEST VIRGINIA

Baking Mix

Use in any recipe that calls for purchased baking mix.

....

Whole wheat baking mix:

7 cups / 1.8 L flour
3 cups / 750 ml whole wheat flour (pastry flour
    recommended)
6 tablespoons baking powder
¼ cup / 60 ml sugar
1½ tablespoon salt
1½ teaspoon cream of tartar
2 cups / 500 ml shortening
2 cups / 500 ml dry milk powder
Combine dry ingredients (except milk powder) in a large bowl. Cut
in shortening with pastry cutter until the mixture is the consistency
of cornmeal. Gently stir in milk powder. Store in an airtight
container in a cool place.

....

Oat-wheat germ baking mix:

3 cups / 750 ml rolled oats
2 cups / 500 ml flour
2 cups / 500 ml whole wheat flour
1 cup / 250 ml wheat germ
3 tablespoons baking powder
2 teaspoons salt
½ teaspoon cream of tartar
2 cups / 500 ml butter, softened
1 cup / 250 ml dry milk powder
Combine dry ingredients (except milk powder) in a large bowl.
Cut in butter with pastry cutter until the mixture is the consistency
of cornmeal. Gently stir in milk powder. Store refrigerated in an
airtight container.

....

For biscuits: Ⓥ Combine 1½ cup / 375 ml baking mix with
½ cup / 125 ml milk. Drop by tablespoons on ungreased
baking sheet and bake in preheated oven at 450° F / 230° C for
8–10 minutes.

....

....

For pancakes: Ⓥ Beat together 1 egg and 1 cup / 250 ml milk. Add 1½ cup / 375 ml baking mix and stir until smooth. Fry in a hot, greased frypan.

....

For dill cheese quick bread: Ⓥ Combine 3 cups / 750 ml baking mix with 1½ cup / 375 ml grated sharp cheddar cheese. In a separate bowl thoroughly combine 1¼ cup / 300 ml milk, 1 beaten egg, 1 teaspoon dried or 1 tablespoon fresh chopped dill, and ½ teaspoon dry mustard. Stir into dry mixture, blending thoroughly, then beat slightly to remove lumps. Pour into well-greased 8 x 4-inch / 1.5-L loaf pan. Bake in preheated oven at 350° F / 180° C until golden, 45–50 minutes.

....

MARY BETH LIND, HARMAN, WEST VIRGINIA
LAURA KEPPLEY, BOYERTOWN, PENNSYLVANIA

Roasted Hazelnuts

Walnuts may also be toasted using these basic methods. Be careful to avoid burning.

....

Oven: Spread shelled hazelnuts in a single layer in a shallow pan and roast at 275° F / 140° C until the skins crack, 20–30 minutes. To remove the skins place warm nuts in a rough cloth and rub between hands.

....

Microwave: Place in a single layer in a shallow, microwave-safe pan. Cook on high until the skins crack, stirring each minute, about 5 minutes total.

....

Stovetop: Place in a single layer in a dry skillet. Cook over medium heat, shaking frequently, until fragrant and lightly colored, 4 minutes or less.

Ⓥ Ⓖⓕ

....

JEANNE HEYERLY, CHENOA, ILLINOIS

Seasoned Bread Crumbs

Scatter on top of casseroles or coat chicken or fish for frying.

....

stale bread
Dry bread thoroughly in a 250° F / 120° C oven. Stir occasionally. (I like to put the stale bread in the oven after I have baked something and have turned the oven off. Often there is enough heat left to dry bread.) To quicken the drying, cut the bread into smaller pieces. After bread is dry, crush in blender or place in a strong plastic bag and crush with a rolling pin. Put crumbs through a coarse sieve. Toss the hard pieces to the birds. Put the fine crumbs into an airtight container and use anywhere bread crumbs are called for, or make seasoned bread crumbs as follows:

1¾ cup / 425 ml dry bread crumbs
1 tablespoon dried parsley
1 teaspoon each salt, paprika, celery salt
½ teaspoon onion salt
⅛ teaspoon pepper
¼ cup / 60 ml Parmesan cheese, grated (optional)
Mix well.

Yields about 2 cups / 500 ml Ⓥ
....

MARY BETH LIND, HARMAN, WEST VIRGINIA

O God, they call it "farm crisis."
Our costs are up and prices for
   our produce down.
The loan is due and there's no
   money to buy this year's seed.
We feel alone, embarrassed in
   our need, like failures in our
   efforts to farm.
The harder we work, the worse it
   seems to get.
There's no laughter or joy
   anymore,
just a constant struggle to
   believe, to hope, and to keep
   trying.

Strengthen us, God.
Keep us gentle and yet firm,
   generous yet open to receive.
Let us see your face in those who
   want to help and don't know
   how.
Grant us perseverance and
   openness to your will.
Hold our family close as we
   do our best to know and act
   according to your will in the
   days ahead.
Amen.
—National Catholic Rural Life
Conference

Herbed Croutons

A fine complement to cream soups or green salads.

. . . .

4 cups / 1 L whole wheat bread cubes
Spread on an ungreased baking sheet and bake in preheated oven at 350° F / 180° C until crisp and dry, 10–15 minutes. Lightly spray dried bread cubes with oil.

1½ tablespoon Parmesan cheese, grated
½ teaspoon dried thyme
¼ teaspoon dried marjoram
2 teaspoons dried parsley
Mix together and toss with the bread cubes. Return the cubes to the oven and bake until crisp, about 5 minutes.

Yields 4 cups / 1 L Ⓥ
. . . .

MALINDA BERRY, NEW YORK, NEW YORK

Polenta

"Growing up, we ate cornmeal mush with honey and butter or milk. We still eat it that way but have also learned to love the Italian version, served with tomato-based sauces or sautéed greens," says contributor Mary Beth Lind.

. . . .

4½–5 cups / 1.1–1.2 L water or milk
1½ cup / 375 ml cornmeal
½ teaspoon salt

Combine in a heavy saucepan, stirring until a smooth consistency is achieved. Cover and cook on very low heat until thick and smooth, about 30 minutes. Stir occasionally with a wooden spoon to avoid scorching. Serve as a thick porridge or pour into a greased 8 x 4-inch / 1.5-L loaf pan. Refrigerate several hours. When ready to use, slice into ¼- to ½-inch / 5- to 10-mm slices. slices. Fry slices in a hot, greased pan until slightly browned or bake in preheated oven at 375° F / 190° C for 15 minutes. Serve topped with Tomato Sauce (p. 200), Greens in Peanut Sauce (p. 233), Summer Garden Ratatouille (p. 152), Greek Fennel Skillet (p. 151), Butternut Skillet (p. 257), chili, or other juicy stews.

Serves 4 Ⓥ Ⓖⓕ

. . . .

Mushroom variation: Use milk instead of water to make the polenta. Separately, sauté in 1 tablespoon oil 2 minced shallots or green onions and 4 ounces / 125 g finely chopped shiitake or other mushrooms. Stir into cooked polenta with ¼ teaspoon crushed hot chilies and 1½ tablespoon grated Parmesan cheese. Mix well, place in loaf pan, chill, and fry or bake as directed above.

. . . .

KELLI BURKHOLDER KING, GOSHEN, INDIANA
MARY BETH LIND, HARMAN, WEST VIRGINIA

Tempeh Gravy

Serve over toast, brown rice, whole wheat noodles, or mashed potatoes.
Delicious with toast made from hearty whole grain sourdough bread!

. . . .

2 (8-ounce / 250-g) packages tempeh, thawed and
chopped in ½-inch / 1-cm cubes or short strips ¼ inch /
5 mm in width
1 cup / 250 ml water
1 teaspoon salt
Place in large nonstick frypan, cover, and steam over medium heat
until water is gone.

1–2 tablespoons olive oil
Remove lid and add, frying until golden brown, stirring occasionally
to turn chunks. Remove tempeh from frypan and set aside.

1–2 onions, chopped
¼ cup / 60 ml whole wheat flour
Add onions to the frypan and sauté until translucent. Stir in flour
and heat gently for 1–2 additional minutes.

2 cups / 500 ml milk or more as needed
Whisk in and heat to a low boil. Stir until thickened then stir in fried
tempeh. (Add ¼ cup / 60 ml or more milk if gravy is too thick.) Add
salt, pepper, and tamari sauce (optional) to taste. Heat through.

Serves 4 ⓥ

. . . .

KRISTIN SHANK ZEHR, HARRISONBURG, VIRGINIA

Modern American culture is fairly empty of any suggestion that one's relationship to the land, to consumption and food, is a religious matter. But it's true; the decision to attend to the health of one's habitat and food chain is a spiritual choice. It's also a political choice, a scientific one, a personal and a convivial one. It's not a choice between living in the country or the town; it is about understanding that every one of us, at the level of our cells and respiration, lives in the country and is thus obliged to be mindful of the distance between ourselves and our sustenance.
—Barbara Kingsolver, author and environmental advocate[9]

Hummus

Serve with pita or whole wheat bread and plenty of fresh vegetables.

. . . .

4 cups / 1 L cooked chickpeas
½ cup / 125 ml lemon juice
½ cup / 125 ml tahini
¼ cup / 60 ml olive oil
3 cloves garlic
salt and pepper to taste
Place in blender along with one of the options listed below.
Purée in blender or food processor until smooth.

Yields 4 cups / 1 L (V) (Gf)
. . . .

Option 1:

2 tablespoons fresh basil or fresh parsley

. . . .

Option 2:

1 large roasted green or red sweet pepper (p. 199)
2 tablespoons low-sodium soy sauce
1 teaspoon crushed hot chilies, more or less to taste
1 teaspoon ground cumin

. . . .

BETHANY SPICHER, WASHINGTON, DISTRICT OF COLUMBIA
SAMIRA MUSLEH, ABBOTSFORD, BRITISH COLUMBIA
DONNA SMITH, PHILIPPI, WEST VIRGINIA

The Earth is rotating on a finely defined axis at an optimum distance from the sun. The moon at just the right orbit controls the tides. The ozone layer is in place to protect us from the sun's dangerous cancer-inducing radiations. The right proportion of carbon dioxide in the atmosphere working with the jet stream and ocean currents gives us balanced weather patterns. The whole thing was designed for us by the Supreme Systems Engineer—one planet for one people.
—Fazlun Khalid, founder of the Islamic Foundation for Ecology and Environmental Sciences[10]

Black Bean Dip

Serve warm or cold as a dip for tortilla chips, wedges of pita bread, or fresh vegetables. Or use as a filling in pita pockets or tortilla wraps. Delicious layered with cheese in quesadillas.

. . . .

Cilantro variation:

1 onion, chopped
2 cups / 500 ml cooked black beans
1 tablespoon sesame seeds, toasted and ground
2–4 tablespoons fresh cilantro, chopped
juice of 1 lime (approx. ¼ cup / 60 ml)
1–2 cloves garlic, minced
salt, Tabasco pepper sauce, and ground cumin to taste
In a frypan, sauté onions in 1 tablespoon olive oil until tender. Add black beans and heat through. Place ½ cup / 125 ml bean mixture in bowl with sesame seeds. Purée remaining beans in blender or food processor. Mix puréed beans and whole beans with sesame seeds. Add remaining ingredients and stir well. Serve warm or cold.

Yields 2 cups / 500 ml Ⓥ ⑼

. . . .

Parsley variation:

2 cups / 500 ml cooked black beans, mashed
⅔ cup / 150 ml fresh parsley, chopped
⅓ cup / 75 ml walnuts, chopped
2 teaspoons lemon juice
1 teaspoon olive oil, or more to taste
1 teaspoon ground cumin
1 clove garlic, minced
½ teaspoon ground coriander
pinch of ground red pepper
salt to taste
Stir together in a mixing bowl.

Yields 2 cups / 500 ml Ⓥ ⑼

. . . .

KRISTIN SHANK ZEHR, HARRISONBURG, VIRGINIA
MIRIAM HUEBERT-STAUFFER, CANTON, KANSAS

Home-Canned Pinto Beans

"I don't always plan far enough ahead to allow for time to cook beans for a meal. I could buy commercially canned beans, and sometimes do, but our family thinks these taste so much better," says contributor Janet Regier. "I can these in winter, when I don't mind heating up the house with the long processing time and when the canning jars are being emptied of their summer-canned contents."

. . . .

8 cups / 2 L dry pinto beans or other beans, sorted and rinsed

Put in large soup pot and cover with cold water. Soak 12–18 hours. Drain. Cover with fresh water and bring beans to a boil; boil 15 minutes. Meanwhile, wash and keep warm five quart-sized canning jars and lids.

½ teaspoon canning salt
¼ teaspoon onion powder (optional)
⅛ teaspoon garlic powder (optional)
⅛ teaspoon ground cumin or other seasonings of choice (optional)

Add to each jar, then fill each jar with hot beans to within 2 inches / 5 cm of the top. Add boiling water or bean cooking liquid within 1 inch / 2.5 cm of the top. Seal with sterilized lids. Process at 10 pounds pressure in pressure canner for 1½ hour.

Yields 5 quarts / 5 L Ⓥ Ⓖⓕ

. . . .

JANET REGIER, NEWTON, KANSAS

It is said: "Before the world was created, the Holy One kept creating worlds and destroying them. Finally He created this one, and was satisfied. He said to Adam: 'This is the last world I shall make. I place it in your hands: hold it in trust.'"
—Midrashic anecdote for Tu Bishvat, the Jewish festival celebrating New Year for Trees

Lord, as we gather at this table,
  we thank you for this food
    and the hands that prepared it.

We also thank you for hands we often forget:
  those of the farmers who raised this food.

Bless the hands of farmers and farmworkers, Lord
  —the calluses, the nicks and scrapes,
    the dirt on these hands.
Thank you for the know-how of these hands
  to prepare, repair, test, and harvest.
Encourage these impatient hands on rainy days
  when they itch to work.
And when their hands wring under financial strain,
  direct them to hope in you.

Bless the hands of farmers, Lord. Amen.

—DIANE ZAERR BRENNEMAN, PARNELL, IOWA

CSAs

Scores of communities now offer CSAs: Community Supported—or Shared—Agriculture, also called subscription farming. In Japan, such an arrangement is called *teikei*, sometimes translated as "food with a farmer's face on it."

In a CSA, subscribers pay the farmer for a share of the season's produce. Each week they receive whatever is ripe. If there's a bumper crop of broccoli, everyone gets extra, but if a late storm destroys the strawberries, well, everyone enjoys plain rhubarb pie. The point is that the farmer doesn't bear the financial risk alone; a bad year doesn't mean losing the farm.

Most CSAs offer organic produce. Some provide meat, eggs, dairy products, honey, or flowers. Subscribers usually pick up their food at a central location or the farm itself. Many CSAs encourage people to visit the farm and participate in seasonal festivals. These occasions build relationships with the farm family and help members to better understand where their food comes from.

The amount of food and length of commitment varies from farm to farm, so explore local options to find one that fits your interests.

Organic

In grocery stores, foods with the "USDA Organic" label have been raised following the U.S. National Organic Program requirements on farms annually inspected by an independent, third-party certifier. These certified farms may not use standard chemical herbicides, synthetic fertilizers, or unapproved pesticides on soil or produce, and their livestock may not be fed antibiotics or growth hormones. "USDA Organic" products also have no genetically modified organisms (GMOs) used in their production.

Canada requires certification of organic products traded across provincial or international borders or that bear the "Canada Organic" logo. General principles behind the Canadian Organic Standards include protecting the environment, maintaining long-term soil fertility, maintaining biological diversity, recycling materials and resources to the greatest extent possible, and caring for the needs of livestock.

Some small farmers have formed regional organizations with unique certification criteria, sometimes more, sometimes less strict than those at the federal level. If you want to know what's in your food—and how it was produced—the best option is getting to know, and asking, your farmer.

Fair trade

Some foods that cannot be grown in cool climates are available through fair trade organizations. Look for the "Fair Trade Certified" label on packages of coffee, tea, chocolate, bananas, mangoes, and coconut, signifying certification by the independent nonprofit Fairtrade Canada or Fair Trade USA. Group inspectors visit production sites annually to ensure that producers work in healthy, cooperative settings; receive a fair and living wage; have access to affordable credit; and use some of the fair trade premium for social, economic, or environmental projects.

Other companies are not certified but work to benefit small farmer co-ops or document specific beneficial practices, such as "bird-friendly" coffee. Fairly traded rice, quinoa, and spices are increasingly available. Many Ten Thousand Villages stores sell fairly traded items, including coffee, tea, chocolate, nuts, dried fruit, and olive oil. More fair trade foods are being procured.

Vegetarian Ⓥ

Vegetarian labels on recipes in this cookbook may contain milk or eggs. If a recipe is to be served over meat, it is not labeled as vegetarian even though the recipe itself may be vegetarian.

Gluten-Free Ⓖⓕ

Wheat products (such as pasta, bread, and flour) contain gluten, which many people avoid for a variety of reasons. In addition to the recipes in this book that are labeled gluten free, many others are easy to adapt to a gluten-free diet. But checking ingredient lists and being aware of hidden sources of gluten are essential. Trace amounts of gluten are possible in a variety of store-bought items.

Gluten-free labels on recipes in this book indicate the general consensus regarding ingredients, but variations on a gluten-free recipe may contain gluten, and cooks preparing food for people on gluten-free diets should carefully check product labels.

These and other items may or may not be gluten free, depending on the brand, so check the labels and find wheat-free options:
- Broth / bouillon / stock
- Dijon mustard
- Fish sauce
- Mayonnaise
- Oyster sauce
- Pasta
- Pork products: ham, ham hocks, sausage
- Prepared dressings
- Soy sauce (look for gluten-free tamari soy sauce as a substitute)
- Worcestershire sauce

Substituting Honey for Sugar

Experiment with using honey in breads, muffins, and desserts. Honey is sweeter than sugar, so you often can use less, sometimes even half the amount of sugar. Here are some tips:

- For every 1 cup / 250 ml of sugar you're replacing, reduce the other liquids in the recipe by ¼ cup / 60 ml.

- In cookie recipes using eggs or recipes without other liquids, add 2 tablespoons flour for every 1 cup / 250 ml honey.

- Add ½ teaspoon baking soda for every 1 cup / 250 ml of honey.

- Reduce the oven temperature by 25° F / 15° C.

- Coat your measuring cup with cooking spray so the honey easily slides out.

Food Preparation and Cooking

Blanch—To plunge food (usually vegetables) into boiling water briefly, then into cold water to stop the cooking process. Used to help preserve vegetables and their nutrients at the peak of ripeness before freezing and to heighten and set color and flavor for "raw" vegetables with a dip.

Broil—To cook food close beneath the flame of an oven, often at 500° F / 260° C or more. Broiling fish and meats is best done with a broiler pan designed for high heat and for handling grease that develops while cooking.

Chop—To cut into pieces; not necessarily uniform.

Cream—To thoroughly blend fat with a dry ingredient such as sugar using an electric mixer, stand mixer, or lots of hand mixing. Creates light texture in baked goods.

Cut in—To mix fat with dry ingredients using a pastry blender, two forks, or fingers. To create the flakiest pastry doughs, use cold fat and work quickly to keep it cool.

Dice—To cut into small, uniform pieces to assure even cooking and pleasant appearance.

Grill—To prepare food on a metal grate over hot coals or other heat source.

Julienne—To slice vegetables into very thin strips.

Marinate—To soak food such as meat or an alternative protein in a seasoned liquid mixture in order to absorb flavor or tenderize.

Mince—To chop as finely as possible so that a food such as garlic blends into a dish.

Preheat oven—To heat the oven to the desired temperature before placing food in the oven. Important when baking breads, cookies, cakes, pies, and egg dishes; however, not necessary for casseroles or most other dishes.

Purée—To blend into a smooth texture by using a blender, food processor, immersion blender, or food mill.

Roast—To oven-cook food in an uncovered pan, a method that usually produces a well-browned exterior and ideally a moist interior.

Sauté—To cook food quickly over high heat in a stovetop pan with a small amount of oil. Best done in a large, broad frypan.

Scald—To heat a liquid, usually milk, just below the boiling point; tiny bubbles start to appear around the edges. Do not bring to a boil, as the milk will scorch. Important to do for raw milk before using in yeast breads or in making yogurt.

Shred—To cut food such as carrots or cheese into narrow strips by using a grater or food processor. Cooked meat can be shredded by pulling it apart with two forks.

Simmer—To cook gently at a low, slow boil. Tiny bubbles should just begin to break the surface.

Steam—To cook food with steam. Often done by placing food in a covered basket or rack over a small amount of boiling water. Steaming does a better job than boiling of retaining a food's flavor and nutrients.

Stir-fry—To quickly cook food in a large frypan or wok over very high heat while constantly and briskly stirring the food. It requires a minimum amount of fat and results in food that is crisp-tender—soft enough for a fork to be inserted but still with a bit of crunch.

Toasted nuts or seeds—Spread nuts or seeds in a single layer in a dry skillet. Cook over medium heat, shaking frequently, until fragrant and lightly colored, usually 4 minutes or less.

Wilt—Gently heat fresh greens until limp. It happens naturally when a warm ingredient is added to greens but can be done by adding them to a hot pan for a short time. Stir to cook evenly.

Food Preservation

CANNING

Canning is a way of preserving foods that relies on sterilization and exclusion of air. Canning foods for year-round enjoyment takes a knowledge of canning basics, top-quality food, and the right equipment. Following is a brief description of the process. Find more detailed instructions in a canning cookbook such as *Saving the Seasons: How to Can, Freeze, or Dry Almost Anything* (Herald Press, 2010).

Most canning is done in glass jars with metal two-part lids—a flat disc and a screw band to hold it in place. Jars should be sterilized if the recipe calls for less than 10 minutes of processing time; sterilizing is unnecessary for processing of more than 10 minutes. Follow the manufacturer's instructions for treating the lids.

Fill jars with the prepared food to within ½–1 inch / 1–2.5 cm of the top. Remove trapped air by running the blade of a table knife between the food and the side of the jar. Clean the rim and cover with the flat disc and screw band. Tighten well. Jars are now ready to process in a boiling water bath (used for canning high-acid foods; low-acid foods must be pressure canned). Fill the canner half full of hot water. Place filled jars on a rack in the canner. Do not crowd. Fill the canner with hot water so the jars are covered with at least 1 inch / 2.5 cm of water. Boil for the recommended amount of time. Remove the jars from the canner and place on a rack or padded surface away from drafts. Allow to cool naturally without moving for 12 hours, then check to make sure all the jars are sealed—lid concave.

DRYING

This process removes enough of the water from fruits and vegetables to preserve it. The goal is to quickly remove the moisture using heat and air without cooking the food. Drying can be as simple as putting vegetables in the sun to dry or as complicated as using a dehydrator. See page 226 for a tip on drying herbs.

FREEZING

This is one of the simplest methods for preserving food. Wash fruits and vegetables well in cold water and drain.

Freezing fruits can be as simple as spreading them in a single layer on a baking sheet and placing them in the freezer until frozen; then removing them, placing in freezer bags or containers, and returning them to the freezer.

Most vegetables should be blanched before freezing so they do not continue to mature; green peppers do not need to be blanched. After blanching and draining, spread vegetables in a single layer on a baking sheet and freeze 3–4 hours until firm. Remove from freezer, place in freezer bags, and return to freezer.

Alternative Proteins

Dried beans and lentils—Sort and discard any pebbles or blemished beans or lentils, then rinse in cold water. Before cooking dried beans, cover them with cold water and soak overnight or 6–8 hours; cook as desired. For the quick-soaking method, cover rinsed beans with fresh water in a saucepan using 4 times more water than beans; heat to boiling, cover, and turn off heat; let sit for 1 hour, then cook as desired. Lentils can be cooked without any presoaking. The familiar brown lentils cook in about 30–40 minutes and small red lentils cook in only 15–20 minutes.

Seitan (say-TAHN)—Chewy form of wheat gluten made from flour; sometimes called "wheat meat." Sold refrigerated in cakes or tubs, often in a marinade, but can be made by hand; also sold in a powdered form that needs to be mixed with water. Used in stir-fries, sandwiches, stews, and so forth. Chunky texture and mild taste; absorbs other flavors somewhat faster than tofu or tempeh.

Soy crumbles—Ready-to-eat food that resembles, and substitutes for, browned hamburger. Available frozen or refrigerated. Use in meat loaf, burgers, tacos, chili, and so forth.

Tofu (bean curd)—Soft food made by curdling hot soymilk (the liquid squeezed from dried soybeans that have been soaked, ground, and cooked) with a coagulant and allowing it to set like yogurt. Comes in blocks, which must be refrigerated. After opening package, store unused tofu submerged in water in a covered container; change water daily and drain before using.

Silken tofu has a smoother, more delicate, custard-like texture; use for puréed foods like dips, dressings, or smoothies.

Firm tofu holds its shape better; use in stir-fries, stews, or kabobs. Will soak in more flavor if pressed: Slice the block in two equal 1-inch / 2.5-cm slabs and place side by side on a plate. Top with a second plate and weigh it down with a full teapot (sides of tofu should bulge but not split). After 20–30 minutes remove weight, pick up both plates (holding tofu firmly in place), and pour off water. Pat dry. Freezing gives firm tofu a chewier, more porous texture good for marinating; after defrosting, squeeze out excess water. Use immediately; defrosted frozen tofu spoils quickly.

Tempeh (TEHM-pay)—A chewy product made from (usually) fermented, partially cooked whole soybeans, often with another grain such as brown rice, wild rice, millet, barley, quinoa, or nuts. Sometimes made locally at restaurants or natural food stores. Comes in fresh (refrigerated) or frozen cakes and has a chunky, chewy texture. Will turn black in the refrigerator so use promptly or freeze; it defrosts quickly and easily. May be grilled, sautéed, braised, panfried, added to stews. Nutty or yeasty flavor (mild but more pronounced than tofu). Least processed and highest protein per ounce of these meat alternatives, plus a good source of iron, calcium, and B vitamins.

Textured soy protein (TSP)—Dry, grainy bits also often used as a substitute for browned hamburger, with larger chunks (big enough to skewer) also available; must be soaked in liquid. Mostly used in soups and stews. May have higher fat content than these other foods.

Whole Grains

Whole grains—Grains are made up of bran, endosperm, and germ. The bran is the outer coating, which is full of good fiber. The germ is the seed, high in nutrients. The endosperm is the initial food for the growing seed; it is mostly carbohydrate and is what most refined grain products are made from. Whole grains include all three parts of the grain, thus retaining all the nutrients.

Barley—Hulled barley has only the outer husk removed and is the most nutritious form of the grain. Pearl barley has had the bran removed.

Brown rice—The entire grain of rice with only the outer husk removed. The nutritious, high-fiber bran coating gives it a light tan color, nutlike flavor, and chewy texture. It takes longer to cook than white rice.

Buckwheat—Unrelated to wheat or other grains, it is the edible fruit seed of a plant related to rhubarb. Close to being a complete protein. Commonly used in combination with wheat flour for pancakes and in pastas.

Cornmeal—Dried corn kernels that have been ground. Most cornmeal has had the husk and germ completely removed. Water-ground (or stone-ground) cornmeal retains some of the hull and germ, so is more nutritious.

Cracked wheat / Bulgur—Produced by cracking whole wheat berries between rollers so they cook more quickly. If they are then hulled, steamed, and roasted they are known as bulgur wheat. Use in grain salads or in stuffings.

Flaxseed—Contains several essential nutrients including calcium, iron, niacin, phosphorous, and vitamin E; it is also a rich source of omega-3 fatty acids. Whole flaxseeds do not digest well because of their hard shells. To get their nutritional benefits, the seeds must be cracked or ground. To make flaxseed meal, process flaxseeds in a blender or coffee grinder. Once ground, flaxseeds go rancid quickly, so store in the refrigerator.

Hominy—Dried white or yellow corn kernels from which the hull and germ have been removed.

Rolled oats / Oat bran—Rolled oats have been toasted, hulled, steamed, and flattened. Oat bran is the outer casing of the oat and is high in soluble fiber.

Quinoa—Tiny, bead-shaped ancient grain that cooks like rice. Contains more protein than any other grain. Use in grain salads, as a stuffing, or with salsas.

Wheat germ—Essentially the embryo of the wheat berry, it is a concentrated source of vitamins, minerals, and protein. Raw wheat germ has a nutty flavor and is oily, which causes it to turn rancid quickly, so store it in the refrigerator. Sprinkle toasted wheat germ on fruit or cereal, or use it in baked goods.

Flours

Whole wheat flour versus white flour—Whole wheat flour is made from the whole berries of wheat, retaining all the nutrients. White all-purpose flour is a mix of hard and soft wheat that has had all the bran and germ removed; unbleached is preferable because it has not been chemically treated.

Bread flour—A high-protein flour (usually 14 percent protein) made from hard wheat. Especially good for making breads.

Pastry flour—A low-protein flour (less than 10 percent protein) usually made from soft wheat. Good for pastry.

Authors

Mary Beth Lind is a registered dietitian and nutritional consultant. She and her husband, Lester, are market gardeners in West Virginia: they grow enough fruits and vegetables for their own year-round needs as well as surplus to sell at local farmers' markets. A member of Philippi Mennonite Church, Lind grew up eating local seasonal foods in the mountains of West Virginia. Her mother loved gardening and her father, a country doctor, was occasionally paid in produce. Lind graduated from Eastern Mennonite University, Harrisonburg, Virginia, with a degree in home economics, and from Oregon State University with a degree in foods and nutrition. She is coauthor of *Recipes from the Old Mill: Baking with Whole Grains*.

"Food is a part of my spirituality," Lind says. **"My garden and kitchen are the places where I am most aware of God's mysterious presence, as well as the places where I flesh out my beliefs and values. For me there is a connection between what I eat and how I pray."**

Cathleen Hockman-Wert is a writer and editor living in Corvallis, Oregon. When producing *Simply in Season*, she was editor for Mennonite Women USA. An Oregon native, she graduated from Goshen College in Indiana and later earned a master's degree in journalism from the University of Oregon. She is a member of Corvallis Mennonite Fellowship and an avid farmers' market shopper.

"My journey with local food entered a new level in the 1990s as my husband, Dave, and I began learning more about environmental issues," Hockman-Wert says. **"We were discovering the many ways in which our lifestyle choices affect God's creation and other people. We gradually became more and more committed to seeking out local, sustainably grown foods. Sometimes this has meant paying more; making that adjustment, for two people ingrained with the frugality ethic, hasn't always been easy. Sometimes we chant a little mantra: 'Cheaper is not always better.' But by now, buying local foods is all joy."**

Acknowledgments

Mary Beth Lind and Cathleen Hockman-Wert, authors:

Simply in Season was created through the gifts, time, and care of hundreds of people. We thank, first of all, the 450 recipe contributors and volunteer recipe testers who submitted some 1,600 recipes for consideration. Most recipes were tested at least twice, in homes, small groups, and at church potlucks. More than 70 people tested at least 10 recipes, thus entering our "Golden Spoon Club." Others provided stories about eating with the seasons, only a fraction of which could be included in these pages. The boundless enthusiasm of all these people infused this book production process with joy.

An advisory group helped us set direction for the book. Many read early drafts of the manuscript, providing invaluable counsel, resources, and encouragement. Group members included: Greg Bowman, Sue Wagner Fields, Tina Hartman, Kelli Burkholder King, Mary Etta King, Eric Kurtz, Joanne Moyer, Meagan Peasgood, Bethany Spicher, Myra Tovar, Dan Wiens, and Levi Miller.

Anita Derstine compiled an outstanding first draft of the fruit and vegetable guide. Marshall V. King and Rick Kulp provided information for the glossary. Story collectors included Sarah Anderson, Angelika Dawson, Marshall V. King, and Rich Preheim.

Nancy Mucklow volunteered her professional indexing services for the original index. Lisa Loewen Ebersole assisted with recipe formatting. Jill Reedy, Ruth Inglis-Widrick, and Carol Spicher offered helpful nutritional advice. Stu Clark of Canadian Foodgrains Bank also was a valued manuscript reader. Warm thanks go as well to editorial consultant Michael A. King.

Staff from Mennonite Central Committee were of great help in producing the original version of this cookbook in 2005. We must especially mention Julie Kauffman, graphic designer of each edition; Fred Yocum, IT support; Kiersten Hoffman, who worked with permissions, formatting, copyediting, and indexing; Rachel Miller Moreland, advisor and copyeditor; and last, but certainly not least, Mark Beach, MCC director of communications, who walked this journey alongside us from proposal to presstime. Julie, Kiersten, Rachel, and Mark no longer work with MCC, but their contributions to *Simply in Season* continue.

Thanks to Mennonite Women USA for granting Cathleen extra flexibility in her work hours, making this big project possible for her. The authors thank Avery Peters and Valerie Weaver-Zercher for their editorial work on this edition.

Thanks and love also to our husbands, Dave Hockman-Wert and Lester Lind, who share our passion for good food, didn't mind a near-constant diet of new recipes, and washed more than their share of the dishes.

Avery Peters, project manager of tenth anniversary edition:

An advisory group was fundamental in determining the new look and feel of *Simply in Season*. This group included Lynne Beth, Emilia Dempc, Tobi Thiessen, Audrey Wichert, Elizabeth Berget, Wendy Hammond, Intisar Awisse, and Patricia Bishop. Many thanks to this advisory group, which provided detailed feedback on recipes, assisted in deciding which recipes to photograph, and generally helped to make the cookbook even more useful to readers. Thanks to Jodi Nisly Hertzler and Ben Mast for indexing the new edition.

NOTES

SPRING

[1] Wendell Berry, *Sabbaths* (San Francisco: North Point Press, 1987), 46.

[2] Montague Yudelman, Annu Ratta, and David Nygaard, "Pest Management and Food Production: Looking to the Future," International Food Policy Research Institute, 1998.

[3] "Coping with Water Scarcity: Challenge of the Twenty-First Century," Food and Agriculture Organization of the United Nations, March 22, 2007, http://www.fao.org/nr/water/docs/escarcity.pdf.

[4] Vandana Shiva, *Stolen Justice: The Hijacking of the Global Food Supply* (Cambridge, MA: South End Press, 2000), 119.

[5] Lawrence Hart, "The Earth Is a Song Made Visible," in *Creation and the Environment: An Anabaptist Perspective on a Sustainable World*, ed. Calvin Redekop (Baltimore: Johns Hopkins University Press, 2000), 174, 179.

[6] Marla Kiley, "Dirt," *Geez* (Winter 2007), 23.

SUMMER

[1] Daniel Rothenberg, *With These Hands: The Hidden World of Migrant Farmworkers Today* (New York: Harcourt Brace and Company, 1998), 204. Reprinted by permission of Harcourt, Inc.

[2] Cheryl Long and Tabitha Alterman, "Meet Real Free-Range Eggs," *Mother Earth News* (October–November 2007).

[3] Gary Gardner and Brian Halweil, *Underfed and Overfed: The Global Epidemic of Malnutrition*, Worldwatch Paper 150 (2000).

[4] "Global Burden of Disease Study," Telegraph (UK), December 13, 2012.

[5] Adam Drewnowski and S.E. Specter, "Poverty and obesity: the role of energy density and energy costs," *American Journal of Clinical Nutrition* (January 2004): 6–16.

[6] Daley, et al., "A review of fatty acid profiles and antioxidant content in grass-fed and grain-fed beef," *Nutrition Journal* 9, no. 10 (2010).

AUTUMN

[1] Calvin B. DeWitt, *Earth-Wise: A Biblical Response to Environmental Issues* (Grand Rapids, MI: Faith Alive Christian Resources, 1994).

[2] Ruth Leonard, "Rice Lessons," *A Common Place* (March–April 2004): 4–5.

[3] Brenda Tiessen-Wiens, "Good Stewardship Begins with Contentment," *Canadian Mennonite* (July 1, 2002), 7.

[4] Michael Pollan, *In Defense of Food: An Eater's Manifesto* (New York: Penguin Press, 2008), 186–87. Updated using information from Centers for Disease Control, "Advance Data," Oct. 27, 2004, http://www.cdc.gov/nchs/data/ad/ad347.pdf. Also, change in data collection noted from "Changed System, New Baseline," http://www.cdc.gov/obesity/data/adult.html.

[5] *Co-op America Quarterly* (Summer 2003). Co-op America, 1-800-58-GREEN, www.coopamerica.org.

[6] Wendell Berry, "Christianity and the Survival of Creation," in *Sex, Economy, Freedom, and Community: Eight Essays* (New York: Pantheon Books, 1993), 103.

WINTER

[1] "United States Dumping on World Agricultural Markets," WTO Cancun Series Paper No. 1, Institute for Agriculture and Trade Policy.

[2] Karen Martens Zimmerly, "Seasons of Celebration and Mystery," *Canadian Mennonite* (August 5, 2000), 6.

[3] A. Azzam, "The Effects of Concentration in the Food Processing Industry on Food Prices," *Cornhusker Economics* (February 6, 2002).

[4] William Kandel. "Economic Research Report Number 60: Profile of Hired Farmworkers, A 2008 Update," United States Department of Agriculture (2008). "Findings from a National Agricultural Workers Survey (NAWS) 2001-2002. A Demographic and Employment Profile of United States Farm Workers," Research Report No. 9 (U.S. Department of Labor, Office of the Assistant Secretary for Policy, Office of Programmatic Policy, March 2005).

[5] John Ikerd, "Who's Paying for Your Food?" *Small Farm Today* (November–December 2003).

[6] Brian Halweil, *Eat Here: Reclaiming Homegrown Pleasures in a Global Supermarket* (Washington, DC: Worldwatch Institute, 2004), 54–55, www.worldwatch.org.

ALL SEASONS

[1] National Farmers Union (Canada), "The Farm Crisis, Bigger Farms, and the Myths of 'Competition' and 'Efficiency'," 2003.

[2] Halweil, *Eat Here*, 45. http://www.mafc.com/blog/where-does-your-food-dollar-go/.

[3] Canadian Foodgrains Bank and Peter Rosset, "The Multiple Functions and Benefits of Small Farm Agriculture," Policy Brief No. 4 (Oakland, CA: Food First/Institute for Food and Development Policy, 1999).

[4] Danielle Nierenberg, "Factory Farming in the Developing World," Worldwatch (May–June 2003), 13.

[5] Alan Durning, "Fat of the Land," World Watch Magazine (May–June 1991).

[6] Quoted in Rothenberg, *With These Hands*, 9.

[7] Cathleen Hockman-Wert, "Around the Circle," *Timbrel* (July–August 2000).

[8] National Catholic Rural Life Conference, "Eating Is a Moral Act" campaign, www.ncrlc.com.

[9] Barbara Kingsolver, foreword to *The Essential Agrarian Reader: The Future of Culture, Community, and the Land*, ed. Norman Wirzba (Berkeley, CA: Counterpoint, 2004), xvii.

[10] Fazlun Khalid, "People, Planet, and Climate Change" (speech, Religions for the Earth Conference, September 18, 2014).

....

Index to writings

Index to recipes

Brownies and bars

Brussels sprouts

Cabbage

Cakes

Canning and preserving

Carrots

Cauliflower